THE WORLD'S CLASSICS

INDIAN SUMMER

WILLIAM DEAN HOWELLS (1837–1920) was born in Ohio, the son of a printer. Despite a scant formal education Howells read widely, and later, while a journalist on the *Ohio State Journal*, began to study languages. In 1860 he wrote a campaign biography of Lincoln, and was rewarded with the consulate in Venice, where he wrote several studies of Italian life and literature. Shortly after his return to America in 1865, he took up the subeditorship of the *Atlantic Monthly*; after five years he became its editor-in-chief and held the post for a decade. During those years he wrote several novels, including *Their Wedding Journey* (1872) and *The Lady of the Aroostook* (1879). The 1880s, after Howells had left the *Atlantic*, saw a shift in emphasis in his fiction towards realism. The major novels from this period include *A Modern Instance* (1882), *The Rise of Silas Lapham* (1885), a masterpiece on Boston society and the self-made businessman, and *Indian Summer* (1886).

In 1889 he moved from Boston to New York, to work on the staff of *Harper's* magazine. His major novel of this period, *A Hazard of New Fortunes* (1890), reflects his increasingly socialist sympathies and his interest in the problems of industrialism.

Throughout his later life Howells was considered the preeminent man of American letters. He continued to write prolifically, producing several volumes of literary criticism (including *Criticism and Fiction*, 1891), over thirty dramas, further novels, autobiographies, travel sketches, and many short stories. He was also enormously influential in promoting the work of other writers, including Henry James, Stephen Crane, and Mark Twain.

TONY TANNER is a Fellow of King's College, Cambridge. His books on American literature include *The Reign of Wonder*, *City of Words*, and *Scenes of Nature, Signs of Men*. He has also edited Melville's *Moby-Dick* for the World's Classics.

JOHN DUGDALE wrote his Cambridge Ph.D. dissertation on the novelist Thomas Pynchon. He is currently working on a study of Sam Shepard.

WILLIAM DEAN HOWELLS (1837–1920) was born in Ohio, the son of a printer. Despite a scant formal education, Howells read widely, and later, while a journalist on the *Ohio State Journal*, began to write. He wrote a campaign biography of Lincoln and was rewarded with the Consulship at Venice, where he pursued studies in Italian life and literature. Shortly after his return to America in 1866, the took up the subeditorship of the *Atlantic Monthly*, after five years becoming its editor-in-chief and holding that post until 1881. During these years, he wrote several novels, including *A Modern Instance* (1882) and *The Rise of Silas Lapham* (1885). *The Minister's Charge* (1886), and *Indian Summer* (1886).

In 1888 he moved from Boston to New York. His work on *A Hazard of New Fortunes* reflects his increasing socialist sympathies and his interest in the problems of the poor.

Throughout his later life, Howells was considered the prime man of American letters. He continued to write prolifically, producing several volumes of fiction. His best known novels are considered to be *A Modern Instance* and *The Rise of Silas Lapham*.

TONY TANNER is a Fellow of King's College, Cambridge. His books on American literature include *The Reign of Wonder* and *City of Words*.

JOHN DUGAN wrote his Cambridge Ph.D. dissertation on the novelist Thomas Pynchon. He lectures on American literature.

THE WORLD'S CLASSICS

WILLIAM DEAN HOWELLS

Indian Summer

with an Introduction by
TONY TANNER
and Explanatory Notes by
JOHN DUGDALE

Oxford   New York
OXFORD UNIVERSITY PRESS
1988

Oxford University Press, Walton Street, Oxford OX2 6DP

Oxford New York Toronto
Delhi Bombay Calcutta Madras Karachi
Petaling Jaya Singapore Hong Kong Tokyo
Nairobi Dar es Salaam Cape Town
Melbourne Auckland

and associated companies in
Berlin Ibadan

Oxford is a trade mark of Oxford University Press

British Library Cataloguing in Publication Data
Howells, W. D. (William Dean), 1837–1920
Indian summer.—(The world's classics).
I. Title
813'.4[F]
ISBN 0-19-281793-0

Library of Congress Cataloging in Publication Data
Howells, William Dean, 1837–1920.
Indian summer / William Dean Howells; with an introduction by
Tony Tanner and explanatory notes by John Dugdale.
p.   cm. — (The World's classics)
Bibliography: p.
I. Dugdale, John. II. Title.
PS2025.I55 1988 813'.4—dc 19   88–3769
ISBN 0-19-281793-0

Set by Grove Graphics
Printed in Great Britain by
Hazell Watson & Viney Ltd.,
Aylesbury, Bucks.

CONTENTS

CONTENTS

INTRODUCTION

'*Make me young, make me young, make me young*' pleads one of the fictional characters to the author at the end of Kurt Vonnengut's *Breakfast of Champions*. When Mark Twain had finished reading the second instalment of *Indian Summer*, he wrote to his old friend Howells:

You are my only author; I am restricted to you; I wouldn't give a damn for the rest . . . I have just read Part II of Indian Summer, & to my mind there isn't a waste line in it, or one that could be improved. I read it yesterday, ending with that opinion; & read it again to-day, ending with the same opinion emphasised . . . It is a beautiful story & makes a body laugh all the time, & cry inside, & feel so old & so forlorn; & gives him gracious glimpses of his lost youth that fill him with a measureless regret, & build up in him a cloudy sense of his having been a prince, once, in some enchanted far-off land, & of being in exile now, & desolate—& lord, no chance ever to get back there again! That is the thing that hurts. Well, you have done it with marvelous facility—& you make all the motives & feelings perfectly clear without analyzing the guts out of them, the way George Eliot does.

This intensely wistful and even rather sentimental effusion was written long before Mark Twian would have reached one of the last conversations in the book, between Colville and Mrs Bowen, which explicitly articulates the theme, the mood, the regret which is constantly adumbrated and sounded in different tones and registers throughout the novel:

'I heard just such singing before I fell asleep the night after that party at Madame Uccelli's, and it filled me with fury.'
'Why should it do that?'
'I don't know. It seemed like voices from our youth—Lina.'
She had no resentment of his use of her name in the tone with which she asked: 'Did you hate that so much?'
'No; the loss of it.'
They both fetched a deep breath.

It is doubtless a theme as universal as it is ancient, but the idealizing, one might even say the fetishizing, of youth and the attendant resistances to, and exaggerated horror at, the signs of age are proclivities and dispositions experienced or indulged with quite peculiar intensity in America. How much this has to do with the privileging of the child in American culture, or with the mythology of Adamic innocence, newness, new beginnings, inextricably intertwined with the nurturing and flaunting of the young republic in the New World, is perhaps idle to speculate. But more than any other national literature, the literature of America has celebrated, mythologized, idolized, cherished, worshipped, recalled, re-created, relived youth—or mourned and lamented the loss of what so many writers imagine it, or want it, or perhaps unconsciously will it, to have been. Needless to say, this inclination or obsession can produce writing of very different degrees of richness and subtlety, with sentimentality an ever-present danger, and lachrymosity not far behind. But it is possible for the obsession or tendency to be submitted to some kind of critical or ironic examination—put in larger and longer perspectives than it itself furnishes or allows—and then you can have a literature of wit, sophistication, even, if one may say it, wisdom. *Indian Summer* is such a work.

Howells was perfectly clear about the organizing intent of the novel, writing to Edmund Gosse in December 1883 that he was 'far into the heart of a new story, the idea of which pleases me greatly. It is that of a man whose youth was broken sharp off in Florence twenty years ago, and who after a busy newspaper life in our West, fancies that he can renew his youth by going back to Italy. There he falls in love with a girl young enough to be his daughter. It is largely a study of the feelings of middle-life in contrast with those of earlier years.' A study of the 'feelings of middle-life' it certainly is, as the opening words of the novel tactfully suggest by positioning Colville 'lounging'—indecisive, suspended, isolated, vague—'Midway of the Ponte Vecchio'. He is in the middle of life's journey and he has indeed lost his way, or rather not found or formed one. What is to happen to him is rather more complicated than Howells suggests in his outline since he only thinks he has fallen in love with Imogene, or, more subtly, thinks he has fallen in love with the idea that she has thought herself into the appropriateness of being in love with him. Imogene is well into the romance of noble self-sacrifice and reparation. 'I want you to feel that *I* am your youth—the youth you were robbed of—given back to you', she cries to Colville. He is not deluded but he feebly capitulates to a situation, in the making of which he has at least culpably colluded, and which he, arguably, irresponsibly provoked and promoted. He complains or confesses to Mr Waters: 'I have lived my life, such as it is. But the child is full of fancies about me that can't be fulfilled. She dreams of restoring my youth somehow, of retrieving the past for me . . . Sometimes I think that the kindest—the least cruel—thing I could do would be to break with her, to leave her. But I know that I shall do nothing of the kind; I shall drift.' There is something hapless about his extreme passivity, and Howells has to enlist a wild horse to trample him into unconsciousness and out of responsibility for a decision which is clearly beyond his capacity. It is Imogene who comes to her senses while he is, appropriately, out of his.

It is a peculiar feature of this state of 'mid-wayness'—this mid-life crisis, perhaps—that life seems definitively elsewhere, while the present seems to be a site of loss, emptiness, formless futility—Carlyle's 'centre of indifference'. Colville comes to Italy from America in quest of renewal, 'drained and feeble', and finds himself in a state of dazed disorientation attendant on unemployment, for his occupation is very decidedly gone. Feeling that 'an objectless life was disgraceful to a man', he nevertheless fails to find any real 'object', any point or project to awaken and sustain motivation and direction. In his state of suspended vacillation he is a man waiting for a motive. He seems to have no volition. He continually contrives to get others to take his decisions for him—most notably and, really, shamefully leaving it to Imogene to decide whether they are formally engaged or not. In what is effectively their last conversation, when she asks him, with some understandable exasperation, 'what do you intend to do?', she has chosen just the right word. Colville has lost all relationship with intentionality. When he limply offers to defer entirely to her wishes, her response again goes to the heart, or heartlessness, of the man: 'Do *you* wish nothing?' He might rationalize his paralysis by maintaining that he is still trying to do the most honourable—the least dishonourable—thing, but what Howells is diagnosing and depicting is a crippling weakness of will, the death of desire. Having decided to leave Florence he allows himself to talk himself out of it. 'Better stay, then, something said to him; and when he answered "I will", something else reminded him that this also was not willing but unwilling.' Colville, corpulent, indolent, finding it difficult to stay awake, and to struggle up out of chairs; fussing about his rheumatism and the room temperature; yawning, bored, and looking at his watch; consuming endless cups of tea in an endless series of rooms, is an American Superfluous Man, with a touch of Oblomov and perhaps a hint of Baudelairean ennui. He is, not surprisingly, particularly happy as a convalescent, easily reconciled to 'a life of inaction and oblivion'. Howells conveys very well Colville's sense of himself 'crumbling away' in random momentary impulses, dissolving 'in one abortive intent and another', trying somehow to clasp and comprehend 'the secret of his failure in life'. It is in this light, I think, that we should see his endless 'banter', his 'tone of persiflage' which Imogene finds, briefly, 'intoxicating', his compulsive facetiousness which so delights little Effie, and which indeed delighted Henry James. 'Theodore Colville, in *Indian Summer*, is so irrepressibly and happily facetious as to make one wonder whether the author is not prompting him a little, and whether he could be quite so amusing without help from outside.' Curiously, I think James has missed a point. Colville's constant recourse to banter is perhaps a mark of some degree of urbanity and sophistication; but it is also self-protective, defensive, anxious, even desperate. Banter is what Colville tries to employ to fill up the gaps and vacancies of feeling, motive, and desire. His 'bantering talk' is, as Howells exactly formulates it, 'a respite from the formless future pressing close upon him'. It is his only occupation. Even Imogene, who feels herself seduced by Colville's mechanical banter, at last cries out against it. 'Oh, don't joke about it! This perpetual joking, I believe it's that that's wearing me out.' The jesting indeed becomes 'dreary' to all concerned, including, particularly, Colville. It is a symptom, not a

relief; a sickness, not a grace. It could be seen as an indication of a more profound impotence.

Howells is fastidious to the point of prudishness about
sexual matters (despite having written about a squalid
divorce case in his previous novel, *A Modern Instance*), and
there is a minimum amount of physicality in this novel. The
turning-point in Colville's relationship with Imogene occurs
when he simply lays his hand on hers. In this world of avoided or denied bodily contacts, this is tantamount to a plea or
a proposition. Consider, then, this description of Colville's
reaction to a small degree of physical initiative from Imogene, some time after he has, in his evasive non-commital
way, 'committed' himself to her, and she to him. 'She pulled
him to the sofa, and put his arm about her waist, with a simple fearlessness and matter-of-course promptness that made
him shudder . . . She took hold of his hand and drew his lax
arm taut.' Howells, I am sure, meant no more than he
wrote, but the spectacle of a beautiful young female trying
to arouse this prematurely aged man to some sort of appropriate masculine 'tautness' surely suggests some deeper
'laxness' or laxity in Colville, a positive fear of all the
energies and entanglements of the erotic. It is his *verbal*
power over Imogene which gives him gratification: 'he felt
the witchery of his power to make this young, radiant, and
beautiful creature hang flattered and bewildered on his talk.'
He is, indeed, playing with Imogene, 'amused at her
seriousness', but he uses talk as much to avoid feelings as to
articulate them, just as he had addressed his young love 'in
words and phrases that, taken in themselves, had no
meaning—that neither committed him nor claimed her'.
This indeed is neutered speech, or talking to neuter, and
Colville's pleasure in the oral (not just banter, for at the
dance we see him 'cramming himself with all the solids and
fluids in sight'—his one hundred and eighty-five pounds are
not surprising!) is surely a compensation and cover for a
profound fear of the sexual. We may think that the lady who
rejected him in his youth and thus saved him from the
disturbing intensities of sexual intimacy was putting it
mildly when she called him 'too much of a mixture'. When

Imogene described him as making you feel 'that he has exhausted all feeling', it provokes one to wonder just how much feeling there was to exhaust.

One particular aspect or result of the onset of the 'feelings of middle life' is the sense of being no longer young but not yet ready to accept the classification of 'old'—however old *old* may be—with all that it is felt to apply. This period of hesitation between generational identity, in which a man 'stands at pause', so to speak, is given an added twist for an American in Europe since America is youth and Europe is, of course, old, old, old. Colville is thus in a paradoxical position. He is an American who, finding life in America dull and insipid (people never go out, there is no real society, etc.), has come to Europe for rejuvenation. To compound the irony it is the benign, Emersonian Mr Waters, happily expatriated in Florence (and among other things, this novel is an early and subtle study of the various modes and manners of American expatriation), who acts as both a counsellor and a warning to Colville. It is he who utters what must be taken as the wisdom of the book in his paean to the felicities of the age of 40 at the middle of the book (in Chapter XI): 'We are in a sort of quiet in which we peacefully enjoy. We have enlarged our perspective sufficiently to perceive things in their true proportion and relation . . . we have got into the habit of life . . . it is a beautiful age.' It is this amiable scourge of the absurdities of puritanism who effectively points Colville in the appropriate direction of Mrs Bowen. But it is also the sight of Mr Waters, immersed and content in his studies, placidly resigned to the solace offered by 'the magic of the book', which provokes a crucial momet of resistance in Colville, just exactly the critical moment.

Colville stared after him; he did not wish to come to just that, either. Life, active life, life of his own day, called to him; he had been one of its busiest children: could he turn his back upon it for any charm or use that was in the past? Again that unnerving doubt, that paralysing distrust, beset him, and tempted him to curse the day in which he had returned to this outworn Old World. Idler on its modern surface, or delver in its deep-hearted past, could he reconcile himself to it? What did he care for the Italians of today, or the history of the Florentines as expressed in their architectural monuments? It was the problems of the vast, tumultuous American life, which he had turned his back on, that really concerned him. Later he might take up the study that fascinated yonder old man, but for the present it was intolerable. He was no longer young, that was true; but with an ache of old regret he felt that he had not yet lived his life, that his was a baffled destiny, an arrested fate.

This is the epiphanic moment of uncertainty which always awaits the figure of the American expatriate and Howells shows real insight and originality in his depiction of it.

Howells generously conceded to Henry James the distinction of having first discerned the potentialities of 'the international theme'—Americans in Europe and the effects they have on each other. In fact, his own first international novel, *A Foregone Conclusion*, is exactly contemporaneous with James's, *Roderick Hudson*—both appearing in 1875. However, there is no point in discussing primacy. The important thing to remember is that Howells produced pioneering and important 'international' novels of his own, including of course *Indian Summer*. In connection with the concluding words of the last long extract, it is particularly interesting and apt that Henry James's *The Ambassadors* owes its origin to a very Colvillean sort of remark made by Howells to a young man in Paris, which provided the inaugural germ. Howells told the young Jonathan Sturges to 'live all you can', adding that for himself it was too late, he was too old, but that Sturges was young and should 'Live!' Sturges told James and James conceived of Lambert Strether, who also tells a young man in Paris to 'Live all you can. It's a shame not to.' Of course the problem is thus posed, what exactly is it to 'live'? James, bolder and more probing than Howells, could see that matters concerning sexual pleasure and fulfilment were both involved and implied. Howells, always more reticent, and perhaps more simply frightened by sexual matters, hardly confronts—indeed conspicuously avoids naming and entering—the zone of the sexual; yet the gentle polemics given to Mr Waters against the damaging effects of the 'hysterical excess of Puritanism' on America suggests that he was well aware of the sexual impoverishment—if not impotence—implied by the pervading sense of loss, unsatisfaction, unnamable frustration, and inarticulate regret experienced by Colville—and the extreme mechanisms of repression which must somewhere lie behind his gasping sense of unfulfilment. And it is perfectly appropriate to see James's Strether as another version of the Colville type, only older and thus perhaps more plausibly disclined to consider— indeed ruling as out of the question—sexual relationships, up to and including marriage by the end. Colville, to be sure, ends by marrying Mrs Bowen and to that extent is notionally admitted into the sexual order. But she is a firm American puritan and we can hardly imagine her so determinedly drawing his 'lax arm taut' like the boisterously adolescent Imogene in her one doomed attempt to arouse him!

As well as a study of the vacillations, hesitations, and temporizings of an expatriate consciousness, the novel is also, of course, a love story. Even, we might say, three love stories, for Colville effectively seeks to enchant Effie with his humour, impress Imogene with his suffering and melancholy maturity, and win Mrs Bowen with his sophistication and gallantry. There is one amusing moment when Colville, by now 'engaged' to, or at least formally involved with, Imogene, finds himself effectively making up to Mrs Bowen and saying words that sound improperly ingratiating, indeed using very much the language of courtship. He stares after his own words in surprise and embar-

rassment, and Howells comments, with that confident aphoristic tone which is a mark of his style, that Colville was 'struggling stupidly with a confusion of desires which every man but no woman will understand. After eighteen hundred years the man is still imperfectly monogamous.' This is almost brave on Howells's part since he is effectively stating that a man can be sexually attracted to more than one woman at the same time, indeed that, at least momentarily, any woman may arouse an interest, an instinct to woo, in a man. It is a mark of his somewhat ponderous gentility that he, as it were, de-eroticizes the declaration by muffling it in the sombre polysyllabicism of 'imperfectly monogamous'. We may take it as a sign of his patriarchal times that he so confidently excludes the possibility that the same truth might obtain in the case of the woman! This possibility of the multiplicity or repetition of desire and attraction across women of different generations was perhaps most remarkably explored in that novel of Thomas Hardy's so admired by Proust, *The Well-Beloved*, in which a man falls successively in love with a woman, her daughter, and her grand-daughter. But Howells gives some intimations of it from the start, when Colville finds Effie and her mother 'bewitchingly alike' and at the conclusion of his first meeting with them 'was rewarded with two pretty smiles, just alike, from mother and her daughter'.

From the start, Howells had made a speciality of studying and scrutinizing American women in a non-romantic light. In this, as in so much else, he was innovative in American fiction, with Henry James, as so often, following in his own unique way. The studies, or portraits, of the witty Kitty Ellison in *A Chance Acquaintance*, the independent Lydia Blood, who is *The Lady of the Aroostock* who sails to Venice unchaperoned, the temperamental Florida Vervain in *A Foregone Conclusion*, the theatrical *femme fatale* Mrs Farrell in *Private Theatricals*, the economically lost Helen Harkness in *A Woman's Reason*, the professional Grace Breen, who gives up medicine for love in *Dr. Breen's Practice*, and, most notably, Marcia Gaylord, the new American 'Medea', in *A Modern Instance*, all these are indicative of and products of Howells's concern with the position and role—and plight and fate—of woman in American society as they were developing after the Civil War. Some of his attitudes to women may now seem somewhat patronizing and deeply bound in convention, but he had precious little to build on in previous American fiction, in which women tend to be angels or allegories or clichés. Contemporary fiction was, to Howells's eye, intolerably and dangerously romantic and sentimental, particularly in its treatment of women, and it was a real achievement on his part to create a series of sympathetic, critical, plausible, and astute portraits of individuated women of authentic contemporary American pedigree. There was a very real social need for this kind of work. As one contemporary admirer of Howells put it, Howells was concerned with the 'emotional anarchy' in

America in which 'an emotion is so sacred a thing that not only no outsider but not even its possessor may presume to undertake its regulation', thus leaving America 'a society without an emotional code'.

It is in the light of this attempt to begin to outline some kind of emotional code that we should appreciate Howells's gentle but firm critique of what he saw as the related temptations and vices of perverse 'self-sacrifice' and myopic egotism. Thus in a note for the novel, Howells stresses that 'Imogene shd typify the fatuous egotism of youth. She never imagines Mrs. B. in love.' And the ending of the novel, over which he took great care, while 'happy' in a conventional sense, in fact includes, or concludes, what has been a subtle but incisive—and fairly devastating—ironic critique of Mrs Bowen. As Edwin Cady noted, she is, in large measure, responsible for the errors of Imogene and even those of Colville, since she knows exactly what is going on and how self-deceived or self-deceiving the other two are, yet out of a perverse pride will do nothing to stop it—indeed does much to promote it. Cady's words are apt: 'The truth is that she has been infected with grand illusions, with an almost monstrous romantic *hubris* . . . she dramatizes herself as the blameless matron, the perfect duenna, antiseptically mounted above the reach of the human emotions to which the girl in charge is subject and from which she must be protected.' At the end, when she initially rejects Colville's proposal with a dramatic 'Never!', she embarks on a discourse of extreme moral outrage, invoking 'self-respect' and complaining histrionically of her 'humiliation', 'degradation'— 'you made me violate every principle that was dear to me'. Striking a pose of high-mindedly sacrificing her love for her dignity, it seems she will let Colville retreat with his tail where it usually is—between his legs. It is only the direct cry of Effie which resolves the perverse and sterile impasse which Mrs Bowen threatens to impose. And the last sentence, describing her reluctant capitulation, shows Howells's irony at its most effective. '"Oh, you must stay!" said Lina, in the self-contemptuous voice of a woman who falls below her ideal of herself.' Howells spent a good deal of his life

campaigning against misplaced and mischievous notions of
'the ideal'—both in art and in life—and his portrait of Mrs
Bowen is one of his most subtle, and powerful, demonstrations of how pride and distorted egotism may be masked by
intense and often self-mystifying invocations of ideals of
'self-sacrifice' which, both in her case and Imogene's, would
in fact have involved self-mutilation. It is not an unsym-
pathetic portrait, however, and indeed his first description of
Mrs Bowen shows Howells at his most delicate, civilized,
and urbane.

Lady-like was the word for Mrs. Bowen throughout—for the turn
of her head, the management of her arm from the elbow, the curve
of her hand from the wrist to finger-tips, the smile, subdued, but
sufficiently sweet, playing about her little mouth, which was yet not
too little, and the refined and indefinite perfume which exhaled
from the ensemble of her silks, her laces, and her gloves, like an
odorous version of that otherwise impalpable quality which women
call style. She had, with all her flexibility, a certain charming stiffness, like the stiffness of a very tall feather. (Ch. II)

The tone and touch are alike impeccable, courteous; and the
concluding simile shows Howells's style at its most felicitous.

The atmosphere of the book is autumnal, wistful, as befits
an Indian summer, and there is much in the book that has
the quality of a late-afternoon idyll with the shadows just
beginning to lengthen. This, and its Florentine setting, con-
tribute greatly to the very real charm and quiet pleasures of
the novel, which remained Howells's personal favourite. It
was to have been called 'September and May' and there are
many references to the seasons, the climate, the temperature
indoors and out (and, by implication, inside the
characters—the fire in the hotel dining-room of which 'the
warmth was potential rather than actual' may be said to
shed a flickering light on the varying capacity for emotional
heat of the characters). The action takes place in winter
moving forward into spring—or is it backwards? By the end
Mrs Bowen looks 'younger and prettier'. Perhaps she, at
least, has drunk of the fountain of youth in the Boboli
Gardens, which Colville sadly recalls. 'The slow, orderly

advance of the Italian spring' is compared to 'the rush of the American spring' and there is some consideration of the joys of the flowers of spring as compared with 'the pleasant little fire on the hearth' which winter ordains. Indeed, there is an unusually large number of references to indoor fires and more than one chapter concludes with a description of just such a fire flaring up or fading to embers—unobtrusively keeping alive the central question of to what extent the fires of youthful intensity of appreciation and desire can be rekindled. The Italian background also glows and fades alternately as Howells fills out the settings with somewhat dogged detailing—there is none of the sheer magic of Henry James's 'sense of place' here. In some ways this is appropriate, since for Colville 'some charm' has gone out of the 'operatic spectacle of Florence'—somewhat wearily inventoried by Howells. Instead of his youthful 'rapture' his response is now 'faint and thin'. There was a straight autobiographical basis for this, as there often is in Howells's fiction.

Howells had first gone to Italy in 1861 when he was 24. He had been awarded the consulate at Venice as a reward for his campaign biography of Lincoln and he did not return to America until 1865 (thus missing the Civil War— something about which he always felt guilty). He immersed himself in Venice and Italian culture (the consular duties were notably unexacting), and if his response was somewhat lower-keyed than Henry James's, it was nevertheless a period of revelation and excitement, of expansion and growth, for the young Howells, who at that time still aspired to be a poet. (His careful, scrupulous documentations of his impressions gathered in this period were published in *Venetian Life* and *Italian Journeys*.) On his return to America he worked for the *Atlantic Monthly*, finally, from 1871 to 1881, as editor. The immeasurable importance of that editorship for American literature, indeed for American culture (encouraging new young writers such as Mark Twain and Henry James, introducing America to the great writers of Europe—Flaubert, Tolstoy, Turgenev, and literally hundreds of others then almost unknown in America), is deservedly a well-known story. In 1881 he became perhaps the first true American man of letters, making his living solely by his pen. He was working on *A Modern Instance* at the time and finishing it left him in a state of exhaustion. His daughter Winifred was also ill, so in 1882 he decided to take his family back to Italy—to rejuvenate himself, rather like Colville. He was disappointed with Venice: 'the poor old place is forlorner and shabbier than ever. I don't think I began to see the misery of it when I lived here', he wrote to Mark Twain. And to Thomas Sergeant Perry: 'I have been . . . putting myself in rapport with Italy again. But I'm not sure that it pays. After all, *we* have the country of the present and the future.' How much of Colville's disillusion is Howells's own may thus be guessed. His age, like his weight, is roughly Howells's own! Howells spent the winter and spring in Florence, gathering material for another travel book, *Tuscan Cities*, but he was very glad to return to America in July of 1883. We may consider *Indian Summer*, with its modulated regrets and nostalgia, the mellow fruit of that return visit. In a way it was Howells's fond valedictory to Italy—and youth.

The tone and timbre of Howells's writing are quite distinctive and represent the sounding of a new note in American literature. 'Describe closely and realistically, keep the tone low', he once wrote to his sister. It has been rather more usual for American writers to keep the tone markedly high, aspiring to new reaches of thought and expression, moving towards the frontiers and edges of experiential possibilities seeking out the further, more remote areas of life and feeling, going—in short—to extremes. In his own way, Howells sought to civilize American writing, to rein in its wildness, chastise and chasten its appetite for romance, educate it out of its deplorable tendency to opt for sentimentality (what he called 'effectism'), open it to the tempered maturity of writers such as Flaubert and Turgenev. That, in his efforts along these lines, he was in danger of making American writing bourgeois, genteel, tame, even of emasculating it, later writers, feeling somehow hampered under the benign

hegemony of his immense authority, would predictably—
and perhaps understandably—claim. Yet he was absolutely indispensable for American literature, indeed for the
bringing of America—the knowable, meetable, measur-
able, tangible, unavoidable, contemporary America—into
literature.

In his first novel, which characteristically was basically
autobiography and travelogue, Howells tried simply to see
the American scene. *Their Wedding Journey* (1871) opens with
Howells self-deprecatingly 'distrusting my fitness for a sustained or involved narration' and promising only 'to talk of
some ordinary traits of American life . . . to speak a little of
well-known and easily accessible places, to present now a bit
of landscape and now a sketch of character'. He is going to
keep the tone low. It is while describing some desultory conversation between a young man and woman on a Hudson
River boat that he makes a declaration which would become
famous. 'Ah! poor Real Life, which I love, can I make
others share the delight I find in thy foolish and insipid face?'
Such an avuncular and cosy—and patronizing—attitude to
'Real Life' will hardly seem a very exciting prescription for
fiction, indeed for any kind of writing, and the degree of
blandness and complacency that we hear in the words is
always a possible danger in Howells's writing; but we should
bear in mind just how little of 'Real' American life was finding its way into fiction at that time. Another incident and comment perhaps indicate more clearly what Howells was attempting to bring about. The couple—Basil and Isabel March (the
slightest of fictional covers for William Dean and Elinor Mead
Howells)—visit the Genesee Falls at Rochester. The Falls are
sublimely beautiful. Basil points out a rock from which one,
Sam Patch, had made a celebrated and fatal leap. Isabel rejects the association: 'Patch! What a name to be linked in our
thoughts with this superb cataract.' This allows Basil to
launch into a Howells manifesto.

Well, Isabel, I think you are very unjust. It's as good a name as
Leander, to my thinking, and it was immortalized in support of a
great idea—the feasibility of all things; while Leander's has come
down to us as that of a weak victim of passion. We shall never have

a poetry of our own till we get over this absurd reluctance from facts, till we make the ideal embrace and include the real, till we consent to face the music in our common names, and put Smith into a lyric and Jones into a tragedy.

There is, perhaps, something a little naïve in the formulation, but it is heartfelt and, quite as sincerely as Whitman, Howells worked and wrote for the true democratization of literature—though Whitman included facts, from which Howells had a particular reluctance. (In an early—1860—essay on Whitman, Howells showed his disquiet, or disgust: 'He has told too much . . . the secrets of the body should be decently hid . . . Whitman goes through his book, like one in an ill-conditioned dream, perfectly nude, with his clothes over his arm.')

It is, however, a mark of Howells's realism that he aimed to keep the tone *particularly* low. When the Marches are enjoying 'A Day's Railroading', Howells makes this comment.

It was in all respects an ordinary carful of human beings, and it was perhaps the more worthy to be studied on that account. As in literature the true artist will shun the use even of real events if they are of an improbable character, so the sincere observer of man will not desire to look upon his heroic or occasional phases, but will seek him in his habitual moods of vacancy and tiresomeness . . . I never perceive him to be so much a man and brother as when I feel the pressure of his vast, natural, unaffected dulness.'

Such a realism is not only low; it is potentially lowering. In seeking to avoid and eradicate the worst excesses of romantic literature, Howells is in danger of narrowing the spectrum of legitimate fictional concerns quite impossibly. But, again, this must be seen as polemical, a redressing of the balance, an insistence on looking at the usually unlooked-at.

Over the years, Howells's concept of realism matured and broadened and deepened (though never, really, to include the sexual). It must be remembered that there was very little coherent theory of fiction available at that time, in America or indeed in England. In his ongoing discussions of realism, Howells was working to formulate the new possibilities and responsibilities of fiction.

In this connection it is worth mentioning an important article by Howells on Henry James which was published in 1882 (while he was on his return trip to Europe) and which is thus from the period just before he started writing *Indian Summer* (published in 1886). In it he made a statement which seems unexceptionable now, but which caused outrage and fury in England at the time.

The art of fiction, has, in fact, become a finer art in our day than it was with Dickens and Thackeray. We would not suffer the confidential attitude of the latter now, nor the mannerism of the former, any more than we could endure the prolixity of a Richardson or the coarseness of Fielding . . . The new school . . . studies human nature much more in its wonted aspects, and finds its ethical and dramatic examples in the operation of lighter but not really less vital motives. The moving accident is certainly not its trade; and it prefers to avoid all manner of dire catastrophes. It is largely influenced by French fiction in form . . . This school, which is so largely of the future as well as the present, finds its chief exemplar in Mr. James . . . Will the reader be content to accept a novel which is an analytic study rather than a story, which is apt to leave him arbiter of the author's creations?

Now 'analyst' was something of a dirty word when it came to discussing novelists around this time. If a novelist was an 'analyst' it usually meant that his work would offer a 'dissection of some moral cancer' and 'a show of stolid indifference to high ideals and "imaginative lift"' (this from Maurice Thompson in 1886 who, we may note, goes on to exonerate Howells from the charge of being a real 'analyst' because he is so 'clean . . . so sane in his imaginings' and has 'one of the finest and sweetest imaginations that America has had'). Though a champion of 'analysts' and analytic fiction, Howells was not really an 'analyst' nor did he regard himself as one. Nevertheless he was criticized because his characters seemed 'clinically studied' and later his own work would be attacked for his air of almost scientific detachment, indeed for being too 'analytic'. It is necessary to remember the resistance to even Howells's 'clean' realism, the antagonism it aroused, to realize what he was up against. An American, Catholic reviewer of *The Rise of Silas Lapham*, for instance, saw Howells's realism as being a form of Darwinism, and that was simply 'the descent to dirt'. More articulately and temperately, a critic named Hamilton Wright Mabie, also reviewing *Silas Lapham* (which, incidentally, was written largely concurrently with *Indian Summer* and in fact published one year earlier) made the case against realism in a way which enables us to understand what was perceived to be at stake.

But modern realism knows nothing of any revelation in human life; of any spiritual facts of which its facts are significant; of any spiritual laws to which they conform in the unbroken order of the Universe. It does more than ignore these things; it denies them. Under the conditions which it imposes art can see nothing but the isolated physical fact before it; there is no infinite blue heaven over it. It forms no part of a universal order; it discovers no common law; it can never be a type of a great class. It is, in a word, practical atheism applied to art. It not only empties the world of the Ideal, but, as Zola frankly says, it denies 'the good God'; it dismisses the old heaven of aspiration and possible fulfillment as an idle dream; it destroys the significance of life and the interpretative quality of art.

Howells kept his distance from Zola, but he certainly wanted to empty the world of all cant about 'the Ideal'. For the rest, he thought that the significance of life would speak for itself, if life was truly and scrupulously represented, and as for interpretation, that should be left to the reader. We now find matters connected with respresentation and 'the real' a good deal more problematic than Howells seems to have done. But he was pointing fiction towards the modern world.

Writing of Howells in 1886, Henry James singled out for praise 'his unerring sentiment of the American character'. 'Other persons have considered and discoursed upon American life, but no one, surely, has *felt* it as completely as he. I will not say that Mr. Howells feels it all equally, for are we not perpetually conscious of how vast and deep it is?— but he is an authority upon many of those parts of it which are most representative.' He adds that 'his work is of a kind of which it is good that there should be much to-day—work of observation, of patient and definite notation'. And he

goes on to provide a fair and generous assessment of
Howells's virtues and predilections and attitudes which can
hardly be bettered.

He is animated by a love of the common, the immediate, the
familiar and vulgar elements of life, and holds that in proportion
as we move into the rare and strange we become vague and
arbitrary; that truth of representation, in a word, can be achieved
only so long as it is in our power to test and measure it. He thinks
scarcely anything too paltry to be interesting, that the small and the
vulgar have been terribly neglected, and would rather see an exact
account of a sentiment or a character he stumbles against every day
than a brilliant evocation of a passion or a type he has never seen
and does not even particularly believe in. He adores the real, the
colloquial, the moderate, the optimistic, the domestic, and the
democratic; looking askance at exceptions and perversities and
superiorities, at surprising and incongruous phenomena in general.
One must have seen a great deal before one concludes; the world
is very large, and life is a mixture of many things; she by no means
eschews the strange, and often risks combinations and effects that
make one rub one's eyes. Nevertheless, Mr. Howells's stand-point
is an excellent one for seeing a large part of the truth, and if it were
less advantageous, there would be a great deal to admire in the
firmness with which he has planted himself.

The good-natured delicacy of the stricture does not conceal
James's sense of the limitations, and possible defects, in
Howells's prescriptions for fiction. He touches on another
notable absence or exclusion a shade more firmly—though
quite as good-naturedly. 'If American life is on the whole,
as I make no doubt whatever, more innocent than that of
any other country, nowhere is the fact more patent than in
Mr. Howells's novels, which exhibit so constant a study of
the actual and so small a perception of evil.' It is perhaps
amusing that in *Indian Summer* the cheerful confidence of
Mr Waters as to the innocence of the carnival and
masquerade—with all the sexual licence and intoxication
which they permit (a very little of which Howells allows into
his book, well diluted and laundered)—prompts Colville to
remember 'reading once in a passage from Swedenborg, that
the most celestial angels had scarcely any power of perceiving evil'. Whether in Howells's own case it was an inability

or a disinclination is necessarily a moot point, but although his outlook on life darkened as he got older, and tensions, corruptions, violence, and widespread economic distress appeared on the surface of American society, James is right—Howells has no real vision of evil. He can see, and conscientiously transcribe, injustice, inequality, squalor, cruelty, hardship, and pain, even murder and slaughter. But there is no sense of *evil*—the real Iago thing. It is why his novels lack an ultimate tension, urgency, force. They are just a little slack, just a shade too at-ease and comfortable with themselves. This effect is compounded by one other tendency which James gently rebuked. 'I should also venture to express a certain regret that Mr. Howells . . . should appear increasingly to hold composition too cheap—by which I mean, should neglect the effect that comes from alternation, distribution, relief.' It would have to be admitted that Howells's theory of fiction and ideas about the art of the novel are crude indeed beside James's.

But none of this matters in connection with *Indian Summer*. The tone is comic, ironic, and elegiac, and corrigible folly rather than irremediable evil is the order of the day. And it is—I think—the most subtly, carefully, and felicitously composed of his novels. It is, thus, perhaps more appropriate to conclude with the appreciative words which Henry James's brother, William, sent to Howells after he finished reading the novel: 'it has given me about as exquisite a kind of delight as anything I ever read in my life, in the line to which it belongs. How you tread the narrow line of nature's truth so infallibly is more than I can understand. Then the profanity, the humor, the humanity, the morality—the everything! In short, 'tis cubical, and set it up any way you please, 't will stand.'

NOTE ON THE TEXT

Indian Summer first appeared in monthly instalments in *Harper's Monthly* in the USA between July 1885 and February 1886. The present text is taken from the first British edition, by David Douglas of Edinburgh, which was published in March 1886. The same plates were used for the first American edition, which was published a month earlier by Ticknor & Co. of Boston.

SELECT BIBLIOGRAPHY

FICTION BY HOWELLS

Selected Edition of W. D. Howells (Bloomington, Indiana: Modern Language Association), ed. E. Cady, R. Gottesman, D. Norloh; in several volumes, and including all the works cited below.

Novels 1875–1886 (New York: Viking Library of America, 2nd printing 1982), includes *A Foregone Conclusion, A Modern Instance, Indian Summer, The Rise of Silas Lapham.*

A Modern Instance (Harmondsworth: Penguin, 1977), introd. Edwin H. Cady.

The Rise of Silas Lapham (New York: Norton Critical Edition, 1982), ed. Don L. Cook.

—— (Harmondsworth: Penguin, 1983), introd. Kermit Vanderbilt.

A Hazard of New Fortunes (London: Oxford University Press, 1965), ed. Tony Tanner.

LETTERS

Mildred Howells (daughter), *A Life in Letters of W. D. Howells* (New York: Doubleday, 1929), 2 vols.

Mark Twain–Howells Letters; the correspondence of S. L. Clemens and W. D. Howells 1872–1910 (Cambridge, Mass.: Belknap Press, 1967), ed. Henry Nash Smith, William Gibson, 2 vols.; the same editors also produced a one-volume selection.

BIOGRAPHY

Edwin H. Cady, *The Road to Realism; the early years, 1837–1885, of William Dean Howells* (Syracuse, New York: Syracuse University Press, 1956).

—— *The Realist at War; the mature years, 1885–1920, of William Dean Howells* (Syracuse, New York: Syracuse University Press, 1958).

Mildred Howells, as above.

Kenneth S. Lynn, *William Dean Howells: an American life* (New York: Harcourt, Brace, Jovanovich, 1971).

CRITICISM

Critical Essays on W. D. Howells, 1866–1920 (Boston: G. K. Hall, 1983), ed. Edwin H. Cady and Norma W. Cady.

Howells; a century of criticism (Dallas: Southern Methodist University

Press, 1962), ed. Kenneth Edle; includes articles on Howells by Twain, James, and Hamlin Garland.

Everett Carter, *Howells and the Age of Realism* (New York: Lippincott, 1954).

John W. Crowley, *The Black Heart's Truth: the early career of W. D. Howells* (Chapel Hill: University of North Carolina Press, 1985).

Olov Fryckstedt, *In Quest of America: a study of Howells's early development as a novelist* (Cambridge, Mass.: Harvard University Press, 1958).

Kermit Vanderbilt, *The Achievement of William Dean Howells; a reinterpretation* (Princeton, NJ: Princeton University Press, 1968).

BIBLIOGRAPHIES

William Gibson and George Arms, *A Bibliography of W. D. Howells* (New York Public Library, 1948).

American Literary Realism, Howells special number (1969), includes extensive bibliographies, with more recent material.

A CHRONOLOGY OF
WILLIAM DEAN HOWELLS

1837   Born in Martinsville, Ohio, the son of William Cooper Howells, a printer and publisher of various papers in Ohio, with Swedenborgian leanings and radical political views.

1853–60   Trained as a printer and largely self-educated, Howells works as a journalist in Cincinatti and other cities in Ohio, and publishes essays, poems, and stories in the major Eastern magazines.

1861–5   As reward for writing Lincoln's campaign biography, he is made US Consul in Venice for the duration of the Civil War. Marries Elinor Mead in 1862.

1866–70   Becomes assistant editor of the *Atlantic Monthly* in Cambridge, Mass., where he moves in literary circles which include Longfellow, Lowell, and Holmes, of the older generation, and William and Henry James. Publishes two Italian travel books.

1871   Becomes editor of the *Atlantic Monthly*, which serializes works by James and Mark Twain, and carries essays by progressive thinkers on social issues.

1872   *Their Wedding Journey* published.

1873   *A Chance Acquaintance.*

1875   *A Foregone Conclusion; Private Theatricals.*

1879   *The Lady of the Aroostock.*

1881   Established as a novelist, Howells resigns as editor of the *Atlantic Monthly*. Publishes *Dr. Breen's Practice*; *A Fearful Responsibility.*

1882   *A Modern Instance.*

1883   *A Woman's Reason.*

1883–4   Writes *Indian Summer* after return to Italy in 1882.

1885   *The Rise of Silas Lapham.*

1886   *Indian Summer.*

1887   Pleads publically for the lives of Chicago anarchists wrongly convicted of murder in the Haymarket Riots.

Indian Summer

I

MIDWAY of the Ponte Vecchio* at Florence, where three
arches break the lines of the little jewellers' booths glittering
on either hand, and open an approach to the parapet, Colville lounged against the corner of a shop and stared out
upon the river. It was the late afternoon of a day in January,
which had begun bright and warm, but had suffered a
change of mood as its hours passed, and now, from a sky
dimmed with flying grey clouds, was threatening rain.
There must already have been rain in the mountains, for the
yellow torrent that seethed and swirled around the piers of
the bridge was swelling momently on the wall of the Lung'
Arno, and rolling a threatening flood toward the Cascine,
where it lost itself under the ranks of the poplars that seemed
to file across its course, and let their delicate tops melt into
the pallor of the low horizon.

The city, with the sweep of the Lung' Arno on either
hand, and its domes and towers hung in the dull air, and the
country with its white villas and black cypresses breaking the
grey stretches of the olive orchards on its hill-sides, had alike
been growing more and more insufferable; and Colville was
finding a sort of vindictive satisfaction in the power to ignore
the surrounding frippery of landscape and architecture. He
isolated himself so perfectly from it, as he brooded upon the
river, that, for any sensible difference, he might have been
standing on the Main Street Bridge at Des Vaches, Indiana,
looking down at the tawny sweep of the Wabash. He had no
love for that stream, nor for the ambitious town on its banks,
but ever since he woke that morning he had felt a growing
conviction that he had been a great ass to leave them. He
had, in fact, taken the prodigious risk of breaking his life
sharp off from the course in which it had been set for many
years, and of attempting to renew it in a direction from
which it had long been diverted. Such an act could be
precipitated only by a strong impulse of conscience or a

profound disgust, and with Colville it sprang from disgust. He had experienced a bitter disappointment in the city to whose prosperity he had given the energies of his best years, and in whose favour he imagined that he had triumphantly established himself.

He had certainly made the Des Vaches *Democrat-Republican* a very good paper; its ability was recognised throughout the State, and in Des Vaches people of all parties were proud of it. They liked every morning to see what Colville said; they believed that in his way he was the smartest man in the State, and they were fond of claiming that there was no such writer on any of the Indianapolis papers. They forgave some political heresies to the talent they admired; they permitted him the whim of free trade, they laughed tolerantly when he came out in favour of civil service reform, and no one had much fault to find when the *Democrat-Republican* bolted the nomination of a certain politician of its party* for Congress. But when Colville permitted his own name to be used by the opposing party, the people arose in their might and defeated him by a tremendous majority. That was what the regular nominee said. It was a withering rebuke to treason, in the opinion of this gentleman; it was a good joke, anyway, with the Democratic managers who had taken Colville up, being all in the Republican family; whichever it was, it was a mortification for Colville which his pride could not brook. He stood disgraced before the community not only as a theorist and unpractical doctrinaire, but as a dangerous man; and what was worse, he could not wholly acquit himself of a measure of bad faith; his conscience troubled him even more than his pride. Money was found, and a printer bought up with it to start a paper in opposition to the *Democrat-Republican*. Then Colville contemptuously offered to sell out to the Republican committee in charge of the new enterprise, and they accepted his terms.

In private life he found much of the old kindness returning to him; and his successful opponent took the first opportunity of heaping coals of fire on his head in the public street, when he appeared to the outer eye to be shaking hands with Colville. During the months that he remained to close up his affairs after the sale of his paper, the *Post-Democrat-Republican* (the newspaper had agglutinated the titles of two of its predecessors, after the fashion of American journals) was fulsome in its complimentary allusions to him. It politely invented the fiction that he was going to Europe for his health, impaired by his journalistic labours, and adventurously promised its readers that they might hope to hear from him from time to time in its columns. In some of its allusions to him Colville detected the point of a fine irony, of which he had himself introduced the practice in the *Democrat-Republican*; and he experienced, with a sense of personal impoverishment, the curious fact that a journalist of strong characteristics leaves the tradition of himself in such degree with the journal he has created that he seems to bring very little away. He was obliged to confess in his own heart that the paper was as good as ever. The assistants, who had trained themselves to write like him, seemed to be writing quite as well, and his honesty would not permit him to receive the consolation offered him by the friends who told him that there was a great falling off in the *Post-Democrat-Republican*. Except that it was rather more Stalwart in its Republicanism, and had turned quite round on the question of the tariff, it was very much what it had always been. It kept the old decency of tone which he had given it, and it maintained the literary character which he was proud of. The new management must have divined that its popularity, with the women at least, was largely due to its careful selections of verse and fiction, its literary news, and its full and piquant criticisms, with their long extracts from new books. It was some time since he had personally looked after this department, and the young fellow in charge of it under him had remained with the paper. Its continued excellence, which he could not have denied if he had wished, seemed to leave him drained and feeble, and it was partly from the sense of this that he declined the overtures, well backed up with money, to establish an independent paper in Des Vaches. He felt that there was not fight enough in him for the work, even if he had not taken that strong disgust for public life which included the place and its people. He

wanted to get away, to get far away, and with the abrupt and
total change in his humour he reverted to a period in his life
when journalism and politics and the ambition of Congress
were things undreamed of.

At that period he was a very young architect, with an inclination toward the literary side of his profession, which
made it seem profitable to linger, with his Ruskin in his
hand,* among the masterpieces of Italian Gothic, when
perhaps he might have been better employed in designing
red-roofed many-verandaed, consciously mullioned seaside
cottages on the New England coast. He wrote a magazine
paper on the zoology of the Lombardic pillars in Verona,
very Ruskinian, very scornful of modern motive. He visited
every part of the peninsula, but he gave the greater part of
his time to North Italy, and in Venice he met the young girl
whom he followed to Florence. His love did not prosper;
when she went away she left him in possession of that
treasure to a man of his temperament, a broken heart. From
that time his vague dreams began to lift, and to let him live
in the clear light of common day; but he was still lingering
at Florence, ignorant of the good which had befallen him,
and cowering within himself under the sting of wounded
vanity, when he received a letter from his elder brother
suggesting that he should come and see how he liked the
architecture of Des Vaches. His brother had been seven
years at Des Vaches, where he had lands, and a lead-mine,
and a scheme for a railroad, and had lately added a daily
newspaper to his other enterprises. He had, in fact, added
two newspapers. For having unexpectedly and almost involuntarily become the owner of the Des Vaches *Republican*,
the fancy of building up a great local journal seized him, and
he bought the *Wabash Valley Democrat*, uniting them under
the name of the *Democrat-Republican*. But he had trouble
almost from the first with his editors, and he naturally
thought of the brother with a turn for writing who had been
running to waste for the last year or two in Europe. His real
purpose was to work Colville into the management of his
paper when he invited him to come out and look at the
architecture of Des Vaches.

Colville went, because he was at that moment in the humour to go anywhere, and because his money was running low, and he must begin work somehow. He was still romantic enough to like the notion of the place a little, because it bore the name given to it by the old French *voyageurs* from a herd of buffalo cows which they had seen grazing on the site of their camp there. But when he came to the place itself he did not like it. He hated it; but he stayed, and as an architect was the last thing any one wanted in Des Vaches since the jail and court-house had been built, he became, half without his willing it, a newspaper man. He learned in time to relish the humorous intimacy of the life about him; and when it was decided that he was no fool—there were doubts, growing out of his Eastern accent and the work of his New York tailor, at first—he found himself the object of a pleasing popularity. In due time he bought his brother out; he became very fond of newspaper life, its constant excitements and its endless variety; and six weeks before he sold his paper he would have scoffed at a prophecy of his return to Europe for the resumption of any artistic purpose whatever. But here he was, lounging on the Ponte Vecchio at Florence, whither he had come with the intention of rubbing up his former studies, and of perhaps getting back to put them in practice at New York ultimately. He had said to himself before coming abroad that he was in no hurry; that he should take it very easily—he had money enough for that; yet he would keep architecture before him as an object, for he had lived long in a community where every one was intensely occupied, and he unconsciously paid to Des Vaches the tribute of feeling that an objectless life was disgraceful to a man.

In the meantime he suffered keenly and at every moment the loss of the occupation of which he had bereaved himself; in thinking of quite other things, in talk of totally different matters, from the dreams of night, he woke with a start to the realisation of the fact that he had no longer a newspaper. He perceived now, as never before, that for fifteen years almost every breath of his life had been drawn with reference to his paper, and that without it he was in some sort lost, and, as it were, extinct. A tide of ridiculous home-sickness, which was an expression of this passionate regret for the life he had put behind him, rather than any longing for Des Vaches, swept over him, and the first passages of a letter to the *Post-Democrat-Republican* began to shape themselves in his mind. He had always, when he left home for New York or Washington, or for his few weeks of summer vacation on the Canadian rivers or the New England coast, written back to his readers, in whom he knew he could count upon quick sympathy in all he saw and felt, and he now found himself addressing them with that frank familiarity which comes to the journalist, in minor communities, from the habit of print. He began by confessing to them the defeat of certain expectations with which he had returned to Florence, and told them that they must not look for anything like the ordinary letters of travel from him. But he was not so singular in his attitude toward the place as he supposed; for any tourist who comes to Florence with the old-fashioned expectation of impressions will probably suffer a disappointment, unless he arrives very young and for the first time. It is a city superficially so well known that it affects one somewhat like a collection of views of itself; they are from the most striking points, of course, but one has examined them before, and is disposed to be critical of them. Certain emotions, certain sensations failed to repeat themselves to Colville at sight of the familiar monuments, which seemed to wear a hardy and indifferent air, as if being stared at so many years by so many thousands of travellers had extinguished in them that sensibility which one likes to fancy in objects of interest everywhere.

The life which was as vivid all about him as if caught by the latest instantaneous process made the same comparatively ineffective appeal. The operatic spectacle was still there. The people, with their cloaks statuesquely draped over their left shoulders, moved down the street, or posed in vehement dialogue on the sidewalks; the drama of bargaining, with the customer's scorn, the shopman's pathos, came through the open shop door. The handsome, heavy-eyed ladies, the bare-headed girls, thronged the ways; the caffés were full of the well-remembered figures over their newspapers and little cups; the officers were as splendid as of old, with their long cigars in their mouths, their swords kicking against their beautiful legs, and their spurs jingling; the dandies, with their little dogs and their flowerlike smiles, were still in front of the confectioners' for the inspection of the ladies who passed; the old beggar still crouched over her scaldino* at the church door, and the young man with one leg, whom he thought to escape by walking fast, had timed him to a second from the other side of the street. There was the wonted warmth in the sunny squares, and the old familiar damp and stench in the deep narrow streets. But some charm had gone out of all this. The artisans coming to the doors of their shallow booths for the light on some bit of carpentering, or cobbling, or tinkering; the crowds swarming through the middle of the streets on perfect terms with the wine-carts and cab horses; the ineffective grandiosity of the palaces huddled upon the crooked thoroughfares; the slight but insinuating cold of the southern winter, gathering in the shade and dispersing in the sun, and denied everywhere by the profusion of fruit and flowers, and by the greenery of gardens showing through the grated portals and over the tops of high walls; the groups of idle poor, permanently or temporarily propped against the bases of edifices with a southern exposure; the priests and monks and nuns in their gliding passage; the impassioned snapping of the cabmen's whips; the clangour of bells that at some hours inundated the city, and then suddenly subsided and left it to the banging of coppersmiths; the open-air frying of cakes, with its primitive smell of burning fat; the tramp of soldiery, and the fanfare of bugles blown to gay measures—these and a hundred other characteristic traits and facts still found a response in the consciousness where they were once a rapture of novelty; but the response was faint and thin; he could not warm over the old mood in which he once treasured them all away as of equal preciousness.

Of course there was a pleasure in recognising some details of former experience in Florence as they recurred. Colville had been met at once by a *festa*,* when nothing could be done, and he was more than consoled by the caressing sympathy with which he was assured that his broken trunk could not be mended till the day after to-morrow; he had quite forgotten about the festas and the sympathy. That night the piazza on which he lodged seemed full of snow to the casual glance he gave it; then he saw that it was the white Italian moonlight, which he had also forgotten. . . . .

II

COLVILLE had reached this point in that sarcastic study of his own condition of mind for the advantage of his late readers in the *Post-Democrat-Republican*, when he was aware of a polite rustling of draperies, with an ensuing well-bred murmur, which at once ignored him, deprecated intrusion upon him, and asserted a common right to the prospect on which he had been dwelling alone. He looked round with an instinctive expectation of style and poise, in which he was not disappointed. The lady, with a graceful lift of the head and a very erect carriage, almost Bernhardtesque* in the backward fling of her shoulders and the strict compression of her elbows to her side, was pointing out the different bridges to the little girl who was with her.

"That first one is the Santa Trinità, and the next is the Carraja, and that one quite down by the Cascine is the iron bridge. The Cascine you remember—the park where we were driving—that clump of woods there——"

A vagueness expressive of divided interest had crept into the lady's tone rather than her words. Colville could feel that she was waiting for the right moment to turn her delicate head, sculpturesquely defined by its toque, and steal an imperceptible glance at him: and he involuntarily afforded her the coveted excuse by the slight noise he made in changing his position in order to be able to go away as soon as he had seen whether she was pretty or not. At forty-one the question is still important to every man with regard to every woman.

"Mr. Colville!"

The gentle surprise conveyed in the exclamation, without time for recognition, convinced Colville, upon a cool review of the facts, that the lady had known him before their eyes met.

"Why, Mrs. Bowen!" he said.

She put out her round, slender arm, and gave him a frank clasp of her gloved hand. The glove wrinkled richly up the sleeve of her dress half-way to her elbow. She bent on his face a demand for just what quality and degree of change he found in hers, and apparently she satisfied herself that his inspection was not to her disadvantage, for she smiled brightly, and devoted the rest of her glance to an electric summary of the facts of Colville's physiognomy; the sufficiently good outline of his visage, with its full, rather close-cut, drabbish-brown beard and moustache, both shaped a little by the ironical self-conscious smile that lurked under them; the non-committal, rather weary-looking eyes; the brown hair, slightly frosted, that showed while he stood with his hat still off. He was a little above the middle height, and if it must be confessed, neither his face nor his figure had quite preserved their youthful lines. They were both much heavier than when Mrs Bowen saw them last, and the latter here and there swayed beyond the strict bounds of symmetry. She was herself in that moment of life when, to the middle-aged observer, at least, a woman's looks have a charm which is wanting to her earlier bloom. By that time her character has wrought itself more clearly out in her face, and her heart and mind confront you more directly there. It is the youth of her spirit which has come to the surface.

"I should have known you anywhere," she exclaimed, with friendly pleasure in seeing him.

"You are very kind," said Colville. "I didn't know that I had preserved my youthful beauty to that degree. But I can imagine it—if you say so, Mrs. Bowen."

"Oh, I assure you that you have!" she protested; and now she began gently to pursue him with one fine question after another about himself, till she had mastered the main facts of his history since they had last met. He would not have known so well how to possess himself of hers, even if he had felt the same necessity; but in fact it had happened that he had heard of her from time to time at not very long intervals. She had married a leading lawyer of her Western city, who in due time had gone to Congress, and after his term was out had "taken up his residence" in Washington, as the newspapers said, "in his elegant mansion at the corner of & Street and Idaho Avenue." After that he remembered reading that Mrs. Bowen was going abroad for the education of her daughter, from which he made his own inferences concerning her marriage. And "You knew Mr. Bowen was no longer living?" she said, with fit obsequy of tone.

"Yes, I knew," he answered, with decent sympathy.

"This is my little Effie,"* said Mrs. Bowen after a moment; and now the child, hitherto keeping herself discreetly in the background, came forward and promptly gave her hand to Colville, who perceived that she was not so small as he had thought her at first; an effect of infancy had possibly been studied in the brevity of her skirts and the immaturity of her corsage, but both were in good taste, and really to the advantage of her young figure. There was reason and justice in her being dressed as she was, for she really was not so old as she looked by two or three years; and there was reason in Mrs. Bowen's carrying in the hollow of her left arm the India shawl sacque* she had taken off and hung there; the deep cherry silk lining gave life to the sombre tints prevailing in her dress, which its removal left free to express all the grace of her extremely lady-like person. Lady-like was the word for Mrs. Bowen throughout— for the turn of her head, the management of her arm from the elbow, the curve of her hand from wrist to finger-tips, the smile, subdued, but sufficiently sweet, playing about her little mouth, which was yet not too little, and the refined and indefinite perfume which exhaled from the ensemble of her silks, her laces, and her gloves, like an odorous version of that otherwise impalpable quality which women call style. She had, with all her flexibility, a certain charming stiffness, like the stiffness of a very tall feather.

"And have you been here a great while?" she asked, turning her head slowly towards Colville, and looking at him with a little difficulty she had in raising her eyelids; when she was younger the glance that shyly stole from under the covert of their lashes was like a gleam of sunshine, and it was still like a gleam of paler sunshine.

Colville, whose mood was very susceptible to the weather, brightened in the ray. "I only arrived last night," he said, with a smile.

"How glad you must be to get back! Did you ever see Florence more beautiful than it was this morning?"

"Not for years," said Colville, with another smile for her pretty enthusiasm. "Not for seventeen years at the least calculation."

"Is it so many?" cried Mrs. Bowen, with lovely dismay. "Yes, it is," she sighed, and she did not speak for an appreciable interval.

He knew that she was thinking of that old love affair of his, to which she was privy in some degree, though he never could tell how much; and when she spoke he perceived that she purposely avoided speaking of a certain person, whom a woman of more tact or of less would have insisted upon naming at once. "I never can believe in the lapse of time when I get back to Italy; it always makes me feel as young as when I left it last."

"I could imagine you'd never left it," said Colville.

Mrs. Bowen reflected a moment. "Is that a compliment?"

"I had an obscure intention of saying something fine; but I don't think I've quite made it out," he owned.

Mrs. Bowen gave her small, sweet smile. "It was very nice of you to try. But I haven't really been away for some time; I've taken a house in Florence, and I've been here two years. Palazzo Pinti, Lung' Arno della Zecca. You must come and see me. Thursdays from four till six."

"Thank you," said Colville.

"I'm afraid," said Mrs. Bowen, remotely preparing to offer her hand in adieu, "that Effie and I broke in upon some very important cogitations of yours." She shifted the silken burden off her arm a little, and the child stirred from the correct pose she had been keeping, and smiled politely.

"I don't think they deserve a real dictionary word like that," said Colville. "I was simply mooning. If there was anything definite in my mind, I was wishing that I was looking down on the Wabash in Des Vaches, instead of the Arno in Florence."

"Oh! And I supposed you must be indulging all sorts of historical associations with the place. Effie and I have been

walking through the Via de' Bardi, where Romola lived,*
and I was bringing her back over the Ponte Vecchio, so as
to impress the origin of Florence on her mind.''

''Is that what makes Miss Effie hate it?'' asked Colville,
looking at the child, whose youthful resemblance to her
mother was in all things so perfect that a fantastic question
whether she could ever have had any other parent swept
through him. Certainly, if Mrs. Bowen were to marry again,
there was nothing in this child's looks to suggest the idea of
a predecessor to the second husband.

''Effie doesn't hate any sort of useful knowledge,'' said
her mother half jestingly. ''She's just come to me from
school at Vevay.''

''Oh, then, I think she might,'' persisted Colville. ''Don't
you hate the origin of Florence a little?'' he asked of the
child.

''I don't know enough about it,'' she answered, with a
quick look of question at her mother, and checking herself
in a possibly indiscreet smile.

''Ah, that accounts for it,'' said Colville, and he laughed.
It amused him to see the child referring even this point of
propriety to her mother, and his thoughts idled off to what
Mrs. Bowen's own untrammelled girlhood must have been
in her Western city. For her daughter there were to be no
buggy rides, or concerts, or dances at the invitation of young
men; no picnics, free and unchaperoned as the casing air; no
sitting on the steps at dusk with callers who never dreamed
of asking for her mother; no lingering at the gate with her
youthful escort home from the ball—nothing of that wild,
sweet liberty which once made American girlhood a long
rapture. But would she be any the better for her privations,
for referring not only every point of conduct, but every
thought and feeling, to her mother? He suppressed a sigh for
the inevitable change, but rejoiced that his own youth had
fallen in the earlier time, and said, ''You will hate it as soon
as you've read a little of it.''

''The difficulty is to read a little of Florentine history. I
can't find anything in less than ten or twelve volumes,'' said
Mrs. Bowen. ''Effie and I were going to Viesseux's Library

again, in desperation, to see if there wasn't something shorter in French.''

She now offered Colville her hand, and he found himself very reluctant to let it go. Something in her looks did not forbid him, and when she took her hand away, he said, ''Let me go to Viesseux's with you, Mrs. Bowen, and give you the advantage of my unprejudiced ignorance in the choice of a book on Florence.''

''Oh, I was longing to ask you!'' said Mrs. Bowen frankly. ''It is really such a serious matter, especially when the book is for a young person. Unless it's very dry, it's so apt to be— objectionable.''

''Yes,'' said Colville, with a smile at her perplexity. He moved off down the slope of the bridge with her, between the jewellers' shops, and felt a singular satisfaction in her company. Women of fashion always interested him; he liked them; it diverted him that they should take themselves seriously. Their resolution, their suffering for their ideal, such as it was, their energy in dressing and adorning themselves, the pains they were at to achieve the trivialities they passed their lives in, were perpetually delightful to him. He often found them people of great simplicity, and sometimes of singularly good sense; their frequent vein of piety was delicious.

Ten minutes earlier he would have said that nothing could have been less welcome to him than this encounter, but now he felt unwilling to leave Mrs. Bowen.

''Go before, Effie,'' she said; and she added, to Colville, ''How very Florentine all this is! If you dropped from the clouds on this spot without previous warning, you would know that you were on the Ponte Vecchio, and nowhere else.''

''Yes, it's very Florentine,'' Colville assented. ''The bridge is very well as a bridge, but as a street I prefer the Main Street Bridge at Des Vaches. I was looking at the jewellery before you came up, and I don't think it's pretty, even the old pieces of peasant jewellery. Why do people come here to look at it? If you were going to buy something for a friend, would you dream of coming here for it?''

"Oh *no!*" replied Mrs. Bowen, with the deepest feeling.

They quitted the bridge, and turning to the left, moved down the street which with difficulty finds space between the parapet of the river and the shops of the mosaicists and dealers in statuary cramping it on the other hand.

"Here's something distinctively Florentine too," said Colville. "These table-tops, and paper-weights, and caskets, and photograph frames, and lockets, and breast-pins; and here, this ghostly glare of undersized Psyches and Hebes and Graces* in alabaster."

"Oh, you mustn't think of any of them!" Mrs. Bowen broke in with horror. "If your friend wishes you to get her something characteristically Florentine, and at the same time very tasteful, you must go——"

Colville gave a melancholy laugh. "My friend is an abstraction, Mrs. Bowen, without sex or any sort of entity."

"Oh!" said Mrs. Bowen. Some fine drops had begun to sprinkle the pavement. "What a ridiculous blunder! It's raining! Effie, I'm afraid we must give up your book for today. We're not dressed for damp weather, and we'd better hurry home as soon as possible." She got promptly into the shelter of a doorway, and gathered her daughter to her, while she flung her sacque over her shoulder and caught her draperies from the ground for the next movement. "Mr. Colville, will you please stop the first closed carriage that comes in sight?"

A figure of *primo tenore** had witnessed the manœuvre from the box of his cab; he held up his whip, and at a nod from Colville he drove abreast of the doorway, his broken-kneed, tremulous little horse gay in brass-mounted harness, and with a stiff turkey feather stuck upright at one ear in his head-stall.

Mrs. Bowen had no more scruple than another woman in stopping travel and traffic in a public street for her convenience. She now entered into a brisk parting conversation with Colville, such as ladies love, blocking the narrow sidewalk with herself, her daughter, and her open carriage door, and making people walk round her cab, in the road, which they did meekly enough, with the Florentine submissiveness to the pretensions of any sort of vehicle. She said a dozen important things that seemed to have just come into her head, and, "Why, how stupid I am!" she called out, making Colville check the driver in his first start, after she had got into the cab. "We are to have a few people tonight. If you have no engagement, I should be so glad to have you come. Can't you?"

"Yes, I can," said Colville, admiring the whole transaction and the parties to it with a passive smile.

After finding her pocket, she found that her card-case was not in it, but in the purse she had given Effie to carry; but she got her address at last, and gave it to Colville, though he said he should remember it without. "Any time between nine and eleven," she said. "It's so nice of you to promise!"

She questioned him from under her half-lifted eyelids, and he added, with a laugh, "I'll come!" and was rewarded with two pretty smiles, just alike, from mother and daughter, as they drove away.

III

TWENTY years earlier, when Mrs. Bowen was Miss Lina Ridgely, she used to be the friend and confidante of the girl who jilted Colville. They were then both so young that they could scarcely have been a year out of school before they left home for the year they were spending in Europe; but to the young man's inexperience they seemed the wisest and maturest of society women. His heart quaked in his breast when he saw them talking and laughing together, for fear they should be talking and laughing about him; he was even a little more afraid of Miss Ridgely than of her friend, who was dashing and effective, where Miss Ridgely was serene and elegant, according to his feeling at that time; but he never saw her after his rejection, and it was not till he read of her marriage with the Hon. Mr. Bowen that certain vague impressions began to define themselves. He then remembered that Lina Ridgely in many fine little ways had shown a kindness, almost a compassion, for him, as for one whose unconsciousness a hopeless doom impended over. He perceived that she had always seemed to like him—a thing that had not occurred to him in the stupid absorption of his passion for the other—and fragments of proof that she had probably defended and advocated him occurred to him, and inspired a vain and retrospective gratitude; he abandoned himself to regrets, which were proper enough in regard to Miss Ridgely, but were certainly a little unlawful concerning Mrs. Bowen.

As he walked away toward his hotel he amused himself with the conjecture whether he, with his forty-one years and his hundred and eighty-five pounds, were not still a pathetic and even a romantic figure to this pretty and kindly woman, who probably imagined him as heart-broken as ever. He was very willing to see more of her, if she wished; but with the rain beginning to fall more thick and chill in the darkening street, he could have postponed their next meeting till a pleasanter evening without great self-denial. He felt a little twinge of rheumatism in his shoulder when he got into his room, for your room in a Florentine hotel is always some degrees colder than outdoors, unless you have fire in it; and with the sun shining on his

windows when he went out after lunch, it had seemed to
Colville ridiculous to have his morning fire kept up. The sun
was what he had taken the room for. It was in it, the
landlord assured him, from ten in the morning till four in the
afternoon; and so, in fact, it was, when it shone; but even
then it was not fully in it, but had a trick of looking in at the
sides of the window, and painting the chamber wall with a
delusive glow. Colville raked away the ashes of his fire-place,
and throwing on two or three fagots of broom and pine
sprays, he had a blaze that would be very pretty to dress by
after dinner, but that gave out no warmth for the present.
He left it, and went down to the reading-room, as it was
labelled over the door, in homage to a predominance of
English-speaking people among the guests; but there was no
fire there; that was kindled only by request, and he shivered
at the bare aspect of the apartment, with its cold piano, its
locked bookcases, and its table, where the London *Times*, the
Neue Freie Presse of Vienna, and the *Italie* of Rome exposed
their titles, one just beyond the margin of the other. He
turned from the door and went into the dining-room, where
the stove was ostentatiously roaring over its small logs and
its lozenges of peat. But even here the fire had been so
recently lighted that the warmth was potential rather than
actual. By stooping down before the stove, and pressing his
shoulder against its brass doors, Colville managed to lull his
enemy, while he studied the figures of the woman-headed,
woman-breasted hounds developing into vines and foliage
that covered the frescoed trellising of the quadrangularly
vaulted ceiling. The waiters, in their veteran dress-coats,
were putting the final touches to the table, and the sound of
voices outside the door obliged Colville to get up. The effort
involved made him still more reluctant about going out to
Mrs. Bowen's.

The door opened, and some English ladies entered, faintly
acknowledging, provisionally ignoring, his presence, and
talking of what they had been doing since lunch. They
agreed that it was really too cold in the churches for any
pleasure in the pictures, and that the Pitti Gallery, where
they had those braziers, was the only place you could

go with comfort. A French lady and her husband came in; a Russian lady followed; an Italian gentleman, an American family, and three or four detached men of the English-speaking race, whose language at once became the law of the table.

As the dinner progressed from soup to fish, and from the *entrée* to the roast and salad, the combined effect of the pleasant cheer and the increasing earnestness of the stove made the room warmer and warmer. They drank Chianti wine from the wicker-covered flasks, tied with tufts of red and green silk, in which they serve table wine at Florence, and said how pretty the bottles were, but how the wine did not seem very good.

"It certainly isn't so good as it used to be," said Colville.

"Ah, then you have been in Florhence before," said the French lady, whose English proved to be much better than the French that he began to talk to her in.

"Yes, a great while ago; in a state of pre-existence, in fact," he said.

The lady looked a little puzzled, but interested. "In a state of prhe-existence?" she repeated.

"Yes; when I was young," he added, catching the gleam in her eye. "When I was twenty-four. A great while ago."

"You must be an Amerhican," said the lady, with a laugh.

"Why do you think so? From my accent?"

"Frhom your metaphysics too. The Amerhicans like to talk in that way."

"I didn't know it," said Colville.

"They like to strhike the key of perhsonality; they can't endure not being interhested. They must rhelate everything to themselves or to those with whom they are talking."

"And the French, no?" asked Colville.

The lady laughed again. "There is a large Amerhican colony in Parhis. Perhaps we have learned to be like you."

The lady's husband did not speak English, and it was probably what they had been saying that she interpreted to him, for he smiled, looking forward to catch Colville's eye in a friendly way, and as if he would not have him take his wife's talk too seriously.

The Italian gentleman on Colville's right was politely offering him the salad, which had been left for the guests to pass to one another. Colville thanked him in Italian, and they began to talk of Italian affairs. One thing led to another, and he found that his new friend, who was not yet his acquaintance, was a member of Parliament, and a republican.*

"That interests me as an American," said Colville. "But why do you want a republic in Italy?"

"When we have a constitutional king, why should we have a king?" asked the Italian.

An Englishman across the table relieved Colville from the difficulty of answering this question by asking him another that formed talk about it between them. He made his tacit observation that the English, since he met them last, seemed to have grown in the grace of facile speech with strangers; it was the American family which kept its talk within itself, and hushed to a tone so low that no one else could hear it. Colville did not like their mumbling; for the honour of the country, which we all have at heart, however little we think it, he would have preferred that they should speak up, and not seem afraid or ashamed; he thought the English manner was better. In fact, he found himself in an unexpectedly social mood; he joined in helping to break the ice; he laughed and hazarded comment with those who were new-comers like himself, and was very respectful of the opinions of people who had been longer in the hotel, when they spoke of the cook's habit of underdoing the vegetables. The dinner at the Hotel d'Atene made an imposing show on the *carte du jour*; it looked like ten or twelve courses, but in fact it was five, and even when eked out with roast chestnuts and butter into six, it seemed somehow to stop very abruptly, though one seemed to have had enough. You could have coffee afterward if you ordered it. Colville ordered it, and was sorry when the last of his commensals, slightly bowing him a good-night, left him alone to it.

He had decided that he need not fear the damp in a cab

rapidly driven to Mrs. Bowen's. When he went to his room
he had his doubts about his dresscoat; but he put it on, and
he took the crush hat* with which he had provided himself in
coming through London. That was a part of the social
panoply unknown in Des Vaches; he had hardly been a
dozen times in evening dress there in fifteen years, and his
suit was as new as his hat. As he turned to the glass he
thought himself personable enough, and in fact he was one
of those men who look better in evening dress than in any
other: the broad expanse of shirt bosom, with its three small
studs of gold dropping, points of light, one below the other,
softened his strong, almost harsh face, and balanced his
rather large head. In his morning coat, people had to look
twice at him to make sure that he did not look common; but
now he was not wrong in thinking that he had an air of
distinction, as he took his hat under his arm and stood before
the pier-glass in his room. He was almost tempted to shave,
and wear his moustache alone, as he used to do: he had let
his beard grow because he found that under the lax social
regimen at Des Vaches he neglected shaving, and went
about days at a time with his face in an offensive stubble.
Taking his chin between his fingers, and peering closer into
the mirror, he wondered how Mrs. Bowen should have
known him; she must have remembered him very vividly.
He would like to take off his beard and put on the
youthfulness that comes of shaving, and see what she would
say. Perhaps, he thought, with a last glance at his toilet, he
was overdoing it, if she were only to have a few people, as
she promised. He put a thick neckerchief over his chest so
as not to provoke that abominable rheumatism by any sort
of exposure, and he put on his ulster instead of the light
spring overcoat that he had gone about with all day.

   He found that Palazzo Pinti, when you came to it, was
rather a grand affair, with a gold-banded porter eating salad
in the lodge at the great doorway, and a handsome gate of
iron cutting you off from the regions above till you had rung
the bell of Mrs. Bowen's apartment, when it swung open of
itself, and you mounted. At her door a man in modified
livery received Colville, and helped him off with his overcoat

so skilfully that he did not hurt his rheumatic shoulder at all; there were half a dozen other hats and coats on the carved chests that stood at intervals along the wall, and some gayer wraps that exhaled a faint, fascinating fragrance on the chilly air. Colville experienced the slight exhilaration, the mingled reluctance and eagerness, of a man who formally re-enters an assemblage of society after long absence from it, and rubbing his hands a little nervously together, he put aside the yellow Abruzzi blanket *portière*,* and let himself into the brilliant interior.

Mrs. Bowen stood in front of the fire in a brown silk of subdued splendour, and with her hands and fan and handkerchief tastefully composed before her. At sight of Colville she gave a slight start, which would have betrayed to him, if he had been another woman, that she had not really believed he would come, and came forward with a rustle and murmur of pleasure to meet him; he had politely made a rush upon her, so as to spare her this exertion, and he was tempted to a long-forgotten foppishness of attitude as he stood talking with her during the brief interval before she introduced him to any of the company. She had been honest with him; there were not more than twenty-five or thirty people there; but if he had overdone it in dressing for so small an affair, he was not alone, and he was not sorry. He was sensible of a better personal effect than the men in frock-coats and cutaways were making, and he perceived with self-satisfaction that his evening dress was of better style than that of the others who wore it; at least no one else carried a crush hat.

At forty-one a man is still very much of a boy, and Colville was obscurely willing that Mrs. Bowen, whose life since they last met at an evening party had been passed chiefly at New York and Washington, should see that he was a man of the world in spite of Des Vaches. Before she had decided which of the company she should first present him to, her daughter came up to his elbow with a cup of tea and some bread and butter on a tray, and gave him good-evening with charming correctness of manner. "Really," he said, turning about to take the cup, "I thought it was you, Mrs. Bowen, who had got round to my side with a sash on. How do you and Miss Effie justify yourselves in looking so bewitchingly alike?"

"You notice it, then?" Mrs. Bowen seemed delighted.

"I did every moment you were together to-day. You don't mind my having been so personal in my observations?"

"Oh, not at all," said Mrs. Bowen, and Colville laughed.

"It must be true," he said, "what a French lady said to me at the *table-d'hôte* dinner to-night: 'the Amerhicans always strhike the note of perhsonality.' " He neatly imitated the French lady's guttural accent.

"I suppose we do," mused Mrs. Bowen, "and that we don't mind it in each other. I wish *you* would say which I shall introduce you to," she said, letting her glance stray invisibly over her company, where all the people seemed comfortably talking.

"Oh, there's no hurry; put it off till to-morrow," said Colville.

"Oh no; that won't do," said Mrs. Bowen, like a woman who has public duties to perform, and is resolute to sacrifice her private pleasure to them. But she postponed them a moment longer. "I hope you got home before the rain," she said.

"Yes," returned Colville. "That is, I don't mind a little sprinkling. Who is the Junonian* young person at the end of the room?"

"Ah," said Mrs. Bowen, "you can't be introduced to *her* first. But *isn't* she lovely?"

"Yes. It's a wonderful effect of white and gold."

"You mustn't say that to her. She was doubtful about her dress, because she says that the ivory white with her hair makes her look just like white and gold furniture."

"Present me at once, then, before I forget not to say it to her."

"No; I must keep you for some other person: anybody can talk to a pretty girl."

Colville said he did not know whether to smile or shed tears at this embittered compliment, and pretended an eagerness for the acquaintance denied him.

Mrs. Bowen seemed disposed to intensify his misery. "Did you ever see a more statuesque creature—with those superb broad shoulders and that little head, and that thick braid brought round over the top? Doesn't her face, with that calm look in those starry eyes, and that peculiar fall of the corners of the mouth, remind you of some of those exquisite great Du Maurier women?* That style of face is very fashionable now: you might think he had made it so."

"Is there a fashion in faces?" asked Colville.

"Why, certainly. You must know that."

"Then why aren't all the ladies in the fashion?"

"It isn't one that can be put on. Besides, every one hasn't got Imogene Graham's figure to carry it off."

"That's her name, then—Imogene Graham. It's a very pretty name."

"Yes. She's staying with me for the winter. Now that's all I can allow you to know for the present. Come! You must!"

"But this is worse than nothing." He made a feint of protesting as she led him away, and named him to the lady she wished him to know. But he was not really sorry; he had his modest misgivings whether he were equal to quite so much young lady as Miss Graham seemed. When he no longer looked at her he had a whimsical impression of her being a heroic statue of herself.

The lady whom Mrs. Bowen left him with had not much to say, and she made haste to introduce her husband, who had a great deal to say. He was an Italian, but master of that very efficient English which the Italians get together with unimaginable sufferings from our orthography, and Colville repeated the republican deputy's saying about a constitutional king, which he had begun to think was neat.

"I might prefer a republic myself," said the Italian, "but I think that gentleman is wrong to be a republican where he is, and for the present. The monarchy is the condition of our unity; nothing else could hold us together, and we must remain united if we are to exist as a nation. It's a necessity, like our army of half a million men. We may not like it in itself, but we know that it is our salvation." He began to speak of the economic state of Italy, of the immense cost of freedom and independence to a people whose political genius enables them to bear quietly burdens of taxation that no other government would venture to impose. He spoke with that fond, that appealing patriotism, which expresses so much to the sympathetic foreigner in Italy: the sense of great and painful uncertainty of Italy's future through the complications of diplomacy, the memory of her sufferings in the past, the spirit of quiet and inexhaustible patience for trials to come. This resolution, which is almost resignation, poetises the attitude of the whole people; it made Colville feel as if he had done nothing and borne nothing yet.

"I am ashamed," he said, not without a remote resentment of the unworthiness of the republican voters of Des Vaches, "when I hear of such things, to think of what we are at home, with all our resources and opportunities."

The Italian would have politely excused us to him, but Colville would have no palliation of our political and moral nakedness; and he framed a continuation of the letter he began on the Ponte Vecchio to the *Post-Democrat-Republican*, in which he made a bitterly ironical comparison of the achievements of Italy and America in the last ten years.*

He forgot about Miss Graham, and had only a vague sense of her splendour as he caught sight of her in the long mirror which she stood before. She was talking to a very handsome young clergyman, and smiling upon him. The company seemed to be mostly Americans, but there were a good many evident English also, and Colville was dimly aware of a question in his mind whether this clergyman was English or American. There were three or four Italians and there were some Germans, who spoke English.

Colville moved about from group to group as his enlarging acquaintance led, and found himself more interested in society than he could ever have dreamed of being again. It was certainly a defect of the life at Des Vaches that people, after the dancing and love-making period, went out rarely or never. He began to see that the time he had spent so busily in that enterprising city had certainly been in some sense wasted.

At a certain moment in the evening, which perhaps

marked its advancement, the tea-urn was replaced by a jug of the rum punch, mild or strong according to the custom of the house, which is served at most Florentine receptions. Some of the people went immediately after, but the young clergyman remained talking with Miss Graham.

Colville, with his smoking glass in his hand, found himself at the side of a friendly old gentleman who had refused the punch. They joined in talk by a common impulse, and the old gentleman said, directly, "You are an American, I presume?"

His accent had already established the fact of his own nationality, but he seemed to think it the part of candour to say, when Colville had acknowledged his origin, "I'm an American myself."

"I've met several of our countrymen since I arrived," suggested Colville.

The old gentleman seemed to like this way of putting it. "Well, yes, we're not unfairly represented here in numbers, I must confess. But I'm bound to say that I don't find our countrymen so aggressive, so loud, as our international novelists* would make out. I haven't met any of their peculiar heroines as yet, sir."

Colville could not help laughing. "I wish *I* had. But perhaps they avoid people of our years and discretion, or else take such a filial attitude toward us that we can't recognise them."

"Perhaps, perhaps," cried the old gentleman, with cheerful assent.

"I was talking with one of our German friends here just now, and he complained that the American girls—especially the rich ones—seem very calculating and worldly and conventional. I told him I didn't know how to account for that. I tried to give him some notion of the ennobling influences of society in Newport,* as I've had glimpses of it."

The old gentleman caressed his elbows, which he was holding in the palms of his hands, in high enjoyment of Colville's sarcasm. "Ah! very good! very good!" he said. "I quite agree with you, and I think the other sort are altogether preferable."

"I think," continued Colville, dropping his ironical tone, "that we've much less to regret in their unsuspecting, unsophisticated freedom than in the type of hard materialism which we produce in young girls, perfectly wide awake, disenchanted, unromantic, who prefer the worldly vanities and advantages deliberately and on principle, recognising something better merely to despise it. I've sometimes seen them——"

Mrs Bowen came up in her gentle, inquiring way. "I'm glad that you and Mr. Colville have made acquaintance," she said to the old gentleman.

"Oh, but we haven't," said Colville. "We're entire strangers."

"Then I'll introduce you to Rev. Mr. Waters. And take you away," she added, putting her hand through Colville's arm with a delicate touch that flattered his whole being, "for your time's come at last, and I'm going to present you to Miss Graham."

"I don't know," he said. "Of course, as there *is* a Miss Graham, I can't help being presented to her, but I had almost worked myself up to the point of wishing there were none. I believe I'm afraid."

"Oh, I don't believe that at all. A simple schoolgirl like that!" Mrs. Bowen's sense of humour had not the national acuteness. She liked joking in men, but she did not know how to say funny things back. "You'll see, as you come up to her."

MISS GRAHAM did, indeed, somehow diminish in the nearer perspective. She ceased to be overwhelming. When Colville lifted his eyes from bowing before her he perceived that she was neither so very tall nor so very large, but possessed merely a generous amplitude of womanhood. But she was even more beautiful, with a sweet and youthful radiance of look that was very winning. If she had ceased to be the goddess she looked across the length of the *salon*, she had gained much by becoming an extremely lovely young girl; and her teeth, when she spoke, showed a fascinating little irregularity that gave her the last charm.

Mrs. Bowen glided away with the young clergyman, but Effie remained at Miss Graham's side, and seemed to have hold of the left hand which the girl let hang carelessly behind her in the volume of her robe. The child's face expressed an adoration of Miss Graham far beyond her allegiance to her mother.

"I began to doubt whether Mrs. Bowen was going to bring you at all," she said frankly, with an innocent nervous laugh, which made favour for her with Colville. "She promised it early in the evening."

"She has used me much worse, Miss Graham," said Colville. "She has kept me waiting from the beginning of time. So that I have grown grey on my way up to you," he added, by an inspiration. "I was a comparatively young man when Mrs. Bowen first told me she was going to introduce me."

"Oh, how *good!*" said Miss Graham joyously. And her companion, after a moment's hesitation, permitted herself a polite little titter. She had made a discovery: she had discovered that Mr. Colville was droll.

"I'm very glad you like it," he said, with a gravity that did not deceive them.

"Oh yes," sighed Miss Graham, with generous ardour.

"Who but an American could say just such things? There's the loveliest old lady here in Florence, who's lived here thirty years, and she's always going back and never getting back, and she's so homesick she doesn't know what to do, and she always says that Americans may not be *better* than other people, but they are *different*."

"That's very pretty. They're different in everything but thinking themselves better. Their native modesty prevents that."

"I don't exactly know what you mean," said Miss Graham, after a little hesitation.

"Well," returned Colville, "I haven't thought it out very clearly myself yet. I may mean that the Americans differ from other people in not thinking well of themselves, or they may differ from them in not thinking well enough. But what I said had a very epigrammatic sound, and I prefer not to investigate it too closely."

This made Miss Graham and Miss Effie both cry out "Oh!" in delighted doubt of his intention. They both insensibly drifted a little nearer to him.

"There was a French lady said to me at the *table-d'hôte* this evening that she knew I was an American, because the Americans always strike the key of personality." He practised these economies of material in conversation quite recklessly, and often made the same incident or suggestion do duty round a whole company.

"Ah, I don't believe that," said Miss Graham.

"Believe what?"

"That the Americans always talk about themselves."

"I'm not sure she meant that. You never can tell what a person means by what he says—or *she*."

"How shocking!"

"Perhaps the French lady meant that we always talk about other people. That's in the key of personality too."

"But I don't believe we do," said Miss Graham. "At any rate, *she* was talking about *us*, then."

"Oh, she accounted for that by saying there was a large American colony in Paris, who had corrupted the French, and taught them our pernicious habit of introspection."

"Do you think we're very introspective?"

"Do you?"

"I know I'm not. I hardly ever think about myself at all. At any rate, not till it's too late. That's the great trouble. I wish I could. But I'm always studying other people. They're so much more interesting."

"Perhaps if you knew yourself better you wouldn't think so," suggested Colville.

"Yes, I know they are. I don't think any young person can be interesting."

"Then what becomes of all the novels? They're full of young persons."

"They're ridiculous. If I were going to write a novel, I should take an old person for a hero—thirty-five or forty. She looked at Colville, and blushing a little, hastened to add, "I don't believe that they begin to be interesting much before that time. Such flat things as young men are always saying! Don't you remember that passage somewhere in Heine's *Pictures of Travel*,* where he sees the hand of a lady coming out from under her mantle, when she's confessing in a church, and he knows that it's the hand of a young person who has enjoyed nothing and suffered nothing, it's so smooth and flower-like? After I read that I hated the look of my hands—I was only sixteen, and it seemed as if I had had no more experience than a child. Oh, I like people to be *through* something. Don't you?"

"Well, yes, I suppose I do. Other people."

"No; but don't you like it for yourself?"

"I can't tell; I haven't been through anything worth speaking of yet."

Miss Graham looked at him dubiously, but pursued with ardour: "Why, just getting back to Florence, after not having been here for so long—I should think it would be so romantic. Oh dear! I wish I were here for the second time."

"I'm afraid you wouldn't like it so well," said Colville. "I wish I were here for the first time. There's nothing like the first time in everything."

"Do you really think so?"

"Well, there's nothing like the first time in Florence."

"Oh, I can't imagine it. I should think that recalling the old emotions would be perfectly fascinating."

"Yes, if they'd come when you do call them. But they're as contrary-minded as spirits from the vasty deep. I've been shouting around here for my old emotions all day, and I haven't had a responsive squeak."

"Oh!" cried Miss Graham, staring full-eyed at him. "How delightful!" Effie Bowen turned away her pretty little head and laughed, as if it might not be quite kind to laugh at a person's joke to his face.

Stimulated by their appreciation, Colville went on with more nonsense. "No; the only way to get at your old emotions in regard to Florence is to borrow them from somebody who's having them fresh. What do *you* think about Florence, Miss Graham?"

"I? I've been here two months."

"Then it's too late?"

"No, I don't know that it is. I keep feeling the strangeness all the time. But I can't tell you. It's very different from Buffalo, I can assure you."

"Buffalo? I can imagine the difference. And it's not altogether to the disadvantage of Buffalo."

"Oh, have you been there?" asked Miss Graham, with a touching little eagerness. "Do you know anybody in Buffalo?"

"Some of the newspaper men; and I pass through there once a year on my way to New York—or used to. It's a lively place."

"Yes, it is," sighed Miss Graham fondly.

"Do the girls of Buffalo still come out at night and dance by the light of the moon?"

"What!"

"Ah, I see," said Colville, peering at her under his thoughtfully knitted brows, "you do belong to another era. You don't remember the old negro minstrel song."*

"No," said Miss Graham. "I can only remember the end of the war."*

"How divinely young!" said Colville. "Well," he added, "I wish that French lady could have overheard us, Miss

Graham. I think she would have changed her mind about Americans striking the note of personality in their talk.''

"Oh!'' exclaimed the girl reproachfully, after a moment of swift reflection and recognition, "I don't see how you could let me do it! You don't suppose that I should have talked so with every one? It was because you were another American, and such an old friend of Mrs. Bowen's.''

"That is what I shall certainly tell the French lady if she attacks me about it,'' said Colville. He glanced carelessly toward the end of the room, and saw the young clergyman taking leave of Mrs. Bowen; all the rest of the company were gone. "Bless me!'' he said, "I must be going.''

Mrs. Bowen had so swiftly advanced upon him that she caught the last words. "Why?'' she asked.

"Because it's to-morrow, I suspect, and the invitation was for one day only.''

"It was a season ticket,'' said Mrs. Bowen, with gay hospitality, "and it isn't to-morrow for half an hour yet. I can't think of letting you go. Come up to the fire, all, and let's sit down by it. It's at its very best.''

Effie looked a pretty surprise and a pleasure in this girlish burst from her mother, whose habitual serenity made it more striking in contrast, and she forsook Miss Graham's hand and ran forward and disposed the easy-chairs comfortably about the hearth.

Colville and Mrs. Bowen suddenly found themselves upon those terms which often succeed a long separation with people who have felt kindly toward each other at a former meeting and have parted friends: they were much more intimate than they had supposed themselves to be, or had really any reason for being.

"Which one of your guests do you wish me to offer up, Mrs. Bowen?'' he asked, from the hollow of the arm-chair, not too low, which he had sunk into. With Mrs. Bowen in a higher chair at his right hand, and Miss Graham intent upon him from the sofa on his left, a sense of delicious satisfaction filled him from head to foot. "There isn't one I would spare if you said the word.''

"And there isn't one I want destroyed, I'm sorry to say,''

answered Mrs. Bowen. "Don't you think they were all very agreeable?"

"Yes, yes; agreeable enough—agreeable enough, I suppose. But they stayed too long. When I think we might have been sitting here for the last half-hour, if they'd only gone sooner, I find it pretty hard to forgive them."

Mrs. Bowen and Miss Graham exchanged glances above his head—a glance which demanded, "Didn't I tell you?" for a glance that answered, "Oh, he *is!*" Effie Bowen's eyes widened; she kept them fastened upon Colville in silent worship.

He asked who were certain of the company that he had noticed, and Mrs. Bowen let him make a little fun of them: the fun was very good-natured. He repeated what the German had said about the worldly ambition of American girls; but she would not allow him so great latitude in this. She said they were no worldlier than other girls. Of course, they were fond of society, and some of them got a little spoiled. But they were in no danger of becoming too conventional.

Colville did not insist. "I missed the military to-night, Mrs. Bowen," he said. "I thought one couldn't get through an evening in Florence without officers?"

"We have them when there is dancing," returned Mrs. Bowen.

"Yes, but they don't know anything but dancing," Miss Graham broke in. "I like some one who can talk something besides compliments."

"You are very peculiar, you know, Imogene," urged Mrs. Bowen gently. "I don't think our young men at home do much better in conversation, if you come to that, though."

"Oh, *young* men, yes! They're the same everywhere. But here, even when they're away along in the thirties, they think that girls can only enjoy flattery. *I* should like a gentleman to talk to me without a single word or look to show that he thought I was good-looking."

"Ah, how could he?" Colville insinuated, and the young girl coloured.

"I mean, if I were pretty. This everlasting adulation is insulting."

"Mr. Morton doesn't flatter," said Mrs. Bowen thought-fully, turning the feather screen she held at her face, now edgewise, now flatwise, toward Colville.

"Oh no," owned Miss Graham. "He's a clergyman."

Mrs Bowen addressed herself to Colville. "You must go to hear him some day. He's very interesting, if you don't mind his being rather Low Church."*

Colville was going to pretend to an advanced degree of ritualism; but it occurred to him that it might be a serious matter to Mrs. Bowen, and he asked instead who was the Rev. Mr. Waters.

"Oh, isn't he lovely?" cried Miss Graham. "There, Mrs. Bowen! Mr. Waters's manner is what I call *truly* complimen-tary. He always talks to you as if he expected you to be interested in serious matters, and as if you were his intellectual equal. And he's so *happy* here in Florence! He gives you the impression of feeling every breath he breathes here a privilege. You ought to hear him talk about Savonarola,* Mr. Colville."

"Well," said Colville, 'I've heard a great many people talk about Savonarola, and I'm rather glad he talked to me about American girls."

"American girls!" uttered Miss Graham, in a little scream. "Did Mr. Waters talk to you about *girls?*"

"Yes. Why not? He was probably in love with one once."

"Mr. Waters?" cried the girl. "What nonsense!"

"Well, then, with some old lady. Would you like that bet-ter?"

Miss Graham looked at Mrs. Bowen for permission, as it seemed, and then laughed, but did not attempt any reply to Colville.

"You find even that incredible of such pyramidal antiquity," he resumed. "Well, it *is* hard to believe. I told him what that German said, and we agreed beautifully about another type of American girl which we said we preferred."

"Oh! What could it be?" demanded Miss Graham.

"Ah, it wouldn't be so easy to say right off-hand," answered Colville indolently.

Mrs. Bowen put her hand under the elbow of the arm holding her screen. "I don't believe I should agree with you so well," she said, apparently with a sort of didactic intention.

They entered into a discussion which is always fruitful with Americans—the discussion of American girlhood, and Colville contended for the old national ideal of girlish liberty as wide as the continent, as fast as the Mississippi. Mrs. Bowen withstood him with delicate firmness. "Oh," he said, "you're Europeanised."

"I certainly prefer the European plan of bringing up girls," she replied steadfastly. "I shouldn't think of letting a daughter of mine have the freedom I had."

"Well, perhaps it will come right in the next generation, then; she will let her daughter have the freedom she hadn't."

"Not if I'm alive to prevent it," cried Mrs. Bowen.

Colville laughed. "Which plan do you prefer, Miss Graham?"

"I don't think it's quite the same now as it used to be," answered the girl evasively.

"Well, then, all I can say is that if I had died before this chance, I had lived a blessed time. I perceive more and more that I'm obsolete. I'm in my dotage; I prattle of the good old times, and the new spirit of the age flouts me. Miss Effie, do you prefer the Amer——"

"No, thank you," said her mother quickly. "Effie is out of the question. It's time you were in bed, Effie."

The child came with instant submissiveness and kissed her mother good-night; she kissed Miss Graham, and gave her hand to Colville. He held it a moment, letting her pull shyly away from him, while he lolled back in his chair, and laughed at her with his sad eyes. "It's past the time *I* should be in bed, my dear, and I'm sitting up merely because there's nobody to send me. It's not that I'm really such a very bad boy. Good night. Don't put me into a disagreeable dream; put me into a nice one." The child bridled at the mild pleasantry, and when Colville released her hand she suddenly stooped forward and kissed him.

"You're so *funny!*" she cried, and ran and escaped beyond the *portière*.

Mrs. Bowen stared in the same direction, but not with severity. "Really, Effie has been carried a little beyond herself."

"Well," said Colville, "that's *one* conquest since I came
to Florence. And merely by being funny! When I was in
Florence before, Mrs. Bowen," he continued, after a
moment, "there were two ladies here, and I used to go about
quite freely with either of them. They were both very pretty,
and we were all very young. Don't you think it was
charming?" Mrs. Bowen coloured a lovely red, and smiled,
but made no other response. "Florence has changed very
much for the worse since that time. There used to be a pretty
flower-girl, with a wide-flapping straw hat, who flung a
heavy bough full of roses into my lap when she met me
driving across the Carraja bridge. I spent an hour looking
for that girl to-day, and couldn't find her. The only flower-
girl I could find was a fat one of fifty, who kept me fifteen
minutes in Via Tornabuoni while she was fumbling away at
my button-hole, trying to poke three second-hand violets
and a sickly daisy into it. Ah, youth! youth! I suppose a
young fellow could have found that other flower-girl at a
glance; but *my* old eyes! No, we belong, each of us, to our
own generation. Mrs. Bowen," he said, with a touch of
tragedy—whether real or affected, he did not well know
himself—in his hardiness, "what has become of Mrs.
Pilsbury?"

"Mrs. Milbury, you mean?" gasped Mrs. Bowen, in
affright at his boldness.

"Milbury, Bilbury, Pilsbury—it's all one, so long as it
isn't——"

"They're living in Chicago!" she hastened to reply, as if
she were afraid he was going to say, "so long as it isn't
Colville," and she could not have borne that.

Colville clasped his hands at the back of his head and
looked at Mrs. Bowen with eyes that let her know that he
was perfectly aware she had been telling Miss Graham of his
youthful romance, and that he had now touched it purposely. "And you wouldn't," he said, as if that were quite
relevant to what they had been talking about—"you
wouldn't let Miss Graham go out walking alone with a
dotard like me?"

"Certainly not," said Mrs. Bowen.

Colville got to his feet by a surprising activity. "Good-bye, Miss Graham." He offered his hand to her with bur-lesque despair, and then turned to Mrs. Bowen. "Thank you for *such* a pleasant evening! What was your day, did you say?"

"Oh, any day!" said Mrs. Bowen cordially, giving her hand.

"Do you know whom you look like?" he asked, holding it.

"No."

"Lina Ridgely."

The ladies stirred softly in their draperies after he was gone. They turned and faced the hearth, where a log burned in a bed of hot ashes, softly purring and ticking to itself, and whilst they stood pressing their hands against the warm fronts of their dresses, as the fashion of women is before a fire, the clock on the mantel began to strike twelve.

"Was that her name?" asked Miss Graham, when the clock had had its say. "Lina Ridgely?"

"No; that was *my* name," answered Mrs. Bowen.

"Oh yes!" murmured the young girl apologetically.

"She led him on; she certainly encouraged him. It was shocking. He was quite wild about it."

"She must have been a cruel girl. How *could* he speak of it so lightly?"

"It was best to speak of it, and have done with it," said Mrs. Bowen. "He knew that I must have been telling you something about it."

"Yes. How bold it was! A *young* man couldn't have done it! Yes, he's fascinating. But how old and sad he looked, as he lay back there in the chair!"

"Old? I don't think he looked old. He looked sad. Yes, it's left its mark on him."

The log burned quite through to its core, and fell asunder, a bristling mass of embers. They had been looking at it with downcast heads. Now they lifted their faces, and saw the pity in each other's eyes, and the beautiful girl impulsively kissed the pretty woman good-night.

V

COLVILLE fell asleep with the flattered sense which abounds
in the heart of a young man after his first successful evening
in society, but which can visit maturer life only upon some
such conditions of long exile and return as had been realised
in his. The looks of these two charming women followed him
into his dreams; he knew he must have pleased them, the
dramatic homage of the child was evidence of that; and
though it had been many years since he had found it sufficient cause of happiness to have pleased a woman, the desire
to do so was by no means extinct in him. The eyes of the girl
hovered above him like stars; he felt in their soft gaze that
he was a romance to her young heart, and this made him
laugh; it also made him sigh.

He woke at dawn with a sharp twinge in his shoulder, and
he rose to give himself the pleasure of making his own fire
with those fagots of broom and pine twigs which he had enjoyed the night before, promising himself to get back into
bed when the fire was well going, and sleep late. While he
stood before the open stove, the jangling of a small bell outside called him to the window, and he saw a procession
which had just issued from the church going to administer
the extreme unction to some dying person across the piazza.
The parish priest went first, bearing the consecrated wafer
in its vessel, and at his side an acolyte holding a yellow silk
umbrella over the Eucharist; after them came a number of
*facchini** in white robes and white hoods that hid their faces;
their tapers burned sallow and lifeless in the new morning
light; the bell jangled dismally.

"They even die dramatically in this country," thought
Colville, in whom the artist was taken with the effectiveness
of the spectacle before his human pity was stirred for the
poor soul who was passing. He reproached himself for that,
and instead of getting back to bed, he dressed and waited for
the mature hour which he had ordered his breakfast for.

When it came at last, picturesquely borne on the open hand of Giovanni, steaming coffee, hot milk, sweet butter in delicate disks, and two white eggs coyly tucked in the fold of a napkin, and all grouped upon the wide salver, it brought him a measure of the consolation which good cheer imparts to the ridiculous human heart even in the house where death is. But the sad incident tempered his mind with a sort of pensiveness that lasted throughout the morning, and quite till lunch. He spent the time in going about the churches; but the sunshine which the day began with was overcast, it was the day before, and the churches were rather too dark and cold in the afternoon. He went to Viesseux's reading-room and looked over the English papers, which he did not care for much; and he also made a diligent search of the catalogue for some book about Florence for little Effie Bowen: he thought he would like to surprise her mother with his interest in the matter. As the day waned toward dark, he felt more and more tempted to take her at her word, when she had said that any day was her day to him, and go to see her. If he had been a younger man he would have anxiously considered this indulgence and denied himself, but after forty a man denies himself no reasonable and harmless indulgence; he has learned by that time that it is a pity and a folly to do so.

Colville found Mrs. Bowen's room half full of arriving and departing visitors, and then he remembered that it was this day she had named to him on the Ponte Vecchio, and when Miss Graham thanked him for coming his first Thursday, he made a merit of not having forgotten it, and said he was going to come every Thursday during the winter. Miss Graham drew him a cup of tea from the Russian samovar which replaces in some Florentine houses the tea-pot of Occidental civilisation, and Colville smiled upon it and upon her, bending over the brazen urn with a flower-like tilt of her beautiful head. She wore an aesthetic dress of creamy camel's-hair, whose colour pleased the eye as its softness would have flattered the touch.

"What a very Tourguéneffish effect the samovar gives!" he said, taking a biscuit from the basket Effie Bowen brought him, shrinking with redoubled shyness from the eyebrows which he arched at her. "I wonder you can keep from calling me Fedor Colvillitch. Where is your mother, Effie Bowenovna?" he asked of the child, with a temptation to say Imogene Grahamovna.

They both looked mystified, but Miss Graham said, "I'm sorry to say you won't see Mrs. Bowen to-day. She has a very bad headache, and has left Effie and me to receive. We feel very incompetent, but she says it will do·us good."

There were some people there of the night before, and Colville had to talk to them. One of the ladies asked him if he had met the Inglehart boys* as he came in.

"The Inglehart boys? No. What are the Inglehart boys?"

"They were here all last winter, and they've just got back. It's rather exciting for Florence." She gave him a rapid sketch of that interesting exodus of a score of young painters from the art school at Munich, under the head of the singular and fascinating genius by whose name they became known. "They had their own school for a while in Munich, and then they all came down into Italy in a body. They had their studio things with them, and they travelled third class, and they made the greatest excitement everywhere, and had the greatest fun. They were a great sensation in Florence. They went everywhere, and were such favourites. I hope they are going to stay."

"I hope so too," said Colville. "I should like to see them."

"Dear me!" said the lady, with a glance at the clock. "It's five! I must be going."

The other ladies went, and Colville aproached to take leave, but Miss Graham detained him.

"What is Tourguéneffish?" she demanded.

"The quality of the great Russian novelist, Tourguéneff," said Colville, perceiving that she had not heard of him.

"Oh!"

"You ought to read him. The samovar sends up its agreeable odour all through his books. Read *Lisa** if you want your heart really broken.

"I'm glad you approve of heart-breaks in books. So many people won't read anything but cheerful books. It's the only quarrel I have with Mrs. Bowen. She says there are so many sad things in life that they ought to be kept out of books."

"Ah, there I perceive a divided duty," said Colville. "I should like to agree with both of you. But if Mrs. Bowen were here I should remind her that if there are so many sad things in life that is a very good reason for putting them in books too."

"Of course I shall tell her what you said."

"Why, I don't object to a certain degree of cheerfulness in books; only don't carry it too far—that's all."

This made the young girl laugh, and Colville was encouraged to go on. He told her of the sight he had seen from his window at daybreak, and he depicted it all very graphically, and made her feel its pathos perhaps more keenly than he had felt it. "Now, that little incident kept with me all day, tempering my boisterous joy in the Giottos, and reducing me to a decent composure in the presence of the Cimabues;* and it's pretty hard to keep from laughing at some of them, don't you think?"

The young people perceived that he was making fun again; but he continued with an air of greater seriousness. "Don't you see what a very good thing that was to begin one's day with? Why, even in Santa Croce, with the thermometer ten degrees below zero in the shade of Alfieri's monument,* I was no gayer than I should have been in a church at home. I suppose Mrs. Bowen would object to having that procession go by under one's window in a book; but I can't really see how it would hurt the reader, or damp his spirits permanently. A wholesome reaction would ensue, such as you see now in me, whom the thing happened to in real life."

He stirred his tea, and shook with an inward laugh as he carried it to his lips.

"Yes," said Miss Graham thoughtfully, and she looked at him searchingly in the interval of silence that ensued. But she only added, "I wish it would get warmer in the churches. I've seen hardly anything of them yet."

"From the way I felt in them to-day," sighed Colville, "I should think the churches would begin to thaw out about the middle of May. But if one goes well wrapped up in furs, and has a friend along to rouse him and keep him walking when he is about to fall into that lethargy which precedes death by freezing, I think they may be visited even now with safety. Have you been in Santa Maria Novella* yet?"

"No," said Miss Graham, with a shake of the head that expressed her resolution to speak the whole truth if she died for it, "not even in Santa Maria Novella."

"What a wonderful old place it is! That curious façade, with the dials and its layers of black and white marble soaked golden-red in a hundred thousand sunsets! That exquisite grand portal!" He gesticulated with the hand that the tea-cup left free, to suggest form and measurement as artists do. "Then the inside! The great Cimabue, with all that famous history on its back—the first divine Madonna by the first divine master, carried through the streets in a triumph of art and religion! Those frescoes of Ghirlandajo's* with real Florentine faces and figures in them, and all lavished upon the eternal twilight of that choir—but I suppose that if the full day were let in on them, once, they would vanish like ghosts at cock-crow! You must be sure to see the Spanish chapel; and the old cloister itself is such a pathetic place. There's a boys' school, as well as a military college, in the suppressed convent now, and the colonnades were full of boys running and screaming and laughing and making a joyful racket; it was so much more sorrowful than silence would have been there. One of the little scamps came up to me, and the young monk that was showing me round, and bobbed us a mocking bow and bobbed his hat off; then they all burst out laughing again and raced away, and the monk looked after them and said, so sweetly and wearily, 'They're at their diversions: we must have patience.' There are only twelve monks left there. All the rest are scattered and gone." He gave his cup to Miss Graham for more tea.

"Don't you think," she asked, drawing it from the samovar, "that it is very sad having the convents suppressed?"*

"It was very sad having slavery abolished—for some people," suggested Colville; he felt the unfairness of the point he had made.

"Yes," sighed Miss Graham.

Colville stood stirring his second cup of tea, when the *portière* parted, and showed Mrs. Bowen wistfully pausing on the threshold. Her face was pale, but she looked extremely pretty there.

"Ah, come in, Mrs. Bowen!" he called gaily to her. "I won't give you away to the other people. A cup of tea will do you good."

"Oh, I'm a great deal better," said Mrs. Bowen, coming forward to give him her hand. "I heard your voice, and I couldn't resist looking in."

"That was very kind of you," said Colville gratefully: and her eyes met his in a glance that flushed her face a deep red. "You find me here—*I* don't know why!—in my character of old family friend, doing my best to make life a burden to the young ladies."

"I wish you would stay to a family dinner with us," said Mrs. Bowen, and Miss Graham brightened in cordial support of the hospitality. "Why can't you?"

"I don't know, unless it's because I'm a humane person, and have some consideration for your headache."

"Oh, that's all gone," said Mrs. Bowen. "It was one of those convenient headaches—if you ever had then, you'd know—that go off at sunset."

"But you'd have another to-morrow."

"No, I'm safe for a whole fortnight from another."

"Then you leave me without an excuse, and I was just wishing I had none," said Colville.

After dinner Mrs. Bowen sent Effie to bed early to make up for the late hours of the night before, but she sat before the fire with Miss Graham rather late, talking Colville over, when he was gone.

"He's very puzzling to me," said Miss Graham. "Sometimes you think he's nothing but an old cynic, from his talk, and then something so sweet and fresh comes out that you don't know what to do. Don't you think he has really a very poetical mind, and that he's putting all the rest on?''

''I think he likes to make little effects,'' said Mrs. Bowen judiciously. ''He always did, rather.''

''Why, was he like this when he was young?''

''I don't consider him very old now.''

''No, of course not. I meant when you knew him before.'' Miss Graham had some needlework in her hand; Mrs. Bowen, who never even pretended to work at that kind of thing, had nothing in hers but the feather screen.

''He is old, compared with you, Imogene; but you'll find, as you live along, that your contemporaries are always young. Mr. Colville is very much improved. He used to be painfully shy, but he put on a bold front, and now the bold front seems to have become a second nature with him.''

''I like it,'' said Miss Graham, to her needle.

''Yes; but I suspect he's still shy, at heart. He used to be very sentimental, and was always talking Ruskin. I think if he hadn't talked Ruskin so much, Jenny Milbury might have treated him better. It was very priggish in him.''

''Oh, I can't imagine Mr. Colville's being priggish!''

''He's very much improved. He used to be quite a sloven in his dress; you know how very slovenly most American gentlemen are in their dress, at any rate. I think that influenced her against him too.''

''He isn't slovenly now,'' suggested Miss Graham.

''Oh no; he's quite swell,'' said Mrs. Bowen, depriving the adjective of slanginess by the refinement of her tone.

''Well,'' said Miss Graham, ''I don't see how you could have endured her after that. It was atrocious.''

''It was better for her to break with him, if she found out she didn't love him, than to marry him. That,'' said Mrs. Bowen, with a depth of feeling uncommon for her, ''would have been a thousand times worse.''

''Yes, but she ought to have found out before she led him on so far.''

''Sometimes girls can't. They don't know themselves; they think they're in love when they're not. She was very impulsive, and of course she was flattered by it; he was so intellectual. But at last she found that she couldn't bear it, and she had to tell him so.''

"Did she ever say why she didn't love him?"

"No; I don't suppose she could. The only thing I remember her saying was that he was 'too much of a mixture.' ''

"What *did* she mean by that?"

"I don't know exactly.''

"Do you think he's insincere?"

"Oh no. Perhaps she meant that he wasn't single-minded.''

"Fickle?"

"No. He certainly wasn't that in her case.''

"Undecided?"

"He was decided enough with her—at last.''

Imogene dropped the hopeless quest, "How can a man ever stand such a thing?" she sighed.

"He stood it very nobly. That was the best thing about it; he took it in the most delicate way. She showed me his letter. There wasn't a word or a hint of reproach in it; he seemed to be anxious about nothing but her feeling badly for him. Of course he couldn't help showing that he was mortified for having pursued her with attentions that were disagreeable to her; but that was delicate too. Yes, it was a very large-minded letter.''

"It was shocking in her to show it.''

"It wasn't very nice. But it was a letter that any girl might have been proud to show.''

"Oh, she *couldn't* have done it to gratify her vanity!"

"Girls are very queer, my dear," said Mrs. Bowen, as if the fact were an abstraction. She mused upon the flat of her screen, while Miss Graham plied her needle in silence.

The latter spoke first. "Do you think he was very much broken by it?"

"You never can tell. He went out west then, and there he has stayed ever since. I suppose his life would have been very different if nothing of the kind had happened. He had a great deal of talent. I always thought I should hear of him in some way.''

"Well, it was a heartless, shameless thing! I don't see how you can speak of it so leniently as you do, Mrs. Bowen. It makes all sorts of coquetry and flirtation more detestable to me than ever. Why, it has ruined his life!"

"Oh, he was young enough then to outlive it. After all, they were a boy and girl."

"A boy and girl! How old were they?"

"He must have been twenty-three or four, and she was twenty."

"*My age*! Do you call that being a girl?"

"She was old enough to know what she was about," said Mrs. Bowen justly.

Imogene fell back in her chair, drawing out her needle the full length of its thread, and then letting her hand fall. "I don't know. It seems as if I never should be grown up, or anything but a child. Yes, when I think of the way young men talk, they do seem boys. Why can't they talk like Mr. Colville? I wish I could talk like him. It makes you forget how old and plain he is."

She remained with her eyelids dropped in an absent survey of her sewing, while Mrs. Bowen regarded her with a look of vexation, impatience, resentment, or the last refinement of these emotions, which she banished from her face before Miss Graham looked up and said, with a smile: "How funny it is to see Effie's infatuation with him! She can't take her eyes off him for a moment, and she follows him round the room so as not to lose a word he is saying. It was heroic of her to go to bed without a murmur before he left to-night."

"Yes, she sees that he is good," said Mrs. Bowen.

"Oh, she sees that he's something very much more. Mr. Waters is good."

Miss Graham had the best of the argument, and so Mrs. Bowen did not reply.

"I feel," continued the young girl, "as if it were almost a shame to have asked him to go to that silly dancing party with us. It seems as if we didn't appreciate him. I think we ought to have kept him for high æsthetic occasions and historical researches."

"Oh, I don't think Mr. Colville was very deeply offended at being asked to go with us."

"No," said Imogene, with another sigh, "He didn't seem so. I suppose there's always an undercurrent of sadness—of tragedy—in everything for him."

"I don't suppose anything of the kind," cried Mrs. Bowen gaily. "He's had time enough to get over it."

"Do people *ever* get over such things?"

"Yes—men."

"It must be because he was young, as you say. But if it had happened *now?*"

"Oh, it *couldn't* happen now. He's altogether too cool and calculating."

"Do you think he's cool and calculating?"

"No. He's too old for a broken heart—a new one."

"Mrs. Bowen," demanded the girl solemnly, "could *you* forgive yourself for such a thing if you had done it?"

"Yes, perfectly well, if I wasn't in love with him."

"But if you'd made him *think* you were?" pursued the girl breathlessly.

"If I were a flirt—yes."

"*I* couldn't," said Imogené, with tragic depth.

"Oh, be done with your intensities, and go to bed, Imogene," said Mrs. Bowen, giving her a playful push.

VI

IT was so long since Colville had been at a dancing party that Mrs. Bowen's offer to take him to Madame Uccelli's had first struck his sense of the ludicrous. Then it had begun to flatter him; it implied that he was still young enough to dance if he would, though he had stipulated that they were not to expect anything of the kind from him. He liked also the notion of being seen and accepted in Florentine society as the old friend of Mrs. Bowen's, for he had not been long in discovering that her position in Florence was, among the foreign residents, rather authoritative. She was one of the very few Americans who were asked to Italian houses, and Italian houses lying even beyond the neutral ground of English-speaking intermarriages. She was not, of course, asked to the great Princess Strozzi ball, where the Florentine nobility appeared in the mediæval pomp—the veritable costumes—of their ancestors; only a rich American banking family went, and their distinction was spoken of under the breath; but any glory short of this was within Mrs. Bowen's reach. So an old lady who possessed herself of Colville the night before had told him, celebrating Mrs. Bowen at length, and boasting of her acceptance among the best English residents, who, next after the natives, seem to constitute the social ambition of Americans living in Italian cities.

It interested him to find that some geographical distinctions which are fading at home had quite disappeared in Florence. When he was there before, people from quite small towns in the East had made pretty Lina Ridgely and her friend feel the disadvantage of having come from the Western side of an imaginary line; he had himself been at the pains always to let people know, at the American watering-places where he spent his vacations, that though presently from Des Vaches, Indiana, he was really born in Rhode Island; but in Florence it was not at all necessary. He found in Mrs. Bowen's house people from Denver, Chicago, St. Louis, Boston, New York, and Baltimore, all meeting as of apparently the same civilisation, and whether Mrs. Bowen's own origin was, like that of the Etruscan cities, lost in the mists of antiquity, or whether she had sufficiently atoned for the error of her birth by subsequent residence in the national capital and prolonged sojourn in New York, it seemed certainly not to be remembered against her among her Eastern acquaintance. The time had been when the fact that Miss Graham came from Buffalo would have gone far to class her with the animal from which her native city had taken its name; but now it made no difference, unless it was a difference in her favour. The English spoke with the same vague respect of Buffalo and of Philadelphia; and to a family of real Bostonians Colville had the courage to say simply that he lived in Des Vaches, and not to seek to palliate the truth in any sort. If he wished to prevaricate at all, it was rather to attribute himself to Mrs. Bowen's city in Ohio.

She and Miss Graham called for him with her carriage the next night, when it was time to go to Madame Uccelli's.

"This gives me a very patronised and effeminate feeling," said Colville, getting into the odorous dark of the carriage, and settling himself upon the front seat with a skill inspired by his anxiety not to tear any of the silken spreading white wraps that inundated the whole interior. "Being come for by ladies!" They both gave some nervous joyful laughs, as they found his hand in the obscurity, and left the sense of a gloved pressure upon it. "Is this the way you used to do in Vesprucius, Mrs. Bowen?"

"Oh no, indeed!" she answered. "The young gentlemen used to find out whether I was going, and came for me with a hack, and generally, if the weather was good, we walked home."

"That's the way we still do in Des Vaches. Sometimes, as a tremendous joke, the ladies come for us in leap-year. How do you go to balls in Buffalo, Miss Graham? Or, no; I withdraw the embarrassing question." Some gleams from the street lamps, as they drove along, struck in through the carriage windows, and flitted over the ladies' faces and were gone again. "Ah! this is very trying. Couldn't you stop him at the next corner, and let me see how radiant you ladies really are? I may be in very great danger; I'd like to know just how much."

"It wouldn't be of any use," cried the young girl gaily. "We're all wrapped up, and you couldn't form any idea of us. You must wait, and let us burst upon you when we come out of the dressing-room at Madame Uccelli's."

"But then it may be too late," he urged. "Is it very far?"

"Yes," said Mrs. Bowen. "It's ridiculously far. It's outside the Roman Gate. I don't see why people live at that distance."

"In order to give the friends you bring the more pleasure of your company, Mrs. Bowen."

"Ah! that's very well. But you're not logical."

"No," said Colville; "you can't be logical and complimentary at the same time. It's too much to ask. How delicious your flowers are!" The ladies each had a bouquet in her hand, which she was holding in addition to her fan, the edges of her cloak, and the skirt of her train.

"Yes," said Mrs. Bowen; "we are so much obliged to you for them."

"Why, I sent you no flowers," said Colville, startled into untimely earnest.

"Didn't you? triumphed Mrs. Bowen. "I thought gentlemen always sent flowers to ladies when they were going to a ball with them. They used to, in Columbus."

"And in Buffalo they always do," Miss Graham added.

"Ah! they don't in Des Vaches," said Colville. They tried to mystify him further about the bouquets; they succeeded in being very gay, and in making themselves laugh a great deal. Mrs. Bowen was even livelier than the young girl.

Her carriage was one of the few private equipages that drove up to Madame Uccelli's door; most people had not even come in a *remise,** but, after the simple Florentine fashion, had taken the little cabs, which stretched in a long line up and down the way; the horses had let their weary

heads drop, and were easing their broken knees by extend-
ing their forelegs while they drowsed; the drivers, huddled
in their great-coats, had assembled around the doorway to
see the guests alight, with that amiable, unenvious interest
of the Italians in the pleasure of others. The deep sky glittered with stars; in the corner of the next villa garden the
black plumes of some cypresses blotted out their space
among them.

"*Isn't* it Florentine?" demanded Mrs. Bowen, giving the
hand which Colville offered in helping her out of the carriage
a little vivid pressure, full of reminiscence and confident
sympathy. A flush of youth warmed his heart; he did not
quail even when the porter of the villa intervened between
her and her coachman, whom she was telling when to come
back, and said that the carriages were ordered for three
o'clock.

"Did you ever sit up so late as that in Des Vaches?" asked
Miss Graham mischievously.

"Oh yes; I was editor of a morning paper," he explained.
But he did not like the imputation of her question.

Madame Uccelli accepted him most hospitably among her
guests when he was presented. She was an American who
had returned with her Italian husband to Italy, and had long
survived him in the villa which he had built with her money.
Such people grow very queer with the lapse of time.
Madame Uccelli's character remained inalienably
American, but her manners and customs had become
largely Italian; without having learned the language
thoroughly, she spoke it very fluently, and its idioms marked
her Philadelphia English. Her house was a menagerie of all
the nationalities; she was liked in Italian society, and there
were many Italians; English-speaking Russians abounded;
there were many genuine English, Germans, Scandina-
vians, Protestant Irish, American Catholics, and then
Americans of all kinds. There was a superstition of her ex-
clusiveness among her compatriots, but one really met every
one there sooner or later; she was supposed to be a convert
to the religion of her late husband, but no one really knew
what religion she was of, probably not even Madame Uccelli

herself. One thing you were sure of at her house, and that was a substantial supper; it is the example of such resident foreigners which has corrupted the Florentines, though many native families still hold out against it.

The dancing was just beginning, and the daughter of Madame Uccelli, who spoke both English and Italian much better than her mother, came forward and possessed herself of Miss Graham, after a polite feint of pressing Mrs. Bowen to let her find a partner for her.

Mrs. Bowen cooed a gracious refusal, telling Fanny Uccelli that she knew very well that she never danced now. The girl had not much time for Colville; she welcomed him, but she was full of her business of starting the dance, and she hurried away without asking him whether she should introduce him to some lady for the quadrille that was forming. Her mother, however, asked him if he would not go out and get himself some tea, and she found a lady to go with him to the supper-room. This lady had daughters whom apparently she wished to supervise while they were dancing, and she brought Colville back very soon. He had to stand by the sofa where she sat till Madame Uccelli found him and introduced him to another mother of daughters. Later he joined a group formed by the father of one of the dancers and the non-dancing husband of a dancing wife. Their conversation was perfunctory; they showed one another they they had no pleasure in it.

Presently the father went to see how his daughter looked while dancing; the husband had evidently no such curiosity concerning his wife; and Colville went with the father, and looked at Miss Graham. She was very beautiful, and she obeyed the music as if it were her breath; her face was rapt, intense, full of an unsmiling delight, which shone in her dark eyes, glowing like low stars. Her *abandon* interested Colville, and then awed him; the spectacle of that young, unjaded capacity for pleasure touched him with a profound sense of loss. Suddenly Imogene caught sight of him, and with the coming of a second look in her eyes the light of an exquisite smile flashed over her face. His heart was in his throat.

"*Your* daughter?" asked the fond parent at his elbow. "That is mine yonder in red."

Colville did not answer, nor look at the young lady in red. The dance was ceasing; the fragments of those kaleidoscopic radiations were dispersing themselves; the tormented piano was silent.

The officer whom Imogene had danced with brought her to Mrs. Bowen, and resigned her with the regulation bow, hanging his head down before him as if submitting his neck to the axe. She put her hand in Colville's arm, where he stood beside Mrs. Bowen. "Oh, *do* take me to get something to eat!"

In the supper-room she devoured salad and ices with a childish joy in them. The place was jammed, and she laughed from her corner at Colville's struggles in getting the things for her and bringing them to her. While she was still in the midst of an ice, the faint note of the piano sounded. "Oh, they're beginning again. It's the Lancers!"* she said, giving him the plate back. She took his arm again; she almost pulled him along on their return.

"Why don't *you* dance?" she demanded mockingly.

"I would if you'd let me dance with you."

"Oh, that's impossible! I'm engaged ever so many deep." She dropped his arm instantly at sight of a young Englishman who seemed to be looking for her. This young Englishman had a zeal for dancing that was unsparing; partners were nothing to him except as a means of dancing; his manner expressed a supreme contempt for people who made the slightest mistake, who danced with less science or less conscience than himself. "I've been looking for you," he said, in a tone of cold rebuke, without looking at her. "We've been waiting."

Colville wished to beat him, but Imogene took his rebuke meekly, and murmured some apologies about not hearing the piano before. He hurried her off without recognising Colville's existence in any way.

The undancing husband of the dancing wife was boring himself in a corner; Colville decided that the chances with him were better than with the fond father, and joined him,

just as a polite officer came up and entreated him to complete a set. "Oh, I never danced in my life," he replied; and
then he referred the officer to Colville. "Don't *you* dance?"

"I used to dance," Colville began, while the officer stood
looking patiently at him. This was true. He used to dance
the Lancers, too, and very badly, seventeen years before. He
had danced it with Lina Ridgely and the other one, Mrs
Milbury. His glance wandered to the vacant place on the
floor; it was the same set which Miss Graham was in; she
smiled and beckoned derisively. A vain and foolish ambition
fired him. "Oh yes, I can dance a little," he said.

A little was quite enough for the eager officer. He had Colville a partner in an instant, and the next he was on the floor.

"Oh, what fun!" cried Miss Graham; but the fun had not
really begun yet.

Colville had forgotten everything about the Lancers. He
walked round like a bear in a pen: he capered to and fro with
a futile absurdity; people poked him hither and thither; his
progress was attended by rending noises from the trains over
which he found his path. He smiled and cringed, and
apologised to the hardening faces of the dancers: even Miss
Graham's face had become very grave.

"This won't do," said the Englishman at last, with cold
insolence. He did not address himself to any one; he merely
stopped; they all stopped, and Colville was effectively expelled the set; another partner was found for his lady, and
he wandered giddily away. He did not know where to turn;
the whole room must have seen what an incredible ass he
had made of himself, but Mrs. Bowen looked as if she had
not seen.

He went up to her, resolved to make fun of himself at the
first sign she gave of being privy to his disgrace. But she only
said, "Have you found your way to the supper-room yet?"

"Oh yes; twice," he answered, and kept on talking with
her and Madame Uccelli. After five minutes or so something
occurred to Colville. "Have *you* found the way to the supper-
room yet, Mrs. Bowen.

"No!" she owned, with a small, pathetic laugh, which
expressed a certain physical faintness, and reproached him

with insupportable gentleness for his selfish obtuseness.

"Let me show you the way," he cried.

"Why, I *am* rather hungry," said Mrs. Bowen, taking his arm, with a patient arrangement first of her fan, her bouquet, and her train, and then moving along by his side with a delicate-footed pace, which insinuated and deprecated her dependence upon him.

There were only a few people in the supper-room and they had it practically to themselves. She took a cup of tea and a slice of buttered bread, with a little salad, which she excused herself from eating because it was the day after her headache. "I shouldn't have thought you *were* hungry, Mrs. Bowen," he said, "if you hadn't told me so," and he recalled that, as a young girl, her friend used to laugh at her for having such a butterfly appetite; she was in fact one of those women who go through life the marvels of such of our brutal sex as observe the ethereal nature of their diet. But in an illogical revulsion of feeling, Colville, who was again cramming himself with all the solids and fluids in reach, and storing up a vain regret against the morrow, preferred her delicacy to the magnificent rapacity of Miss Graham: Imogene had passed from salad to ice, and at his suggestion had frankly reverted to salad again and then taken a second ice, with the robust appetite of perfect health and perfect youth. He felt a desire to speak against her to Mrs. Bowen, he did not know why and he did not know how; he veiled his feeling in an open attack. "Miss Graham has just been the cause of my playing the fool, with her dancing. She dances so superbly that she makes you want to dance too—she made me feel as if I *could* dance."

"Yes," said Mrs. Bowen; "it was very kind of you to complete the set. I saw you dancing," she added, without a glimmer of guilty consciousness in her eyes.

It was very sweet, but Colville had to protest. "Oh no; you didn't see me *dancing;* you saw me *not* dancing. I am a ruined man, and I leave Florence to-morrow; but I have the sad satisfaction of reflecting that I don't leave an unbroken train among the ladies of that set. And I have made one

young Englishman so mad that there is a reasonable hope of
his not recovering.''

''Oh no; you *don't* think of going away for that!'' said
Mrs. Bowen, not heeding the rest of his joking.

''Well, the time had been when I have left Florence for
less,'' said Colville, with the air of preparing himself to listen
to reason.

''You mustn't,'' said Mrs. Bowen briefly.

''Oh, very well, then, I won't,'' said Colville whimsically,
as if that settled it.

Mrs. Bowen would not talk of the matter any more; he
could see that with her kindness, which was always more
than her tact, she was striving to get away from the subject.
As he really cared for it no longer, this made him persist in
clinging to it; he liked this pretty woman's being kind to
him. ''Well,'' he said finally, ''I consent to stay in Florence
on condition that you suggest some means of atonement for
me which I can also make a punishment to Miss Graham.''

Mrs. Bowen did not respond to the question of placating
and punishing her *protégée* with sustained interest. They went
back to Madame Uccelli, and to the other elderly ladies in
the room that opened by archways upon the dancing-room.

Imogene was on the floor, dancing not merely with
unabated joy, but with a zest that seemed only to freshen
from dance to dance. If she left the dance, it was to go out
on her partner's arm to the supper-room. Colville could not
decently keep on talking to Mrs. Bowen the whole evening;
it would be too conspicuous; he devolved from frump to
frump; he bored himself; he yawned in his passage from one
of these mothers or fathers to another. The hours passed; it
was two o'clock; Imogene was going out to the supper-room
again. He was taking out his watch. She saw him, and ''Oh,
don't!'' she cried, laughing, as she passed.

The dancing went on; she was waltzing now in the interminable german.* Some one had let down a window in the
dancing-room, and he was feeling it in his shoulder. Mrs.
Bowen, across the room, looked heroically patient, but
weary. He glanced down at the frump on the sofa near, and
realised that she had been making a long speech to him,

which, he could see from her look, had ended in some sort
of question.

Three o'clock came, and they had to wait till the german
was over. He felt that Miss Graham was behaving badly,
ungratefully, selfishly; on the way home in the carriage he
was silent from utter boredom and fatigue, but Mrs. Bowen
was sweetly sympathetic with the girl's rapture. Imogene did
not seem to feel his moodiness; she laughed, she joked, she
told a number of things that happened, she hummed the air
of the last waltz. "Isn't it divine?" she asked. "*Oh!* I feel as
if I could dance for a week." She was still dancing; she gave
Colville's foot an accidental tap in keeping time on the floor
of the carriage to the tune she was humming. No one said
anything about a next meeting when they parted at the gate
of Palazzo Pinti, and Mrs. Bowen bade her coachman drive
Colville to his hotel. But both the ladies' voices called good-
night to him as he drove away. He fancied a shade of mocking in Miss Graham's voice.

The great outer door of the hotel was locked, of course,
and the poor little porter kept Colville thumping at it some
time before he unlocked it, full of sleepy smiles and apologies. "I'm sorry to wake you up," said Colville kindly.

"It is my duty," said the porter, with amiable heroism.
He discharged another duty by lighting a whole new candle,
which would be set down to Colville's account, and went
before him to his room, up the wide stairs, cold in their
white linen path, and on through the crooked corridors
haunted by the ghosts of extinct *tables d'hôte*, and full of
goblin shadows. He had recovered a noonday suavity by the
time he reached Colville's door, and bowed himself out,
after lighting the candles within, with a sweet plenitude of
politeness, which Colville, even in his gloomy mood, could
not help admiring in a man in his shirt sleeves, with only one
suspender up.

If there had been a fire, Colville would have liked to sit
down before it, and taken an account of his feelings, but the
atmosphere of a bed-chamber in a Florentine hotel at half-
past three o'clock on a winter morning is not one that invites
to meditation; and he made haste to get into bed, with

nothing clearer in his mind than a shapeless sense of having been trifled with. He ought not to have gone to a dancing party, to begin with, and then he certainly ought not to have attempted to dance; so far he might have been master of the situation, and was responsible for it; but he was, over and above this, aware of not having wished to do either, of having been wrought upon against his convictions to do both. He regarded now with supreme loathing a fantastic purpose which he had formed while tramping round on those women's dresses, of privately taking lessons in dancing, and astonishing Miss Graham at the next ball where they met. Miss Graham? What did he care for that child? Or Mrs. Bowen either, for the matter of that? Had he come four thousand miles to be used, to be played with, by them? At this point Colville was aware of the brutal injustice of his mood. They were ladies, both of them, charming and good, and he had been a fool; that was all. It was not the first time he had been a fool for women. An inexpressible bitterness for that old wrong, which, however he had been used to laugh at it and despise it, had made his life solitary and barren, poured upon his soul; it was as if it had happened to him yesterday.

A band of young men burst from one of the narrow streets leading into the piazza and straggled across it, letting their voices flare out upon the silence, and then drop extinct one by one. A whole world of faded associations flushed again in Colville's heart. This was Italy; this was Florence; and he execrated the hour in which he had dreamed of returning.

VII

THE next morning's sunshine dispersed the black mood of
the night before; but enough of Colville's self-disgust remained to determine him not to let his return to Florence be
altogether vain, or his sojourn so idle as it had begun being.
The vague purpose which he had cherished of studying the
past life and character of the Florentines in their architecture
shaped itself anew in the half-hour which he gave himself
over his coffee; and he turned it over in his mind with that
mounting joy in its capabilities which attends the contemplation of any sort of artistic endeavour. No people had ever
more distinctly left the impress of their whole temper in their
architecture, or more sharply distinguished their varying
moods from period to period in their palaces and temples.
He believed that he could not only supply that brief
historical sketch of Florence which Mrs. Bowen had
lamented the want of, but he could make her history speak
an unintelligible, an unmistakeable tongue in every monument of the past, from the Etruscan wall at Fiesole* to the
cheap, plain, and tasteless shaft raised to commemorate
Italian Unity in the next piazza. With sketches from his own
pencil, illustrative of points which he could not otherwise
enforce, he could make such a book on Florence as did not
exist, such a book as no one had yet thought of making.
With this object in his mind, making and keeping him
young, he could laugh with any one who liked at the vanity
of the middle-aged Hoosier* who had spoiled a set in the
Lancers at Madame Uccelli's party; he laughed at him now
alone, with a wholly impersonal sense of his absurdity.

After breakfast he went without delay to Viesseux's
reading-room, to examine his catalogue, and see what there
was in it to his purpose. While he was waiting his turn to pay
his subscription, with the people who surrounded the pro-
prietor, half a dozen of the acquaintants he had made at
Mrs. Bowen's passed in and out. Viesseux's is a place where

sooner or later you meet every one you know among the
foreign residents at Florence; the natives in smaller proportion resort there too; and Colville heard a lady asking for a
book in that perfect Italian which strikes envy to the heart
of the stranger sufficiently versed in the language to know
that he never shall master it. He rather rejoiced in his
despair, however, as an earnest of his renewed intellectual
life. Henceforth his life would be wholly intellectual. He did
not regret his little excursion into society; it had shown him
with dramatic sharpness how unfit for it he was.

"Good *morning!*" said some one in a bland undertone full
of a pleasant recognition of the claims to quiet of a place
where some others were speaking in their ordinary tones.

Colville looked round on the Rev. Mr. Waters, and took
his friendly hand. "Good morning—glad to see you," he
answered.

"Are you looking for that short Florentine history for
Mrs. Bowen's little girl?" asked Mr. Waters, inclining his
head slightly for the reply. "She mentioned it to me."

By day Colville remarked more distinctly that the old
gentleman was short and slight, with a youthful eagerness in
his face surviving on good terms with the grey locks that fell
down his temples from under the brim of his soft felt hat.
With the boyish sweetness of his looks blended a sort of appreciative shrewdness, which pointed his smiling lips slightly
aslant in what seemed the expectation rather than the intention of humour.

"Not exactly," said Colville, experiencing a difficulty in
withholding the fact that in some sort he was just going to write
a short Florentine history, and finding a certain pleasure in
Mrs. Bowen's having remembered that he had taken an interest in Effie's reading. He had a sudden wish to tell Mr.
Waters of his plan, but this was hardly the time or place.

They now found themselves face to face with the librarian,
and Mr. Waters made a gesture of waiving himself in Colville's favour.

"No, no!" said the latter; "You had better ask. I am
going to put this gentleman through rather an extended
course of sprouts."*

The librarian smiled with the helplessness of a foreigner, who knows his interlocutor's English, but not the meaning of it.

"Oh, I merely wanted to ask," said Mr. Waters, addressing the librarian, and explaining to Colville, "whether you had received that book on Savonarola yet. The German one."

"I shall see," said the librarian, and he went upon a quest that kept him some minutes.

"You're not thinking of taking Savonarola's life, I suppose?" suggested Colville.

"Oh no. Villari's book* has covered the whole ground for ever, it seems to me. It's a wonderful book. You've read it?"

"Yes. It's a thing that makes you feel that, after all, the Italians have only to make a real effort in any direction, and they go ahead of everybody else. What biography of the last twenty years can compare with it?"

"You're right, sir—you're right," cried the old man enthusiastically. "They're a gifted race, a people of genius."

"I wish for their own sakes they'd give their minds a little to generalship," said Colville, pressed by the facts to hedge somewhat. "They did get so badly smashed in their last war, poor fellows."

"Oh, I don't think I should like them any better if they were better soldiers. Perhaps the lesson of noble endurance that they've given our times is all that we have the right to demand of them in the way of heroism; no one can say they lack courage. And sometimes it seems to me that in simply outgrowing the different sorts of despotism that had fastened upon them, till their broken bonds fell away without positive effort on their part, they showed a greater sublimity than if they had violently conquered their freedom. Most nations sink lower and lower under tyranny; the Italians grew steadily more and more civilised, more noble, more gentle, more grand. It was a wonderful spectacle—like a human soul perfected through suffering and privation. Every period of their history is full of instruction. I find my ancestral puritanism* particularly appealed to by the puritanism of Savonarola."

"Then Villari hasn't satisfied you that Savonarola wasn't a Protestant?"

"Oh yes, he has. I said his puritanism. Just now I'm interested in justifying his failure to myself, for it's one of the things in history that I've found it hardest to accept. But no doubt his puritanic state fell because it was dreary and ugly, as the puritanic state always has been. It makes its own virtues intolerable; puritanism won't let you see how good and beautiful the Puritans often are. It was inevitable that Savonarola's enemies should misunderstand and hate him."

"You are one of the last men I should have expected to find among the *Arrabiati*,"* said Colville.

"Oh, there's a great deal to be said for the Florentine Arrabiati, as well as for the English Malignants,* though the Puritans in neither case would have known how to say it. Savonarola perished because he was excessive. I am studying him in this aspect; it is fresh ground. It is very interesting to inquire just at what point a man's virtues become mischievous and intolerable."

These ideas interested Colville; he turned to them with relief from the sense of his recent trivialities. In this old man's earnestness he found support and encouragement in the new course he had marked out for himself. Sometimes it had occurred to him not only that he was too old for the interests of his youth at forty, but that there was no longer time for him to take up new ones. He considered Mr. Waters's grey hairs, and determined to be wiser. "I should like to talk these things over with you—and some other things," he said.

The librarian came toward them with the book for Mr. Waters, who was fumbling near-sightedly in his pocket-book for his card. "I shall be very happy to see you at my room," he said. "Ah, thank you," he added, taking his book, with a simple relish as if it were something whose pleasantness was sensible to the touch. He gave Colville the scholar's far-off look as he turned to go: he was already as remote as the fifteenth century through the magic of the book, which he opened and began to read at once. Colville stared after him; he did not wish to come to just that yet, either. Life, active

life, life of his own day, called to him; he had been one of
its busiest children: could he turn his back upon it for any
charm or use that was in the past? Again that unnerving
doubt, that paralysing distrust, beset him, and tempted him
to curse the day in which he had returned to this outworn
Old World. Idler on its modern surface, or delver in its
deep-hearted past, could he reconcile himself to it? What did
he care for the Italians of to-day, or the history of the Florentines as expressed in their architectural monuments? It was
the problems of the vast, tumultuous American life, which
he had turned his back on, that really concerned him. Later
he might take up the study that fascinated yonder old man,
but for the present it was intolerable.

He was no longer young, that was true; but with an ache
of old regret he felt that he had not yet lived his life, that his
was a baffled destiny, an arrested fate. A lady came up and
took his turn with the librarian, and Colville did not stay for
another. He went out and walked down the Lung' Arno
toward the Cascine.* The sun danced on the river, and
bathed the long line of pale buff and grey houses that followed
its curve, and ceased in the mist of leafless tree-tops where
the Cascine began. It was not the hour of the promenade,
and there was little driving; but the sidewalks were peopled
thickly enough with persons, in groups, or singly, who had
the air of straying aimlessly up or down, with no purpose but
to be in the sun, after the rainy weather of the past week.
There were faces of invalids, wistful and thin, and here and
there a man, muffled to the chin, lounged feebly on the
parapet and stared at the river. Colville hastened by them;
they seemed to claim him as one of their ailing and aging
company, and just then he was in the humour of being very
young and strong.

A carriage passed before him through the Cascine gates,
and drove down the road next the river. He followed, and
when it had got a little way it stopped at the roadside, and
a lady and little girl alighted, who looked about and caught
sight of him, and then obviously waited for him to come
up with them. It was Imogene and Effie Bowen, and the
young girl called to him. "We *thought* it was you. Aren't

you astonished to find us here at this hour?'' she demanded, as soon as he came up, and gave him her hand. "Mrs Bowen sent us for our health—or Effie's health—and I was just making the man stop and let us out for a little walk.''

"My health is very much broken too, Miss Effie,'' said Colville. "Will you let me walk with you?'' The child smiled, as she did at Colville's speeches, which she apparently considered all jokes, but diplomatically referred the decision to Imogene with an upward glance.

"We shall be very glad indeed,'' said the girl.

"That's very polite of you. But Miss Effie makes no effort to conceal her dismay,'' said Colville.

The little girl smiled again, and her smile was so like the smile of Lina Ridgely, twenty years ago, that his next words were inevitably tinged with reminiscence.

"Does one still come for one's health to the Cascine? When I was in Florence before, there was no other place if one went to look for it with young ladies—the Cascine or the Boboli Gardens.* Do they keep the fountain of youth turned on here during the winter still?''

"I've never seen it,'' said Imogene gaily.

"Of course not. You never looked for it. Neither did I when I was here before. But it wouldn't escape me now.''

Since he had met them he had aged again, in spite of his resolutions to the contrary; somehow, beside their buoyancy and bloom, the youth in his heart faded.

Imogene had started forward as soon as he joined them, and Colville, with Effie's gloved hand stolen shyly in his, was finding it quite enough to keep up with her in her elastic advance.

She wore a long habit of silk, whose fur-trimmed edge wandered diagonally across her breast and down to the edge of her walking dress. To Colville, whom her girlish slimness in her ball costume had puzzled after his original impressions of Junonian abundance, she did not so much dwindle as seem to vanish from the proportions his visions had assigned her that first night when he saw her standing before the mirror. In this outdoor avatar, this companionship with the sun and breeze, she was new to him again, and he found himself.

searching his consciousness for his lost acquaintance with her, and feeling as if he knew her less and less. Perhaps, indeed, she had no very distinctive individuality; perhaps at her age no woman has, but waits for it to come to her through life, through experience. She was an expression of youth, of health, of beauty, and of the moral loveliness that comes from a fortunate combination of these; but beyond this she was elusive in a way that seemed to characterise her even materially. He could not make anything more of the mystery as he walked at her side, and he went thinking— formlessly, as people always think—that with the child or with her mother he would have had a community of interest and feeling which he lacked with this splendid girlhood; he was both too young and too old for it. And then, while he answered this or that to Imogene's talk aptly enough, his mind went back to the time when this mystery was no mystery, or when he was contemporary with it, and if he did not understand it, at least accepted it as if it were the most natural thing in the world. It seemed a longer time now since it had been in his world than it was since he was a child.

"Should you have thought," she asked, turning her face back toward him, "that it would be so hot in the sun today? *Oh*, that beautiful river! How it twists and writhes along! Do you remember that sonnet of Longfellow's*—the one he wrote in Italian about the Ponte Vecchio, and the Arno twisting like a dragon underneath it? They say that Hawthorne* used to live in a villa just behind the hill over there; we're going to look it up as soon as the weather is settled. Don't you think his books are perfectly fascinating?"

"Yes," said Colville; "only I should want a good while to say it."

"*I* shouldn't!" retorted the girl. "When you've said fascinating, you've said everything. There's no other word for them. Don't you like to talk about the books you've read?"

"I would if I could remember the names of the characters. But I get them mixed up."

"Oh, *I* never do! I remember the least one of them, and all they do and say."

"I used to."

"It seems to me you *used* to do everything."

"It seems to me as if I did.

> " 'I remember, when I think,
> That my youth was half divine.' "*

"Oh, Tennyson—yes! *He's* fascinating. Don't you think he's fascinating?"

"Very," said Colville. He was wondering whether this were the kind of talk that he thought was literary when he was a young fellow.

"How perfectly weird the 'Vision of Sin' is!" Imogene continued. "Don't you like *weird* things?"

"Weird things?" Colville reflected. "Yes; but I don't see very much in them any more. The fact is, they don't seem to come to anything in particular."

"Oh, *I* think they do! I've had dreams that I've lived on for days. Do you ever have prophetic dreams?"

"Yes; but they never come true. When they do, I know that I didn't have them."

"What *do* you mean?"

"I mean that we are all so fond of the marvellous that we can't trust ourselves about any experience that seems supernatural. If a ghost appeared to me I should want him to prove it by at least two other reliable, disinterested witnesses before I believed my own account of the matter."

"Oh!" cried the girl, half puzzled, half amused. "Then of course you don't believe in ghosts?"

"Yes; I expect to be one myself some day. But I'm in no hurry to mingle with them."

Imogene smiled vaguely, as if the talk pleased her, even when it mocked the fancies and whims which, after so many generations that have indulged them, she was finding so fresh and new in her turn.

"Don't you like to walk by the side of a river?" she asked, increasing her eager pace a little. "I feel as if it were bearing me along."

"I feel as if I were carrying it," said Colville. "It's as fatiguing as walking on railroad ties."

"Oh, that's too bad!" cried the girl. "How can you be so prosaic? Should you ever have believed that the sun could be so hot in January? And look at those ridiculous green hillsides over the river there! Don't you like it to be winter when it is winter?"

She did not seem to have expected anything from Colville but an impulsive acquiescence, but she listened while he defended the mild weather. "I think it's very well for Italy," he said. "It has always seemed to me—that is, it seems to me now for the first time, but one has to begin the other way—as if the seasons here had worn themselves out like the turbulent passions of the people. I dare say the winter was much fiercer in the times of the Bianchi and Neri."*

"Oh, how delightful! Do you really believe that?"

"No, I don't know that I do. But I shouldn't have much difficulty in proving it, I think, to the sympathetic understanding."

"I wish you would prove it to mine. It sounds so pretty, I'm sure it must be true."

"Oh, then, it isn't necessary. I'll reserve my arguments for Mrs. Bowen."

"You had better. She isn't at all romantic. She says it's very well for me she isn't—that her being matter-of-fact lets me be as romantic as I like."

"Then Mrs. Bowen isn't as romantic as she would like to be if she hadn't charge of a romantic young lady?"

"Oh, I don't say that. Dear me! I'd no idea it *could* be so hot in January." As they strolled along beside the long hedge of laurel, the carriage slowly following them at a little distance, the sun beat strong upon the white road, blotched here and there with the black irregular shadows of the ilexes. The girl undid the pelisse across her breast, with a fine impetuosity, and let it swing open as she walked. She stopped suddenly. "Hark! What bird was that?"

" 'It was the nightingale, and not the lark,' "* suggested Colville lazily.

"Oh, *don't* you think *Romeo and Juliet* is divine?" demanded

Imogene, promptly dropping the question of the bird.

"I don't know about Romeo," returned Colville, "but it's sometimes occurred to me that Juliet was rather forth-putting."

"You *know* she wasn't. It's my favourite play. I could go every night. It's perfectly amazing to me that they can play anything else."

"You would like it five hundred nights in the year, like *Hazel Kirke?** That would be a good deal of Romeo, not to say Juliet."

"They ought to do it out of respect to Shakespeare. Don't you like Shakespeare?"

"Well, I've seen the time when I preferred Alexander Smith,"* said Colville evasively.

"Alexander Smith? Who in the world is Alexander Smith?"

"How recent you are! Alexander Smith was an immortal who flourished about the year 1850."

"That was before I was born. How could I remember him? But I don't feel so very recent for all that."

"Neither do I, this morning," said Colville. "I was up at one of Pharaoh's balls last night, and I danced too much."

He gave Imogene a droll glance, and then bent it upon Effie's discreet face. The child dropped her eyes with a blush like her mother's, having first sought provisional counsel of Imogene, who turned away. He rightly inferred that they all had been talking him over at breakfast, and he broke into a laugh which they joined in, but Imogene said nothing in recognition of the fact.

With what he felt to be haste for his relief she said, "Don't you hate to be told to read a book?"

"I used to—quarter of a century ago," said Colville, recognising that this was the way young people talked, even then.

"Used to?" she repeated. "Don't you now?"

"No; I'm a great deal more tractable now. I always say that I shall get the book out of the library. I draw the line at buying. I still hate to *buy* a book that people recommend."

"What kind of books *do* you like to buy?"

"Oh, no kind. I think we ought to get all our books out of the library."

"Do you never like to talk in earnest?"

"Well, not often," said Colville. "Because, if you do, you can't say with a good conscience afterward that you were only in fun."

"Oh! And do you always like to talk so that you can get out of things afterward?"

"No. I didn't say that, did I?"

"Very nearly, I should think."

"Then I'm glad I didn't quite."

"I like people to be outspoken—to say everything they think," said the girl, regarding him with a puzzled look.

"Then I foresee that I shall become a favourite," answered Colville. "I say a great deal more than I think."

She looked at him again with envy, with admiration, qualifying her perplexity. They had come to a point where some moss-grown, weather-beaten statues stood at the corners of the road that traversed the bosky stretch between the avenues of the Cascine. "Ah, how beautiful they are!" he said, halting, and giving himself to the rapture that a blackened garden statue imparts to one who beholds it from the vantage-ground of sufficient years and experience.

"Do you remember that story of Heine's,"* he resumed, after a moment, "of the boy who steals out of the old castle by moonlight, and kisses the lips of the garden statue, fallen among the rank grass of the ruinous parterres? And long afterward, when he looks down on the sleep of the dying girl where she lies on the green sofa, it seems to him that she and that statue are the same?"

"Oh!" deeply sighed the young girl. "No, I never read it. Tell me what it is. I *must* read it."

"The rest is all talk—very good talk; but I doubt whether it would interest you. He goes on to talk of a great many things—of the way Bellini* spoke French, for example. He says it was blood-curdling, horrible, cataclysmal. He brought out the poor French words and broke them upon the wheel, till you thought the whole world must give way with a thunder-crash. A dead hush reigned in the room; the women did not know whether to faint or fly; the men looked down at their pantaloons, and tried to realise what they had on.''

"Oh, how perfectly delightful! how shameful!" cried the girl. "I *must* read it. What is it in? What is the name of the story?"

"It isn't a story," said Colville. "Did you ever see anything lovelier than these statues?"

"No," said Imogene. "*Are* they good?"

"They are much better than good—they are the very worst rococo."*

"What makes you say they are beautiful, then?"

"Why, don't you see? They commemorate youth, gaiety, brilliant, joyous life. That's what that kind of statues was made for—to look on at rich, young, beautiful people and their gallantries; to be danced before by fine ladies and gentlemen playing at shepherd and shepherdesses; to be driven past by marcheses and contessinas flirting in carriages. To be hung with scarfs and wreaths; to be parts of eternal *fêtes champêtres*.* Don't you see how bored they look? When I first came to Italy I should have detested and ridiculed their bad art; but now they're exquisite—the worse, the better."

"I don't know what in the world you *do* mean," said Imogene, laughing uneasily.

"Mrs. Bowen would. It's a pity Mrs. Bowen isn't here with us. Miss Effie, if I lift you up to one of those statues, will you kindly ask it if it doesn't remember a young American signor who was here just before the French Revolution? I don't believe it's forgotten me."

"No, no," said Imogene. "It's time we were walking back. Don't you like Scott!" she added. "I should think you would if you like those romantic things. I used to like Scott so *much*. When I was fifteen I wouldn't read anything but Scott. Don't you like Thackeray? Oh, he's so *cynical!* It's perfectly delightful."

"Cynical?" repeated Colville thoughtfully. "I was looking into *The Newcomes** the other day, and I thought he was rather sentimental."

"Sentimental! Why, what an idea! That is the strangest thing I ever heard of. Oh!" she broke in upon her own amazement, "don't you think Browning's 'Statue and the Bust'* is splendid? Mr. Morton read it to us—to Mrs. Bowen, I mean."

Colville resented this freedom of Mr. Morton's, he did not know just why; then his pique was lost in sarcastic recollection of the time when he too used to read poems to ladies. He had read that poem to Lina Ridgely and the other one.

"Mrs. Bowen asked him to read it," Imogene continued.

"Did she?" asked Colville pensively.

"And then we discussed it afterward. We had a long discussion. And then he read us the 'Legend of Pornic,' and we had a discussion about that. Mrs. Bowen says it was real gold they found in the coffin; but I think it was the girl's 'gold hair.' I don't know which Mr. Morton thought. Which do you? Don't you think the 'Legend of Pornic'* is splendid?"

"Yes, it's a great poem, and deep," said Colville. They had come to a place where the bank sloped invitingly to the river. "Miss Effie," he asked, "wouldn't you like to go down and throw stones into the Arno? That's what a river is for," he added, as the child glanced toward Imogene for authorisation, "to have stones thrown into it."

"Oh, let us!" cried Imogene, rushing down to the brink. "I don't want to throw stones into it, but to get near it—to get near to any bit of nature. They do pen you up so from it in Europe!" She stood and watched Colville skim stones over the current. "When you stand by the shore of a swift river like this, or near a railroad train when it comes whirling by, don't you ever have a morbid impulse to fling yourself forward?"

"Not at my time of life," said Colville, stooping to select a flat stone. "Morbid impulses are one of the luxuries of youth." He threw the stone, which skipped triumphantly far out into the stream. "That was beautiful, wasn't it, Miss Effie?"

"Lovely!" murmured the child.

He offered her a flat pebble. "Would you like to try one?"

"It would spoil my gloves," she said, in deprecating refusal.

"Let *me* try it!" cried Imogene. "I'm not afraid of my gloves."

Colville yielded the pebble, looking at her with the thought of how intoxicating he should once have found this bit of wilful *abandon*, but feeling rather sorry for it now. "Oh, perhaps not?" he said, laying his hand upon hers, and looking into her eyes.

She returned his look, and then she dropped the pebble and put her hand back in her muff, and turned and ran up the bank. "There's the carriage. It's time we should be going." At the top of the bank she became a mirror of dignity, a transparent mirror to his eye. "Are you going back to town, Mr. Colville?" she asked, with formal state. "We could set you down anywhere!"

"Thank you, Miss Graham. I shall be glad to avail myself of your very kind offer. Allow me." He handed her ceremoniously to the carriage; he handed Effie Bowen even more ceremoniously to the carriage, holding his hat in one hand while he offered the other. Then he mounted to the seat in front of them. "The weather has changed," he said.

Imogene hid her face in her muff, and Effie Bowen bowed hers against Imogene's shoulder.

A sense of the girl's beauty lingered in Colville's thought all day, and recurred to him again and again; and the ambitious intensity and enthusiasm of her talk came back in touches of amusement and compassion. How divinely young it all was, and how lovely! He patronised it from a height far aloof.

He was not in the frame of mind for the hotel table, and he went to lunch at a restaurant. He chose a simple trattoria, the first he came to, and he took his seat at one of the bare, rude tables, where the joint saucers for pepper and salt, and a small glass for toothpicks, with a much-scraped porcelain box for matches, expressed an uncorrupted Florentinity of custom. But when he gave his order in off-hand Italian, the waiter answered in the French which waiters get together for the traveller's confusion in Italy, and he resigned himself to whatever chance of acquaintance might befall him. The place had a companionable smell of stale tobacco, and the dim light showed him on the walls of a space dropped a step or two lower, at the end of the room, a variety of sketches and caricatures. A waiter was laying a large table in this space, and when Colville came up to examine the drawings he jostled him, with due apologies, in the haste of a man working against time for masters who will brook no delay. He was hurrying still when a party of young men came in and took their places at the table, and began to rough him for his delay. Colville could recognise several of them in the vigorous burlesques on the walls, and as others dropped in the grotesque portraitures made him feel as if he had seen them before. They all talked at once, each man of his own interests, except when they joined in a shout of mockery and welcome for some new-comer. Colville, at his *risotto*, almost the room's length away, could hear what they thought, one and another, of Botticelli and Michelangelo; of Old Piloty's things at Munich;* of the dishes they had served to them, and of the quality of the Chianti; of the respective merits of German and Italian tobacco; of whether Inglehart had probably got to Venice yet; of the personal habits of Billings, and of the question whether the want of modelling in Simmons's nose had anything to do with his style of snoring; of the overrated colouring of some of those Venetian fellows; of the delicacy of Mino da Fiesole, and of the genius of Babson's tailor. Babson was there to defend the cut of his trousers, and Billings and Simmons were present to answer for themselves at the expense of the pictures of those who had called their habits and features into question. When it came to this all the voices joined in jolly uproar. Derision and denial broke out of the tumult, and presently they were all talking quietly of a reception which some of them were at the day before. Then Colville heard one of them saying that he would like a chance to paint some lady whose name he did not catch, and "She looks awfully sarcastic," one of the young fellows said.

"They say she *is*," said another. "They say she's awfully intellectual."

"Boston?" queried a third.

"No, Kalamazoo. The centre of culture is out there now."

"She knows how to dress, anyhow," said the first commentator. "I wonder what Parker would talk to her about when he was painting her. He's never read anything but Poe's 'Ullalume.' "*

"Well, that's a good subject—'Ullalume.' "

"I suppose she's read it?"

"She's read 'most everything, they say."

"What's an Ullalume, anyway, Parker?"

One of the group sprang up from the table and drew on the wall what he labelled "An Ullalume." Another rapidly depicted Parker in the moment of sketching a young lady; her portrait had got as far as the eyes and nose when some one protested: "Oh, hello! No personalities."

The draughtsman said, "Well, all right!" and sat down again.

"Hall talked with her the most. What did she say, Hall?"

"Hall can't remember words in three syllables, but he says it was mighty brilliant and mighty deep."

"They say she's a niece of Mrs. Bowen's. She's staying with Mrs. Bowen."

Then it was the wisdom and brilliancy and severity of Imogene Graham that these young men stood in awe of! Colville remembered how the minds of girls of twenty had once dazzled him. "And yes," he mused, "she must have believed that we were talking literature in the Cascine. Certainly I should have thought it an intellectual time when I was at that age," he owned to himself with forlorn irony.

The young fellows went on to speak of Mrs. Bowen, whom it seemed they had known the winter before. She had been very polite to them; they praised her as if she were quite an old woman.

"But she must have been a very pretty girl," one of them put in.

"Well, she has a good deal of style yet."

"Oh yes, but she never could have been a beauty like the other one."

On her part, Imogene was very sober when she met Mrs. Bowen, though she had come in flushed and excited from the air and the morning's adventure. Mrs. Bowen was sitting by the fire, placidly reading; a vase of roses on the little table near her diffused the delicate odour of winter roses through the room; all seemed very still and dim, and of another time, somehow.

Imogene kept away from the fire, sitting down, in the provisional fashion of women, with her things on; but she unbuttoned her pelisse and flung it open. Effie had gone to her room.

"Did you have a pleasant drive?" asked Mrs. Bowen.

"Very," said the girl.

"Mr. Morton brought you these roses," continued Mrs. Bowen.

"Oh," said Imogene, with a cold glance at them.

"The Flemmings have asked us to a party Thursday. There is to be dancing."

"The Flemmings?"

"Yes." As if she now saw reason to do so, Mrs. Bowen laid the book face downward in her lap. She yawned a little, with her hand on her mouth. "Did you meet any one you knew?"

"Yes; Mr. Colville." Mrs. Bowen cut her yawn in half. "We got out to walk in the Cascine, and we saw him coming in at the gate. He came up and asked if he might walk with us."

"Did you have a pleasant walk?" asked Mrs. Bowen, a breath more chillily than she had asked if they had a pleasant drive.

"Yes, pleasant enough. And then we came back and went down the river bank, and he skipped stones, and we took him to his hotel."

"Was there anybody you knew in the Cascine?"

"Oh no; the place was a howling wilderness. I never saw it so deserted," said the girl impatiently. "It was terribly hot walking. I thought I should burn up."

Mrs. Bowen did not answer anything; she let the book lie in her lap.

"What an odd person Mr. Colville is!" said Imogene, after a moment. "Don't you think he's very different from other gentlemen?"

"Why?"

"Oh, he has such a peculiar way of talking."

"What peculiar way?"

"Oh, I don't know. Plenty of the young men I see talk cynically, and I do sometimes myself—desperately, don't you know. But then I know very well we don't mean anything by it."

"And do you think Mr. Colville does? Do you think he talks cynically?"

Imogene leaned back in her chair and reflected. "No," she returned slowly, "I can't say that he does. But he talks lightly, with a kind of touch and go that makes you feel that he has exhausted all feeling. He doesn't parade it at all. But you hear between the words, don't you know, just as you read between the lines in some kinds of poetry. Of course it's everything in knowing what he's been through. He's perfectly unaffected; and don't you think he's good?"

"Oh yes," sighed Mrs. Bowen. "In his way."

"But he sees through you. Oh, quite! Nothing escapes him, and pretty soon he lets out that he has seen through you, and then you feel so *flat!* Oh, it's perfectly intoxicating to be with him. I would give the world to talk as he does."

"What was your talk all about?"

"Oh, I don't know. I suppose it would have been called rather intellectual."

Mrs. Bowen smiled infinitesimally. But after a moment she said gravely, "Mr. Colville is very much older than you. He's old enough to be your father."

"Yes, I know that. You feel that he feels old, and it's perfectly tragical. Sometimes when he turns that slow, dull, melancholy look on you, he seems a thousand years old."

"I don't mean that he's positively old," said Mrs. Bowen. "He's only old comparatively."

"Oh yes; I understand that. And I don't mean that he

really seems a thousand years old. What I meant was, he seems a thousand years off, as if he were still young, and had got left behind somehow. He seems to be on the other side of some impassable barrier, and you want to get over there and help him to our side, but you can't do it. I suppose his talking in that light way is merely a subterfuge to hide his feeling, to make him forget.''

Mrs. Bowen fingered the edges of her book. "You mustn't let your fancy run away with you, Imogene," she said, with a little painful smile.

"Oh, I *like* to let it run away with me. And when I get such a subject as Mr. Colville, there's no stopping. I can't stop, and I don't *wish* to stop. Shouldn't you have thought that he would have been perfectly crushed at the exhibition he made of himself in the Lancers last night? He wasn't the least embarrassed when he met me, and the only allusion he made to it was to say that he had been up late, and had danced too much. Wasn't it wonderful he could do it? Oh, if *I* could do that!''

"I wish he could have avoided the occasion for his bravado," said Mrs. Bowen.

"I think I was a little to blame, perhaps," said the girl. "I beckoned him to come and take the vacant place.''

"I don't see that that was an excuse," returned Mrs. Bowen primly.

Imogene seemed insensible to the tone, as it concerned herself; it only apparently reminded her of something. "Guess what Mr. Colville said, when I had been silly, and then tried to make up for it by being very dignified all of a sudden?''

"I don't know. How had you been silly?''

The servant brought in some cards. Imogene caught up the pelisse which she had been gradually shedding as she sat talking to Mrs. Bowen, and ran out of the room by another door.

They did not recur to the subject. But that night, when Mrs. Bowen went to say good night to Effie, after the child had gone to bed, she lingered.

"Effie," she said at last, in a husky whisper, "what

did Imogene say to Mr. Colville to-day that made him laugh?''

''I don't know,'' said the child. ''They kept laughing at so many things.''

''Laughing?''

''Yes; he laughed. Do you mean toward the last, when he had been throwing stones into the river?''

''It must have been then.''

The child stretched herself drowsily. ''Oh I couldn't understand it all. She wanted to throw a stone in the river, but he told her she had better not. But that didn't make *him* laugh. She was so very stiff just afterward that he said the weather had changed, and that made *us* laugh.''

''Was that all?''

''We kept laughing ever so long. I never saw any one like Mr. Colville. How queerly the fire shines on your face! It gives you such a beautiful complexion.''

''Does it?''

''Yes, lovely.'' The child's mother stooped over and kissed her. ''You're the prettiest mamma in the world,'' she said, throwing her arms round her neck. ''Sometimes I can't tell whether Imogene is prettier or not, but to-night I'm certain you are. Do you like to have me think that?''

''Yes—yes. But don't pull me down so; you hurt my neck. Good night.''

The child let her go. ''I haven't said my prayer yet, mamma. I was thinking.''

''Well, say it now, then,'' said the mother gently.

When the child had finished she turned upon her cheek. ''Good night, mamma.''

Mrs. Bowen went about the room a little while, picking up its pretty disorder. Then she sat down in a chair by the hearth, where a log was still burning. The light of the flame flickered upon her face, and threw upon the ceiling a writhing, fantastic shadow, the odious caricature of her gentle beauty.

VIII

In that still air of the Florentine winter, time seems to share
the arrest of the natural forces, the repose of the elements.
The pale blue sky is frequently overcast, and it rains two
days out of five; sometimes, under extraordinary provoca-
tion from the north a snow-storm whirls along under the low
grey dome, and whitens the brown roofs, where a growth of
spindling weeds and grass clothes the tiles the whole year
round, and shows its delicate green above the gathered flakes.
But for the most part the winds are laid, and the sole change
is from quiet sun to quiet shower. This at least is the impression which remains in the senses of the sojourning stranger,
whose days slip away with so little difference one from
another that they seem really not to have passed, but, like
the grass that keeps the hillsides fresh round Florence all the
winter long, to be waiting some decisive change of season
before they begin.

The first of the Carnival sights that marked the lapse of
a month since his arrival took Colville by surprise. He could
not have believed that it was February yet if it had not been
for the straggling maskers in armour whom he met one day
in Via Borgognissanti, with their visors up for their better
convenience in smoking. They were part of the chorus at one
of the theatres, and they were going about to eke out their
salaries with the gifts of people whose windows the festival
season privileged them to play under. The silly spectacle
stirred Colville's blood a little, as any sort of holiday
preparation was apt to do. He thought that it afforded him
a fair occasion to call at Palazzo Pinti, where he had not
been so much of late as in the first days of his renewed
acquaintance with Mrs. Bowen. He had at one time had the
fancy that Mrs. Bowen was cool toward him. He might very
well have been mistaken in this; in fact, she had several
times addressed him the politest reproaches for not coming,
but he made some evasion, and went only on the days when

she was receiving other people, and when necessarily he saw very little of the family.

Miss Graham was always very friendly, but always very busy, drawing tea from the samovar, and looking after others. Effie Bowen dropped her eyes in re-established strangeness when she brought the basket of cake to him. There was one moment when he suspected that he had been talked over in family council, and put under a certain regimen. But he had no proof of this, and it had really nothing to do with his keeping away, which was largely accidental. He had taken up, with as much earnestness as he could reasonably expect of himself, that notion of studying the architectural expression of Florentine character at the different periods. He had spent a good deal of money in books, he had revived his youthful familiarity with the city, and he had made what acquaintance he could with people interested in such matters. He met some of these in the limited but very active society in which he mingled daily and nightly. After the first strangeness to any sort of social life had worn off, he found himself very fond of the prompt hospitalities which his introduction at Mrs. Bowen's had opened to him. His host—or more frequently it was his hostess—had sometimes merely an apartment at a hotel; perhaps the family was established in one of the furnished lodgings which stretch the whole length of the Lung' Arno on either hand, and abound in all the new streets approaching the Cascine, and had set up the simple and facile housekeeping of the sojourner in Florence for a few months; others had been living in the villa or the palace they had taken for years.

The more recent and transitory people expressed something of the prevailing English and American æstheticism in the decoration of their apartments, but the greater part accepted the Florentine drawing-room as their landlord had imagined it for them, with furniture and curtains in yellow satin, a cheap ingrain carpet thinly covering the stone floor, and a fire of little logs ineffectually blazing on the hearth, and flickering on the carved frames of the pictures on the wall and the nakedness of the frescoed allegories in the ceiling. Whether of longer or shorter stay, the sojourners were bound together by a common language and a common social tradition; they all had a Day, and on that day there was tea and bread and butter for every comer. They had one another to dine; there were evening parties, with dancing and without dancing. Colville even went to a fancy ball, where he was kept in countenance by several other Florentines of the period of Romola. At all these places he met nearly the same people, whose alien life in the midst of the native community struck him as one of the phases of modern civilisation worthy of note, if not particular study; for he fancied it destined to a wider future throughout Europe, as the conditions in England and America grow more tiresome and more onerous. They seemed to see very little of Italian society, and to be shut out from practical knowledge of the local life by the terms upon which they had themselves insisted. Our race finds its simplified and cheapened London or New York in all its Continental resorts now, but nowhere has its taste been so much studied as in Italy, and especially in Florence. It was not, perhaps, the real Englishman or American who had been considered, but a *forestiere** conventionalised from the Florentine's observation of many Anglo-Saxons. But he had been so well conjectured that he was hemmed round with a very fair illusion of his national circumstances.

It was not that he had his English or American doctor to prescribe for him when sick, and his English or American apothecary to compound his potion; it was not that there was an English tailor and an American dentist, an English bookseller and an English baker, and chapels of every shade of Protestantism, with Catholic preaching in English every Sunday. These things were more or less matters of necessity, but Colville objected that the barbers should offer him an American shampoo; that the groceries should abound in English biscuit and our own canned fruit and vegetables, and that the grocers' clerks should be ambitious to read the labels of the Boston baked beans. He heard—though he did not prove this by experiment—that the master of a certain trattoria had studied the doughnut of New England till he had actually surpassed the original in the qualities that have undermined our digestion as a people. But above all it interested him to see that intense expression of American civilisation, the horse-car, triumphing along the magnificent avenues that mark the line of the old city walls; and he recognised an instinctive obedience to an abtruse natural law in the fact that whereas the omnibus, which the Italians have derived from the English, was not filled beyond its seating capacity, the horse-car was overcrowded without and within at Florence, just as it is with us who invented it.

"I wouldn't mind even that," he said one day to the lady who was drawing him his fifth or sixth cup of tea for that afternoon, and with whom he was naturally making this absurd condition of things a matter of personal question; "but you people here pass your days in a round of unbroken English, except when you talk with your servants. I'm not sure you don't speak English with the shop people. I can hardly get them to speak Italian to me."

"Perhaps they think you can speak English better," said the lady.

This went over Florence; in a week it was told to Colville as something said to some one else. He fearlessly reclaimed it as said to himself, and this again was told. In the houses where he visited he had the friendly acceptance of any intelligent and reasonably agreeable person who comes promptly and willingly when he is asked, and seems always to have enjoyed himself when he goes away. But besides this sort of general favour, he enjoyed a very pleasing little personal popularity which came from his interest in other people, from his good-nature, and from his inertness. He slighted no acquaintance, and talked to every one with the same apparent wish to be entertaining. This was because he was incapable of the cruelty of open indifference when his lot was cast with a dull person, and also because he was mentally too lazy to contrive pretences for getting away; besides he did not really find anybody altogether a bore, and he had no wish to shine. He listened without shrinking to stories that he had heard before, and to things that had already been said to him; as has been noted, he had himself the habit of repeating his ideas with the recklessness of maturity, for he had lived long enough to know that this can be done with almost entire safety.

He haunted the studios a good deal, and through a retrospective affinity with art, and a human sympathy with the sacrifice which it always involves, he was on friendly terms with sculptors and painters who were not in every case so friendly with one another. More than once he saw the scars of old rivalries, and he might easily have been an adherent of two or three parties. But he tried to keep the freedom of the different camps without taking sides; and he felt the pathos of the case when they all told the same story of the disaster which the taste for bric-à-brac had wrought to the cause of art; how people who came abroad no longer gave orders for statues and pictures, but spent their money on curtains and carpets, old chests and chairs, and pots and pans. There were some among these artists whom he had known twenty years before in Florence, ardent and hopeful beginners; and now the backs of their grey or bald heads, as they talked to him with their faces towards their work, and a pencil or a pinch of clay held thoughtfully between their fingers, appealed to him as if he had remained young and prosperous, and they had gone forward to age and hard work. They were very quaint at times. They talked the American slang of the war days and of the days before the war; without a mastery of Italian, they often used the idioms of that tongue in their English speech. They were dim and vague about the country, with whose affairs they had kept up through the newspapers. Here and there one thought he was going home very soon; others had finally relinquished all thoughts of return. These had, perhaps without knowing it, lost the desire to come back. They cowered before the expensiveness of life in America, and doubted of a future with which, indeed, only the young can hopefully grapple. But in spite of their accumulated years, and the evil times on which they had fallen, Colville thought them mostly very happy men, leading simple and innocent lives in a world of the ideal, and rich in the inexhaustible beauty of the city, the sky, the air. They all, whether they were ever going back or

not, were fervent Americans, and their ineffaceable nationality marked them, perhaps, all the more strongly for the
patches of something alien that overlaid it in places. They
knew that he was or had been a newspaper man; but if they
secretly cherished the hope that he would bring them to the
dolce lume of print,* they never betrayed it; and the author-
ship of his letter about the American artists in Florence,
which he printed in the *American Register* at Paris, was not
traced to him for a whole week.

Colville was a frequent visitor of Mr. Waters, who had a
lodging in Piazza San Marco, of the poverty which can
always be decent in Italy. It was bare, but for the books that
furnished it; with a table for his writing, on a corner of which
he breakfasted, a wide sofa with cushions in coarse white
linen that frankly confessed itself a bed by night, and two
chairs of plain Italian walnut; but the windows, which had
no sun, looked out upon the church and the convent sacred
to the old Socinian* for the sake of the meek, heroic mystic
whom they keep alive in all the glory of his martyrdom. No
two minds could well have been further apart than the New
England minister and the Florentine monk, and no two souls
nearer together, as Colville recognised with a not irreverent
smile.

When the old man was not looking up some point of his
saint's history in his books, he was taking with the
hopefulness of youth and the patience of age a lesson in colloquial Italian from his landlady's daughter, which he pro-
nounced with a scholarly scrupulosity and a sincere atonic
Massachusetts accent. He practised the language wherever
he could, especially at the trattoria where he dined, and
where he made occasions to detain the waiter in conversation. They humoured him, out of their national good-
heartedness and sympathy, and they did what they could to
realise a strange American dish for him on Sundays—a combination of stockfish and potatoes boiled, and then fried
together in small cakes. They revered him as a foreign
gentleman of saintly amiability and incomprehensible
preferences; and he was held in equal regard at the next
green-grocer's where he spent every morning five centessimi

for a bunch of radishes and ten for a little pat of butter to
eat with his bread and coffee; he could not yet accustom
himself to mere bread and coffee for breakfast, though he
conformed as completely as he could to the Italian way of living. He respected the abstemiousness of the race; he held
that it came from a spirituality of nature to which the North
was still strange, with all its conscience and sense of in-
dividual accountability. He contended that he never suffered
in his small dealings with these people from the dishonesty
which most of his countrymen complained of; and he praised
their unfailing gentleness of manner; this could arise only
from goodness of heart, which was perhaps the best kind of
goodness after all.

None of these humble acquaintance of his could well have
accounted for the impression they all had that he was some
sort of ecclesiastic. They could never have understood—nor,
for that matter, could any one have understood through
European tradition—the sort of sacerdotal office that Mr.
Waters had filled so long in the little deeply book-clubbed
New England village where he had outlived most of his
flock, till one day he rose in the midst of the surviving
dyspeptics and consumptives and, following the example of
Mr. Emerson,* renounced his calling for ever. By that time
even the pale Unitarianism thinning out into paler doubt
was no longer tenable with him. He confessed that while he
felt the Divine goodness more and more, he believed that it
was a mistake to preach any specific creed or doctrine, and
he begged them to release him from their service. A young
man came to fill his place in their pulpit, but he kept his
place in their hearts. They raised a subscription of seventeen
hundred dollars and thirty-five cents; another being submitted to the new button manufacturer, who had founded
his industry in the village, he promotly rounded it out to
three thousand, and Mr. Waters came to Florence. His
people parted with him in terms of regret as delicate as
they were awkward, and their love followed him. He
corresponded regularly with two or three ladies, and his letters were sometimes read from his pulpit.

Colville took the Piazza San Marco in on his way to

Palazzo Pinti on the morning when he had made up his mind to go there, and he stood at the window looking out with the old man, when some more maskers passed through the place—two young fellows in old Florentine dress, with a third habited as a nun.

"Ah," said the old man gently, "I wish they hadn't introduced the nun! But I suppose they can't help signalising their escape from the domination of the Church on all occasions. It's a natural reaction. It will all come right in time."

"You preach the true American gospel," said Colville.

"Of course; there is no other gospel. That *is* the gospel."

"Do you suppose that Savonarola would think it had all come out right," asked Colville, a little maliciously, "if he could look from the window with us here and see the wicked old Carnival, that he tried so hard to kill* four hundred years ago, still alive? And kicking?" he added, in cognisance of the caper of one of the maskers.

"Oh yes; why not? By this time he knows that his puritanism was all a mistake, unless as a thing for the moment only. I should rather like to have Savonarola here with us; he would find these costumes familiar; they are of his time. I shall make a point of seeing all I can of the Carnival, as part of my study of Savonarola, if nothing else."

"I'm afraid you'll have to give yourself limitations," said Colville, as one of the maskers threw his arm round the mock-nun's neck. But the old man did not see this, and Colville did not feel it necessary to explain himself.

The maskers had passed out of the piazza now, and "Have you seen our friends at Palazzo Pinti lately?" said Mr. Waters.

"Not very," said Colville. "I was just on my way there."

"I wish you would make them my compliments. Such a beautiful young creature."

"Yes," said Colville; "she is certainly a beautiful girl."

"I meant Mrs. Bowen," returned the old man quietly.

"Oh, I thought you meant Miss Graham. Mrs. Bowen is my contemporary, and so I didn't think of her when you said young. I should have called her pretty rather than beautiful."

"No; she's beautiful. The young girl is good-looking—I don't deny that; but she is very crude yet."

Colville laughed. "Crude in looks? I should have said Miss Graham was rather crude in mind, though I'm not sure I wouldn't have stopped at saying *young*."

"No," mildly persisted the old man; "she couldn't be crude in mind without being crude in looks."

"You mean," pursued Colville, smiling, but not wholly satisfied, "that she hasn't a lovely nature?"

"You never can know what sort of nature a young girl has. Her nature depends so much upon that of the man whose fate she shares."

"The woman is what the man makes her? That is convenient for the woman, and relieves her of all responsibility."

"The man is what the woman makes him, too, but not so much so. The man was cast into a deep sleep, you know——"

"And the woman was what he dreamed her. I wish she were."

"In most cases she is," said Mr. Waters.

They did not pursue the matter. The truth that floated in the old minister's words pleased Colville by its vagueness, and flattered the man in him by its implication of the man's superiority. He wanted to say that if Mrs. Bowen were what the late Mr. Bowen had dreamed her, then the late Mr. Bowen, when cast into his deep sleep, must have had Lina Ridgely in his eye. But this seemed to be personalising the fantasy unwarrantably, and pushing it too far. For like reason he forbore to say that if Mr. Waters's theory were correct, it would be better to begin with some one whom nobody else had dreamed before; then you could be sure at least of not having a wife to somebody else's mind rather than your own. Once on his way to Palazzo Pinti, he stopped, arrested by a thought that had not occurred to him before in relation to what Mr. Waters had been saying, and then pushed on with the sense of security which is the compensation the possession of the initiative brings to our sex along with many responsibilities. In the enjoyment of this, no man stops to consider the other side, which must wait his initiative, however they mean to meet it.

In the Por San Maria Colville found masks and dominoes filling the shop windows and dangling from the doors. A devil in red and a clown in white crossed the way in front of him from an intersecting street; several children in pretty masquerading dresses flashed in and out among the crowd. He hurried to the Lung' Arno, and reached the palace where Mrs. Bowen lived, with these holiday sights fresh in his mind. Imogene turned to meet him at the door of the apartment, running from the window where she had left Effie Bowen still gazing.

"We saw you coming," she said gaily, without waiting to exchange formal greetings. "We didn't know at first but it might be somebody else disguised as you. We've been watching the maskers go by. Isn't it exciting?"

"Awfully," said Colville, going to the window with her, and putting his arm on Effie's shoulder, where she knelt in a chair looking out. "What have you seen?"

"Oh, only two Spanish students with mandolins," said Imogene; "but you can see they're *beginning* to come."

"They'll stop now," murmured Effie, with gentle disappointment; "it's commencing to rain."

"Oh, too bad!" wailed the young girl. But just then two mediæval men-at-arms came in sight, carrying umbrellas. "Isn't that too delicious? Umbrellas and chain-armour!"

"You can't expect them to let their chain-armour get rusty," said Colville. "You ought to have been with me— minstrels in scale-armour, Florentines of Savonarola's times, nuns, clowns, demons, fairies—no end to them."

"It's very well saying we ought to have been with you; but we can't go anywhere alone."

"I didn't say alone," said Colville. "Don't you think Mrs. Bowen would trust you with me to see these Carnival beginnings?" He had not meant at all to do anything of this kind, but that had not prevented his doing it.

"How do we know, when she hasn't been asked?" said Imogene, with a touch of burlesque dolor, such as makes a dignified girl enchanting, when she permits it to herself. She took Effie's hand in hers, the child having faced round from the window, and stood smoothing it, with her lovely head pathetically tilted on one side.

"What haven't I been asked yet?" demanded Mrs. Bowen, coming lightly toward them from a door at the side of the *salon*. She gave her hand to Colville with the prettiest grace, and a cordiality that brought a flush to her cheek. There had really been nothing between them but a little unreasoned coolness, if it were even so much as that; say rather a dryness, aggravated by time and absence, and now, as friends do, after a thing of that kind, they were suddenly glad to be good to each other.

"Why, you haven't been asked how you have been this long time," said Colville.

"I have been wanting to tell you for a whole week," returned Mrs. Bowen, seating the rest and taking a chair for herself. "Where have you been?"

"Oh, shut up in my cell at Hotel d'Atene, writing a short history of the Florentine people for Miss Effie."

"Effie, take Mr. Colville's hat," said her mother. "We're going to make you stay to lunch," she explained to him.

"Is that so?" he asked, with an effect of polite curiosity.

"Yes." Imogene softly clapped her hands, unseen by Mrs. Bowen, for Colville's instruction that all was going well. If it delights women to pet an undangerous friend of our sex, to use him like one of themselves, there are no words to paint the soft and flattered content with which his spirit purrs under their caresses. "You must have nearly finished the history," added Mrs. Bowen.

"Well, I could have finished it," said Colville, "If I had only begun it. You see, writing a short history of the Florentine people is such quick work that you have to be careful how you actually put pen to paper, or you're through with it before you've had any fun out of it."

"I think Effie will like to read that kind of history," said her mother.

The child hung her head, and would not look at Colville; she was still shy with him; his absence must have seemed longer to a child, of course.

At lunch they talked of the Carnival sights that had begun

to appear. He told of his call upon Mr. Waters, and of the old minister's purpose to see all he could of the Carnival in order to judge intelligently of Savonarola's opposition to it.

"Mr. Waters is a very good man," said Mrs. Bowen, with the air of not meaning to approve him quite, nor yet to let any notion of his be made fun of in her presence. "But for my part I wish there were not going to be any Carnival; the city will be in such an uproar for the next two weeks."

"O Mrs. Bowen!" cried Imogene reproachfully; Effie looked at her mother in apparent anxiety lest she should be meaning to put forth an unquestionable power and stop the Carnival.

"The last Carnival, I thought there was never going to be any end to it; I was so glad when Lent came."

"Glad when *Lent* came!" breathed Imogene, in astonishment; but she ventured upon nothing more insubordinate, and Colville admired to see this spirited girl as subject to Mrs. Bowen as her own child. There is no reason why one woman should establish another woman over her, but nearly all woman do it in one sort or another, from love of a voluntary submission, or from a fear of their own ignorance, if they are younger and more inexperienced than their lieges. Neither the one passion nor the other seems to reduce them to a like passivity as regards their husbands. They must apparently have a fetish of their own sex. Colville could see that Imogene obeyed Mrs. Bowen not only as a *protégée* but as a devotee.

"Oh, I suppose *you* will have to go through it all," said Mrs. Bowen, in reward of the girl's acquiescence.

"You're rather out of the way of it up here," said Colville. "You had better let me go about with the young ladies—if you can trust them to the care of an old fellow like me."

"Oh, I don't think you're so very old, at all times," replied Mrs. Bowen, with a peculiar look, whether indulgent or reproachful he could not quite make out.

But he replied, boldly, in his turn: "I have certainly my moments of being young still; I don't deny it. There's always a danger of their occurrence."

"I was thinking," said Mrs. Bowen, with a graceful effect of not listening, "that you would let me go too. It would be quite like old times."

"Only too much honour and pleasure," returned Colville, "if you will leave out the old times. I'm not particular about having them along." Mrs. Bowen joined in laughing at the joke, which they had to themselves. "I was only consulting an explicit abhorrence of yours in not asking you to go at first," he explained.

"Oh yes; I understand that."

The excellence of the whole arrangement seemed to grow upon Mrs. Bowen. "Of course," she said, "Imogene ought to see all she can of the Carnival. She may not have another chance, and perhaps if she had, *he* wouldn't consent."

"I'll engage to get *his* consent," said the girl. "What I was afraid of was that I couldn't get yours, Mrs. Bowen."

"Am I so severe as that?" asked Mrs. Bowen softly.

"Quite," replied Imogene.

"Perhaps," thought Colville, "it isn't always silent submission."

For no very good reason that any one could give, the Carnival that year was not a brilliant one. Colville's party seemed to be always meeting the same maskers on the street, and the maskers did not greatly increase in numbers. There were a few more of them after nightfall, but they were then a little more bacchanal, and he felt it was better that the ladies had gone home by that time. In the pursuit of the tempered pleasure of looking up the maskers he was able to make the reflection that their fantastic and vivid dresses sympathised in a striking way with the architecture of the city, and gave him an effect of Florence which he could not otherwise have had. There came by and by a little attempt at a *corso** in Via Cerratani and Via Tornabuoni. There were some masks in carriages, and from one they actually threw plaster *confetti;* half a dozen bare-legged boys ran before and beat one another with bladders. Some people, but not many, watched the show from the windows, and the footways were crowded.

Having proposed that they should see the Carnival

together, Colville had made himself responsible for it to the Bowen household. Imogene said, "Well is *this* the famous Carnival of Florence?"

"It certainly doesn't compare with the Carnival last year," said Mrs. Bowen.

"Your reproach is just, Mrs. Bowen," he acknowledged. "I've managed it badly. But you know I've been out of practice a great while there in Des Vaches."

"Oh, poor Mr. Colville!" cried Imogene. "He isn't altogether to blame."

"I don't know," said Mrs. Bowen, humouring the joke in her turn. "It seems to me that if he had consulted us a little earlier, he might have done better."

He drove home with the ladies, and Mrs. Bowen made him stay to tea. As if she felt that he needed to be consoled for the failure of his Carnival, she was especially indulgent with him. She played to him on the piano some of the songs that were in fashion when they were in Florence together before. Imogene had never heard them; she had heard her mother speak of them. One or two of them were negro songs, such as very pretty young ladies used to sing without harm to themselves or offence to others; but Imogene decided that they were rather rowdy. "Dear me, Mrs. Bowen! Did *you* sing such songs? You wouldn't let Effie!"

"No, I wouldn't let Effie. The times are changed. I wouldn't let Effie go to the theatre alone with a young gentleman."

"The times are changed for the worse," Colville began. "What harm ever came to a young man from a young lady's going alone to the theatre with him?"

He stayed till the candles were brought in, and then went away only because, as he said, they had not asked him to stay to dinner.

He came nearly every day, upon one pretext or another, and he met them oftener than that at the teas and on the days of other ladies in Florence; for he was finding the busy idleness of the life very pleasant, and he went everywhere. He formed the habit of carrying flowers to the Palazzo Pinti, excusing himself on the ground that they were so cheap and so abundant as to be impersonal. He brought violets to Effie and roses to Imogene; to Mrs. Bowen he always brought a bunch of the huge purple anemones which grow so abundantly all winter long about Florence. "I wonder why *purple* anemones?" he asked her one day in presenting them to her.

"Oh, it is quite time I should be wearing purple," she said gently.

"Ah, Mrs. Bowen!" he reproached her. "Why do I bring purple violets to Miss Effie?"

"You must ask Effie!" said Mrs. Bowen, with a laugh.

After that he stayed away forty-eight hours, and then appeared with a bunch of the red anemones, as large as tulips, which light up the meadow grass when it begins to stir from its torpor in the spring. "They grew on purpose to set me right with you," he said, "and I saw them when I was in the country."

It was a little triumph for him, which she celebrated by putting them in a vase on her table, and telling people who exclaimed over them that they were some Mr. Colville gathered in the country. He enjoyed his privileges at her house with the futureless satisfaction of a man. He liked to go about with the Bowens; he was seen with the ladies driving and walking, in most of their promenades. He directed their visits to the churches and the galleries; he was fond of strolling about with Effie's daintily-gloved little hand in his. He took her to Giocosa's and treated her to ices; he let her choose from the confectioner's prettiest caprices in candy; he was allowed to bring the child presents in his pockets. Perhaps he was not as conscientious as he might have been in his behaviour with the little girl. He did what he could to spoil her, or at least to relax the severity of the training she had received; he liked to see the struggle that went on in the mother's mind against this, and then the other struggle with which she overcame her opposition to it. The worst he did was to teach Effie some picturesque Western phrases, which she used with innocent effectiveness; she committed the crimes against convention which he taught her with all the conventional elegance of her training. The most that he ever gained for her were some concessions in going out in weather that her mother thought unfit, or sitting up for half-hours after her bed-time. He ordered books for her from Goodban's, and it was Colville now, and not the Rev. Mr. Morton, who read poetry aloud to the ladies on afternoons when Mrs. Bowen gave orders that she and Miss Graham should be denied to all other comers.

It was an intimacy; and society in Florence is not blind, and especially it is not dumb. The old lady who had celebrated Mrs. Bowen to him the first night at Palazzo Pinti led a life of active questions as to what was the supreme attraction to Colville there, and she referred her doubt to every friend with whom she drank tea. She philosophised the situation very scientifically, and if not very conclusively, how few are the absolute conclusions of science upon any point!

"He is a bachelor, and there is a natural affinity between bachelors and widows—much more than if he were a widower too. If he were a widower I should say it was undoubtedly mademoiselle. If he were a little *bit* younger, I should have no doubt it was madame; but men of that age have such an ambition to marry young girls! I suppose that they think it proves they are not so very old, after all. And certainly he isn't too old to marry. If he were wise—which he probably isn't, if he's like other men in such matters— there wouldn't be any question about Mrs. Bowen. Pretty creature! And so much sense! Too much for him. Ah, my dear, how we are wasted upon that sex!"

Mrs. Bowen herself treated the affair with masterly frankness. More than once in varying phrase, she said: "You are very good to give us so much of your time, Mr. Colville, and I won't pretend I don't know it. You're helping me out with a very hazardous experiment. When I undertook to see Imogene through a winter in Florence, I didn't reflect what a very gay time girls have at home, in Western towns especially. But I haven't heard her breathe Buffalo once. And I'm sure it's doing her a great deal of good here. She's naturally got a very good mind; she's very ambitious to be cultivated. She's read a good deal, and she's anxious to know history and art; and your advice and criticism are the greatest possible advantage to her.''

''Thank you,'' said Colville, with a fine, remote dissatisfaction. ''I supposed I was merely enjoying myself.''

He had lately begun to haunt his banker's for information in regard to the Carnival balls, with the hope that something might be made out of them. But either there were to be no great Carnival balls, or it was a mistake to suppose that his banker ought to know about them. Colville went experimentally to one of the people's balls at a minor theatre, which he found advertised on the house walls. At half-past ten the dancing had not begun, but the masks were arriving; young women in gay silks and dirty white gloves; men in women's dresses, with enormous hands; girls as pages; clowns, pantaloons, old women, and the like. They were all very good-humoured; the men, who far outnumbered the women, danced contentedly together. Colville liked two cavalry soldiers who waltzed with each other for an hour, and then went off to a battery on exhibition* in the pit, and had as much electricity as they could hold. He liked also two young citizens who danced together as long as he stayed, and did not leave off even for electrical refreshment. He came away at midnight, pushing out of the theatre through a crowd of people at the door, some of whom were tipsy. This certainly would not have done for the ladies, though the people were civilly tipsy.

IX

THE next morning Paolo, when he brought up Colville's breakfast, brought the news that there was to be a veglione* at the Pergola Theatre. This news revived Colville's courage. "Paolo," he said, "you ought to open a banking-house." Paolo was used to being joked by foreigners who could not speak Italian very well; he smiled as if he understood.

The banker had his astute doubts of Paolo's intelligence; the banker in Europe doubts all news not originating in his house; but after a day or two the advertisements in the newspapers carried conviction even to the banker.

When Colville went to the ladies with news of the veglione, he found that they had already heard of it. "Should you like to go?" he asked Mrs. Bowen.

"I don't know. What do you think?" she asked in turn.

"Oh, it's for you to do the thinking. I only know what I want."

Imogene said nothing, while she watched the internal debate as it expressed itself in Mrs. Bowen's face.

"People go in boxes," she said thoughtfully; "but you would feel that a box wasn't the same thing exactly?"

"*We* went on the floor," suggested Colville.

"It was very different then. And, besides, Mrs. Finlay had absolutely *no* sense of propriety." When a woman has explicitly condemned a given action, she apparently gathers courage for its commission under a little different conditions. "Of course, if we went upon the floor, I shouldn't wish it to be known at all, though foreigners can do almost anything they like."

"Really," said Colville, "when it comes to that, I don't see any harm in it."

"And you say go?"

"I say whatever you say."

Mrs. Bowen looked from him to Imogene. "I don't

either," she said finally, and they understood that she meant the harm which he had not seen.

"Which of us has been so good as to deserve this?" asked Colville.

"Oh, you have all been good," she said. "We shall go in masks and dominoes,"* she continued. "Nothing will happen, and who should know us if anything did?" They had received tickets to the great Borghese ball, which is still a fashionable and desired event of the Carnival to foreigners in Florence; but their preconceptions of the veglione threw into the shade the entertainment which the gentlemen of Florence offered to favoured sojourners.

"Come," said Mrs. Bowen, "you must go with us and help us choose our dominoes."

A prudent woman does not do an imprudent thing by halves. Effie was to be allowed to go to the veglione too, and she went with them to the shop where they were to hire their dominoes. It would be so much more fun, Mrs. Bowen said, to choose the dresses in the shop than to have them sent home for you to look at. Effie was to be in black; Imogene was to have a light blue domino, and Mrs. Bowen chose a purple one; even where their faces were not to be seen they considered their complexions in choosing the colours. If you happened to find a friend, and wanted to unmask, you would not want to look horrid. The shop people took the vividest interest in it all, as if it were a new thing to them, and these were the first foreigners they had ever served with masks and dominoes. They made Mrs. Bowen and Imogene go into an inner room and come out for the mystification of Colville, hulking about in the front shop with his mask and domino on.

"Which is which?" the ladies both challenged him, in the mask's conventional falsetto, when they came out.

With a man's severe logic he distinguished them according to their silks, but there had been time for them to think of changing, and they took off their masks to laugh in his face.

They fluttered so airily about among the pendent masks and dominoes, from which they shook a ghostly perfume of old carnivals, that his heart leaped.

"Ah, you'll never be so fascinating again!" he cried. He wanted to take them in his arms, they were both so delicious; a man has still only that primitive way of expressing his supreme satisfaction in women. "Now, which am I?" he demanded of them, and that made them laugh again. He had really put his arm about Effie.

"Do you think you will know your papa at the veglione?" asked one of the shop-women, with a mounting interest in the amiable family party.

They all laughed; the natural mistake seemed particularly droll to Imogene.

"Come," cried Mrs. Bowen; "it's time we should be going."

That was true; they had passed so long a time in the shop that they did not feel justified in seriously attempting to beat down the price of their dresses. They took them at the first price. The woman said with reason that it was Carnival, and she could get her price for the things.

They went to the veglione at eleven, the ladies calling for Colville, as before, in Mrs. Bowen's carriage. He felt rather sheepish, coming out of his room in his mask and domino, but the corridors of the hotel were empty, and for the most part dark; there was no one up but the porter, who wished him a pleasant time in as matter-of-fact fashion as if he were going out to an evening party in his dress coat. His spirits mounted in the atmosphere of adventure which the ladies diffused about them in the carriage; Effie Bowen laughed aloud when he entered, in childish gaiety of heart.

The narrow streets roared with the wheels of cabs and carriages coming and going; the street before the theatre was so packed that it was some time before they could reach the door. Masks were passing in and out; the nervous joy of the ladies expressed itself in a deep-drawn quivering sigh. Their carriage door was opened by a servant of the theatre, who wished them a pleasant veglione, and the next moment they were in the crowded vestibule, where they paused a moment, to let Imogene and Effie really feel that they were part of a masquerade.

"Now, keep all together," said Mrs. Bowen, as they

passed through the inner door of the vestibule, and the
brilliantly lighted theatre flashed its colours and splendours
upon them. The floor of the pit had been levelled to that of
the stage, which, stripped of the scenic apparatus, opened
vaster spaces for the motley crew already eddying over it in
the waltz. The boxes, tier over tier, blazed with the light of
candelabra which added their sparkle to that of the gas jets.

"You and Effie go before," said Mrs. Bowen to Imogene.
She made them take hands like children, and mechanically
passed her own hand through Colville's arm.

A mask in red from head to foot attached himself to the
party, and began to make love to her in excellent
pantomime.

Colville was annoyed. He asked her if she should tell the
fellow to take himself off.

"Not on any account!" she answered. "It's perfectly
delightful. It wouldn't be the veglione without it. Did you
ever see such good acting?"

"I don't think it's remarkable for anything but its fervour," said Colville.

"I should like to see *you* making love to some lady," she
rejoined mischievously.

"I will make love to you, if you like," he said, but he felt
in an instant that his joke was in bad taste.

They went the round of the theatre. "That is Prince
Strozzi, Imogene," said Mrs. Bowen, leaning forward to
whisper to the girl. She pointed out other people of historic
and aristocratic names in the boxes, where there was a
democracy of beauty among the ladies, all painted and
powdered to the same marquise effect.

On the floor were gentlemen in evening dress, without
masks, and here and there ladies waltzing, who had masks
but no dominoes. But for the most part people were in
costume; the theatre flushed and flowered in gay variety of
tint that teased the eye with its flow through the dance.

Mrs. Bowen had circumscribed the adventure so as to exclude
dancing from it. Imogene was not to dance. One might go to the
veglione and look on from a box; if one ventured further and
went on the floor, decidedly one was not to dance.

This was thoroughly understood beforehand, and there were to be no petitions or murmurs at the theatre. They found a quiet corner, and sat down to look on.

The mask in red followed, and took his place at a little distance, where, whenever Mrs. Bowen looked that way, he continued to protest his passion.

"You're sure he doesn't bore you?" suggested Colville.

"No, indeed. He's very amusing."

"Oh, all right!"

The waltz ceased; the whirling and winding confusion broke into an irregular streaming hither and thither, up and down. They began to pick out costumes and characters that interested them. Clowns in white, with big noses, and harlequins in their motley, with flat black masks, abounded. There were some admirable grasshoppers in green, with long antennæ quivering from their foreheads. Two or three Mephistos* reddened through the crowd. Several knights in armour got about with difficulty, apparently burdened by their greaves and breastplates.

A group of leaping and dancing masks gathered around a young man in evening dress, with long hair, who stood leaning against a pillar near them, and who underwent their mockeries with a smile of patience, half amused, half tormented.

When they grew tired of baiting him, and were looking about for other prey, the red mask redoubled his show of devotion to Mrs. Bowen, and the other masks began to flock round and approve.

"Oh, *now*," she said, with a little embarrassed laugh, in which there was no displeasure, "I think you may ask him to go away. But don't be harsh with him," she added, at a brusque movement which Colville made toward the mask.

"Oh, why should I be harsh with him? We're not rivals." This was not in good taste either, Colville felt. "Besides, I'm an Italian too," he said, to retrieve himself. He made a few paces toward the mask, and said in a low tone, with gentle suggestion, "Madame finds herself a little incommoded."

The mask threw himself into an attitude of burlesque despair, bowed low with his hand on his heart, in token of

submission, and vanished into the crowd. The rest dispersed
with cries of applause.

"How very prettily you did it, both of you!" said Mrs.
Bowen. "I begin to believe you *are* an Italian, Mr. Colville.
I shall be afraid of you."

"You weren't afraid of *him*."

"Oh, he was a *real* Italian."

"It seems to me that mamma is getting all the good of the
veglione," said Effie, in a plaintive murmur. The well-
disciplined child must have suffered deeply before she lifted
this seditious voice.

"Why, so I am, Effie," answered her mother, "and I
don't think it's fair myself. What shall we do about it?"

"I should like something to eat," said the child.

"So should I," said Colville. "That's reparation your
mother owes us all. Let's make her take us and get us
something. Wouldn't you like an ice, Miss Graham?"

"Yes, an *ice*," said Imogene, with an effect of adding,
"Nothing more for worlds," that made Colville laugh. She
rose slowly, like one in a dream, and cast a look as impassioned as a look could be made through a mask on the scene
she was leaving behind her. The band was playing a waltz
again, and the wide floor swam with circling couples.

The corridor where the tables were set was thronged with
people, who were drinking beer and eating cold beef and
boned turkey and slices of huge round sausages. "Oh, how
can they?" cried the girl, shuddering.

"I didn't know you were so ethereal-minded about these
things," said Colville. "I thought you didn't object to the
salad at Madame Uccelli's."

"Oh, but at the veglione!" breathed the girl for all
answer. He laughed again, but Mrs. Bowen did not laugh
with him; he wondered why.

When they returned to their corner in the theatre they
found a mask in a black domino there, who made place for
them, and remained standing near. They began talking
freely and audibly, as English-speaking people incorrigibly
do in Italy, where their tongue is all but the language of the
country.

"Really," said Colville, "I think I shall stifle in this mask. If you ladies will do what you can to surround me and keep me secret, I'll take it off a moment."

"I believe I will join you, Mr. Colville," said the mask near them. He pushed up his little visor of silk, and discovered the mild, benignant features of Mr. Waters.

"Bless my soul!" cried Colville.

Mrs. Bowen was apparently too much shocked to say anything.

"You didn't expect to meet me here?" asked the old man, as if otherwise it should be the most natural thing in the world. After that they could only unite in suppressing their astonishment. "It's extremely interesting," he went on, "extremely! I've been here ever since the exercises began, and I have not only been very greatly amused, but greatly instructed. It seems to me the key to a great many anomalies in the history of this wonderful people."

If Mr. Waters took this philosophical tone about the Carnival, it was not possible for Colville to take any other.

"And have you been able to divine from what you have seen here," he asked gravely, "the grounds of Savonarola's objection to the Carnival?"

"Not at all," said the old man promptly. "I have seen nothing but the most harmless gaiety throughout the evening."

Colville hung his head. He remembered reading once in a passage from Swedenborg,* that the most celestial angels had scarcely any power of perceiving evil.

"Why aren't you young people dancing?" asked Mr. Waters, in a cheerful general way, of Mrs. Bowen's party.

Colville was glad to break the silence. "Mrs. Bowen doesn't approve of dancing at vegliones."

"No?—why not?" inquired the old man, with invincible simplicity.

Mrs. Bowen smiled her pretty, small smile below her mask.

"The company is apt to be rather mixed," she said quietly.

"Yes," pursued Mr. Waters; "but you could dance with one another. The company seems very well behaved."

"Oh, quite so," Mrs. Bowen assented.

"Shortly after I came," said Mr. Waters, "one of the masks asked me to dance. I was really sorry that my age and traditions forbade my doing so. I tried to explain, but I'm afraid I didn't make myself quite clear."

"Probably it passed for a joke with her," said Colville, in order to say something.

"Ah, very likely; but I shall always feel that my impressions of the Carnival would have been more definite if I could have danced. Now, if I were a young man like you——"

Imogene turned and looked at Colville through the eyeholes of her mask; even in that sort of isolation he thought her eyes expressed surprise.

"It never occurred to you before that I was a young man," he suggested gravely.

She did not reply.

After a little interval, "Imogene," asked Mrs. Bowen, "would you like to dance?"

Colville was astonished. "The veglione has gone to your head, Mrs. Bowen," he tacitly made his comment. She had spoken to Imogene, but she glanced at him as if she expected him to be grateful to her for this stroke of liberality.

"What would be the use?" returned the girl.

Colville rose. "After my performance in the Lancers, I can't expect you to believe me; but I really *do* know how to waltz." He had but to extend his arms, and she was hanging upon his shoulder, and they were whirling away through a long orbit of delight to the girl.

"Oh, why have you let me do you such injustice?" she murmured intensely. "I never shall forgive myself."

"It grieved me that you shouldn't have divined that I was really a magnificent dancer in disguise, but I bore it as best I could," said Colville, really amused at her seriousness. "Perhaps you'll find out after a while that I'm not an old fellow either, but only a 'Lost Youth.' "

"Hush," she said; "I don't like to hear you talk so."

"How?"

"About—age!" she answered. "It makes me feel——
Don't to-night!"

Colville laughed. "It isn't a fact that my blinking is going
to change materially. You had better make the most of me
as a lost youth. I'm old enough to be two of them."

She did not answer, and as they wound up and down
through the other orbing couples, he remembered the
veglione of seventeen years before, when he had dreamed
through the waltz with the girl who jilted him; she was very
docile and submissive that night; he believed afterward that
if he had spoken frankly then, she would not have refused
him. But he had veiled his passion in words and phrases
that, taken in themselves, had no meaning—that neither
committed him nor claimed her. He could not help it; he
had not the courage at any moment to risk the loss of her for
ever, till it was too late, till he must lose her.

"Do you believe in pre-existence?" he demanded of
Imogene.

"Oh yes!" she flashed back. "This very instant it was just
as if I had been here before, long ago."

"Dancing with me?"

"With you? Yes—yes—I think so."

He had lived long enough to know that she was making
herself believe what she said, and that she had not lived long
enough to know this.

"Then you remember what I said to you—tried to say to
you—that night?" Through one of those psychological jug-
gles which we all practise with ourselves at times, it amused
him, it charmed him, to find her striving to realise this past.

"No; it was so long ago? What was it?" she whispered
dreamily.

A turn of the waltz brought them near Mrs. Bowen; her
mask seemed to wear a dumb reproach. He began to be
weary; one of the differences between youth and later life is
that the latter wearies so soon of any given emotion.

"Ah, I can't remember, either! Aren't you getting rather
tired of the waltz and me?"

"Oh no; go on!" she deeply murmured. "Try to
remember."

The long, pulsating stream of the music broke and fell. The dancers crookedly dispersed in wandering lines. She took his arm; he felt her heart leap against it; those innocent, trustful throbs upbraided him. At the same time his own heart beat with a sort of fond, protecting tenderness; he felt the witchery of his power to make this young, radiant, and beautiful creature hang flattered and bewildered on his talk; he liked the compassionate worship with which his tacit confidence had inspired her, even while he was not without some satirical sense of the crude sort of heart-broken hero he must be in the fancy of a girl of her age.

"Let us go and walk in the corridor a moment," he said. But they walked there till the alluring melancholy music of the waltz began again. In a mutual caprice, they rejoined the dance.

It came into his head to ask, "Who is *he?*" and as he had got past denying himself anything, he asked it.

"He? What he?"

"He that Mrs. Bowen thought might object to your seeing the Carnival?"

"Oh!—oh yes! That was the not impossible he."

"Is that all?"

"Yes."

"Then he's not even the not improbable he?"

"No, indeed."

They waltzed in silence. Then, "Why did you ask me that?" she murmured.

"I don't know. Was it such a strange question?"

"I don't know. You ought to."

"Yes, if it was wrong, I'm old enough to know better."

"You promised not to say 'old' any more."

"Then I suppose I mustn't. But you mustn't get me to ignore it, and then laugh at me for it."

"Oh!" she reproached him, "you think I could do that?"

"You could if it was you who were here with me once before."

"Then I know I wasn't."

Again they were silent, and it was he who spoke first. "I wish you would tell me why you object to the interdicted topic?"

"Because—because I like every time to be perfect in itself."

"Oh! And this wouldn't be perfect in itself if I were—not so young as some people?"

"I didn't mean that. No; but if you didn't mention it, no one else would think of it or care for it."

"Did any one ever accuse you of flattering, Miss Graham?"

"Not till now. And you are unjust."

"Well, I withdraw the accusation."

"And will you ever pretend such a thing again?"

"Oh, never!"

"Then I have your promise."

The talk was light word-play, such as depends upon the talker's own mood for its point or its pointlessness. Between two young people of equal years it might have had meanings to penetrate, to sigh over, to question. Colville found it delicious to be pursued by the ingenuous fervour of this young girl, eager to vindicate her sincerity in prohibiting him from his own ironical depreciation. Apparently, she had a sentimental mission of which he was the object; he was to be convinced that he was unnecessarily morbid; he was to be cheered up, to be kept in heart.

"I must believe in you after this," he said, with a smile which his mask hid.

"Thanks," she breathed. It seemed to him that her hand closed convulsively upon his in their light clasp.

The pressure sent a real pang to his heart. It forced her name from his lips. "Imogene! Ah, I've no right to call you that."

"Yes."

"From this out I promise to be twenty years younger. But no one is to know it but you. Do you think you will know it? I shouldn't like to keep the secret to myself altogether."

"No; I will help you. It shall be *our* secret."

She gave a low laugh of delight. He convinced himself that she had entered into the light spirit of banter in which he believed that he was talking.

The music ceased again. He whirled her to the seat where he had left Mrs. Bowen. She was not there, nor the others.

Colville felt the meanness of a man who had betrayed his trust, and his self-contempt was the sharper because the trust had been as tacit and indefinite as it was generous. The effect of Mrs. Bowen's absence was as if she had indignantly flown, and left him to the consequences of his treachery.

He sat down rather blankly with Imogene to wait for her return. It was the only thing they could do.

It had grown very hot. The air was thick with dust. The lights burned through it as through a fog.

"I believe I will take off my mask," she said. "I can scarcely breathe."

"No, no," protested Colville; "that won't do."

"I feel faint," she gasped.

His heart sank. "Don't,' he said incoherently. "Come with me into the vestibule, and get a breath of air."

He had almost to drag her through the crowd, but in the vestibule she revived, and they returned to their place again. He did not share the easy content with which she recognised the continued absence of Mrs. Bowen.

"Why, they must be lost. But isn't it perfect sitting here and watching the maskers?"

"Perfect," said Colville distractedly.

"Don't you like to make romances about the different ones?"

It was on Colville's tongue to say that he had made all the romances he wished for that evening, but he only answered, "Oh, very."

"Poor Mrs. Bowen," laughed the girl. "It will be such a joke on her, with her punctilious notions, getting lost from her *protégée* at a Carnival ball! I shall tell every one."

"Oh no, don't," said Colville, in horror that his mask scarcely concealed.

"Why not?"

"It wouldn't be at all the thing."

"Why, are *you* becoming Europeanised too?" she demanded. "I thought you went in for all sorts of unconventionalities.

Recollect your promise. You must be as impulsive as I am."

Colville, staring anxiously about in every direction, made for the first time the reflection that most young girls probably conform to the proprieties without in the least knowing why.

"Do you think," he asked, in desperation, "that you would be afraid to be left here a moment while I went about in the crowd and tried to find them?"

"Not at all," she said. But she added, "Don't be gone long."

"Oh no," he answered, pulling off his mask. "Be sure not to move from here on any account."

He plunged into the midst of the crowd that buffeted him from side to side as he struck against its masses. The squeaking and gibbering masks* mocked in their falsetto at his wild-eyed, naked face thrusting hither and thither among them.

"I saw your lady wife with another gentleman," cried one of them, in a subtle misinterpretation of the cause of his distraction.

The throng had immensely increased; the clowns and harlequins ran shrieking up and down, and leaped over one another's heads.

It was useless. He went back to Imogene with a heart-sickening fear that she too might have vanished.

But she was still there.

"You ought to have come sooner," she said gaily. "That red mask has been here again. He looked as if he wanted to make love to *me* this time. But he didn't. If you'd been here you might have asked him where Mrs. Bowen was."

Colville sat down. He had done what he could to mend the matter, and the time had come for philosophical submission. It was now his duty to keep up Miss Graham's spirits. They were both Americans, and from the national standpoint he was simply the young girl's middle-aged bachelor friend. There was nothing in the situation for him to beat his breast about.

"Well, all that we can do is to wait for them," he said.

"Oh yes," she answered easily. "They'll be sure to come back in the course of time."

They waited a half-hour, talking somewhat at random, and still the others did not come. But the red mask came again. He approached Colville, and said politely—

"*La signora è partita.*"

"The lady gone?" repeated Colville, taking this to be part of the red mask's joke.

"*La bambina pareva poco bene.*"

"The little one not well?" echoed Colville again, rising. "Are you joking?"

The mask made a deep murmur of polite deprecation. "I am not capable of such a thing in a serious affair. Perhaps you know me?" he said, taking off his mask; and in further sign of good faith he gave the name of a painter sufficiently famous in Florence.

"I beg your pardon, and thank you," said Colville. He had no need to speak to Imogene; her hand was already trembling on his arm.

They drove home in silence through the white moonlight of the streets, filled everywhere with the gay voices and figures of the Carnival.

Mrs. Bowen met them at the door of her apartment, and received them with a manner that justly distributed the responsibility and penalty for their escapade. Colville felt that a meaner spirit would have wreaked its displeasure upon the girl alone. She made short, quiet answers to all his eager inquiries. Most probably it was some childish indisposition; Effie had been faint. No, he need not go for the doctor. Mr. Waters had called the doctor, who had just gone away. There was nothing else that he could do for her. She dropped her eyes, and in everything but words dismissed him. She would not even remain with him till he could decently get himself out of the house. She left Imogene to receive his adieux, feigning that she heard Effie calling.

"I'm—I'm very sorry," faltered the girl, "that we didn't go back to her at once."

"Yes; I was to blame," answered the humiliated hero of her Carnival dream. The clinging regret with which she kept his hand at parting scarcely consoled him for what had happened.

"I will come round in the morning," he said. "I must know how Effie is."

"Yes; come."

X

COLVILLE went to Palazzo Pinti next day with the feeling that he was defying Mrs. Bowen. Upon a review of the facts he could not find himself so very much to blame for the occurrences of the night before, and he had not been able to prove to his reason that Mrs. Bowen had resented his behaviour. She had not made a scene of any sort when he came in with Imogene; it was natural that she should excuse herself, and should wish to be with her sick child: she had done really nothing. But when a woman has done nothing she fills the soul of the man whose conscience troubles him with an instinctive apprehension. There is then no safety, his nerves tell him, except in bringing the affair, whatever it is, to an early issue—in having it out with her. Colville subdued the cowardly impulse of his own heart, which would have deceived him with the suggestion that Mrs. Bowen might be occupied with Effie, and it would be better to ask for Miss Graham. He asked for Mrs. Bowen, and she came in directly.

She smiled in the usual way, and gave her hand, as she always did. But her hand was cold, and she looked tired, though she said Effie was quite herself again, and had been asking for him. "Imogene has been telling her about your adventure last night, and making her laugh."

If it had been Mrs. Bowen's purpose to mystify him, she could not have done it more thoroughly than by this bold treatment of the affair. He bent a puzzled gaze upon her. "I'm glad any of you have found it amusing," he said. "I confess that I couldn't let myself off so lightly in regard to it." She did not reply, and he continued: "The fact is, I don't think I behaved very well. I abused your kindness to Miss Graham."

"Abused my kindness to Miss Graham?"

"Yes. When you allowed her to dance at the veglione, I ought to have considered that you were stretching a point. I ought to have taken her back to you very soon, instead of tempting her to go and walk with me in the corridor."

"Yes," said Mrs. Bowen. "So it was you who proposed it? Imogene was afraid that she had. What exemplary young people you are! The way each of you confesses and assumes all the blame would leave the severest chaperone without a word."

Her gaiety made Colville uncomfortable. He said gravely, "What I blame myself most for is that I was not there to be of use to you when Effie——"

"Oh, you mustn't think of that at all. Mr. Waters was most efficient. My admirer in the red mask was close at hand, and between them they got Effie out without the slightest disturbance. I fancy most people thought it was a Carnival joke. Please don't think of that again."

Nothing could be politer than all this.

"And you won't allow me to punish myself for not being there to give you even a moral support?"

"Certainly not. As I told Imogene, young people *will* be young people; and I knew how fond you were of dancing."

Though it pierced him, Colville could not help admiring the neatness of this thrust. "I didn't know you were so ironical, Mrs. Bowen."

"Ironical? Not at all."

"Ah! I see I'm not forgiven."

"I'm sure I don't know what you mean."

Imogene and Effie came in. The child was a little pale, and willingly let him take her on his knee, and lay her languid head on his shoulder. The girl had not aged over-night like himself and Mrs. Bowen; she looked as fresh and strong as yesterday.

"Miss Graham," said Colville, "if a person to whom you had done a deadly wrong insisted that you hadn't done any wrong at all, should you consider yourself forgiven?"

"It would depend upon the person," said the girl, with innocent liveliness, recognising the extravagance in his tone.

"Yes," he said, with an affected pensiveness, "so very much depends upon the person in such a case."

Mrs. Bowen rose. "Excuse me a moment; I will be back

directly. Don't get up, please," she said, and prevented him with a quick withdrawal to another room, which left upon his sense the impression of elegant grace, and a smile and sunny glance. But neither had any warmth in it.

Colville heaved an involuntary sigh. "Do you feel very much used up?" he asked Imogene.

"Not at all," she laughed. "Do you?"

"Not in the least. My veglione hasn't ended yet. I'm still practically at the Pergola. It's easy to keep a thing of that sort up if you don't sleep after you get home."

"Didn't you sleep? I expected to lie awake a long time thinking it over; but I dropped asleep at once. I suppose I was very tired. I didn't even dream."

"You must have slept hard. You're pretty apt to dream when you're waking."

"How do you know?"

"Ah, I've noticed when you've been talking to me. Better not! It's a bad habit; it gives you false views of things. I used——"

"But you mustn't say you *used!* That's forbidden now. Remember your promise!"

"My promise? What promise?"

"Oh, if you've forgotten already."

"I remember. But that was last night."

"No, no! It was for all time. Why should dreams be so very misleading? I think there's ever so much in dreams. The most wonderful thing is the way you make people talk in dreams. It isn't strange that you should talk yourself, but that other people should say this and that when you aren't at all expecting what they say."

"That's when you're sleeping. But when you're waking, you make people say just what you want. And that's why day dreams are so bad. If you make people say what you want, they probably don't mean it."

"Don't you think so?"

"Half the time. Do you ever have day dreams?" he asked Effie, pressing her cheek against his own.

"I don't know what they are," she murmured, with a soft

little note of polite regret for her ignorance, if possibly it incommoded him.

"You will by and by," he said, "and then you must look out for them. They're particularly bad in this air. I had one of them in Florence once that lasted three months."

"What was it about?" asked the child.

Imogene involuntarily bent forward.

"Ah, I can't tell you now. She's trying to hear us."

"No, no," protested the girl, with a laugh. "I was thinking of something else."

"Oh, we know her, don't we?" he said to the child, with a playful appeal to that passion for the joint possession of a mystery which all children have.

"We might whisper it," she suggested.

"No; better wait for some other time." They were sitting near a table where a pencil and some loose leaves of paper lay. He pulled his chair a little closer, and, with the child still upon his knee, began to scribble and sketch at random. "Ah, there's San Miniato," he said, with a glance from the window. "Must get its outline in. You've heard how there came to be a church up there? No? Well, it shows the sort of man San Miniato really was. He was one of the early Christians, and he gave the poor pagans a great deal of trouble. They first threw him to the wild beasts in the amphitheatre, but the moment those animals set eyes on him they saw it would be of no use; they just lay down and died. Very well, then; the pagans determined to see what effect the axe would have upon San Miniato: but as soon as they struck off his head he picked it up, set it back on his shoulders again, waded across the Arno, walked up the hill, and when he came to a convenient little oratory up there he knelt down and expired. Isn't that a pretty good story? It's like fairies, isn't it?"

"Yes," whispered the child.

"What nonsense!" said Imogene. "You made it up."

"Oh, did I? Perhaps I built the church that stands there to commemorate the fact. It's all in the history of Florence. Not in all histories; some of them are too proud to put such stories in, but I'm going to put every one I can find into the history I'm writing for Effie. San Miniato was beheaded where the church of Santa Candida stands now, and he walked all that distance.''

"Did he have to die when he got to the oratory?" asked the child, with gentle regret.

"It appears so," said Colville, sketching. "He would have been dead by this time, anyway, you know."

"Yes," she reluctantly admitted.

"I never quite like those things, either, Effie," he said, pressing her to him. "There were people cruelly put to death two or three hundred years ago that I can't help feeling would be alive yet if they had been justly treated. There are a good many fairy stories about Florence; perhaps they used to be true stories; the truth seems to die out of stories after a while, simply because people stop believing them. Saint Ambrose of Milan restored the son of his host to life when he came down here to dedicate the Church of San Giovanni. Then there was another saint, San Zenobi, who worked a very pretty miracle after he was dead. They were carrying his body from the Church of San Giovanni to the Church of Santa Reparata, and in Piazza San Giovanni his bier touched a dead elm-tree that stood there, and the tree instantly sprang into leaf and flower, though it was in the middle of the winter. A great many people took the leaves home with them, and a marble pillar was put up there, with a cross and an elm-tree carved on it. Oh, the case is very well authenticated.''

"I shall really begin to think you believe such things," said Imogene. "Perhaps you *are* a Catholic."

Mrs. Bowen returned to the room, and sat down.

"There's another fairy story, prettier yet," said Colville, while the little girl drew a long deep breath of satisfaction and expectation. "You've heard of the Buondelmonti?"* he asked Imogene.

"Oh, it seems to me as if I'd had *nothing* but the Buondelmonti dinned into me since I came to Florence!" she answered in lively despair.

"Ah, this happened some centuries before the Buondelmonte you've been bored with was born. This was

Giovanni Gualberto of the Buondelmonti, and he was riding along one day in 1003, near the Church of San Miniato, when he met a certain man named Ugo, who had killed one of his brothers. Gualberto stopped and drew his sword; Ugo saw no other chance of escape, and he threw himself face downward on the ground, with his arms stretched out in the form of the cross. 'Gualberto, remember Jesus Christ, who died upon the cross praying for His enemies.' The story says that these words went to Gualberto's heart; he got down from his horse, and in sign of pardon lifted his enemy and kissed and embraced him. Then they went together into the church, and fell on their knees before the figure of Christ upon the cross, and the figure bowed its head in sign of approval and pleasure in Gualberto's noble act of Christian piety.''

''Beautiful!'' murmured the girl; the child only sighed.

''Ah, yes; it's an easy matter to pick up one's head from the ground, and set it back on one's shoulders, or to bring the dead to life, or to make a tree put forth leaves and flowers in midwinter; but to melt the heart of a man with forgiveness in the presence of his enemy—that's a different thing; *that's* no fairy story; that's a real miracle; and I believe this one happened—it's so impossible.''

''Oh yes, it must have happened,'' said the girl.

''Do you think it's so very hard to forgive, then?'' asked Mrs. Bowen gravely.

''Oh, not for ladies,'' replied Colville.

She flushed, and her eyes shone when she glanced at him.

''I'm sorry to put you down,'' he said to the child; ''but I can't take you with me, and I must be going.''

Mrs. Bowen did not ask him to stay to lunch; he thought afterward that she might have relented as far as that but for the last little thrust, which he would better have spared.

''Effie dear,'' said her mother, when the door closed upon Colville, ''don't you think you'd better lie down a while? You look so tired.''

''Shall I lie down on the sofa here?''

''No, on your bed.''

''Well.''

"I'll go with you, Effie," said Imogene, "and see that you're nicely tucked in."

When she returned alone, Mrs. Bowen was sitting where she had left her, and seemed not to have moved. "I think Effie will drop off to sleep," she said; "she seems drowsy." She sat down, and after a pensive moment continued, "I wonder what makes Mr. Colville seem so gloomy."

"Does he seem gloomy?" asked Mrs. Bowen unsympathetically.

"No, not gloomy exactly. But different from last night. I wish people could always be the same! He was so gay and full of spirits; and now he's so self-absorbed. He thinks you're offended with him, Mrs. Bowen."

"I don't think he was very much troubled about it. I only thought he was flighty from want of sleep. At your age you don't mind the loss of a night."

"Do you think Mr. Colville seems so very old?" asked Imogene anxiously.

Mrs. Bowen appeared not to have heard her. She went to the window and looked out. When she came back, "Isn't it almost time for you to have a letter from home?" she asked.

"Why, no. I had one from mother day before yesterday. What made you think so?"

"Imogene," interrupted Mrs. Bowen, with a sudden excitement which she tried to control, but which made her lips tremble, and break a little from her restraint, "you know that I am here in the place of your mother, to advise you and look after you in every way?"

"Why, yes, Mrs. Bowen," cried the girl, in surprise.

"It's a position of great responsibility in regard to a young lady. I can't have anything to reproach myself with afterward."

"No."

"Have I always been kind to you, and considerate of your rights and your freedom? Have I ever interfered with you in any way that you think I oughtn't?"

"What an idea! You've been loveliness itself, Mrs. Bowen!"

"Then I want you to listen to me, and answer me frankly, and not suspect my motives."

"Why, how *could* I do that?"

"Never mind!" cried Mrs. Bowen impatiently, almost angrily. "People can't help their suspicions! Do you think Mr. Morton cares for you?"

The girl hung her head.

"Imogene, answer me!"

"I don't know," answered Imogene coldly; "but if you're troubled about that, Mrs. Bowen, you needn't be; I don't care anything for Mr. Morton."

"If I thought you were becoming interested in any one, it would be my duty to write to your mother and tell her."

"Of course; I should expect you to do it."

"And if I saw you becoming interested in any one in a way that I thought would make you unhappy, it would be my duty to warn you."

"Yes."

"Of course, I don't mean that any one would knowingly try to make you unhappy?"

"No."

"Men don't go about nowadays trying to break girls' hearts. But very good men can be thoughtless and selfish."

"Yes; I understand that," said Imogene, in a falling accent.

"I don't wish to prejudice you against any one. I should consider it very wrong and wicked. Besides, I don't care to interfere with you to that degree. You are old enough to see and judge for yourself."

Imogene sat silent, passing her hand across the front of her dress. The clock ticked audibly from the mantel.

"I will not have it left to me!" cried Mrs. Bowen. "It is hard enough, at any rate. Do you think I like to speak to you?"

"No."

"Of course it makes me seem inhospitable, and distrustful, and detestable."

"I never thought of accusing you," said the girl, slowly lifting her eyes.

"I will never, never speak to you of it again," said Mrs. Bowen, "and from this time forth I insist upon your feeling just as free as if I hadn't spoken." She trembled upon the verge of a sob, from which she repelled herself.

Imogene sat still, with a sort of serious, bewildered look.

"You shall have every proper opportunity of meeting any one you like."

"Oh yes."

"And I shall be only too gl-glad to take back everything!"

Imogene sat motionless and silent. Mrs. Bowen broke out again with a sort of violence; the years teach us something of self-control, perhaps, but they weaken and unstring the nerves. In this opposition of silence to silence, the woman of the world was no match for the inexperienced girl.

"Have you nothing to say, Imogene?"

"I never thought of him in that way at all. I don't know what to say yet. It—confuses me. I—I can't imagine it. But if you think that he is trying to amuse himself——"

"I never said that!"

"No, I know it."

"He likes to make you talk, and to talk with you. But he is perfectly idle here, and—there is too much difference, every way. The very good in him makes it the worse. I suppose that after talking with him everyone else seems insipid."

"Yes."

Mrs. Bowen rose and ran suddenly from the room.

Imogene remained sitting cold and still.

No one had been named since they spoke of Mr. Morton.

XI

COLVILLE had not done what he meant in going to Mrs. Bowen's; in fact, he had done just what he had not meant to do, as he distinctly perceived in coming away. It was then that in a luminous retrospect he discovered his motive to have been a wish to atone to her for behaviour that must have distressed her, or at least to explain it to her. She had not let him do this at once; an instant willingness to hear and to condone was not in a woman's nature; she had to make him feel, by the infliction of a degree of punishment, that she had suffered. But before she ended she had made it clear that she was ready to grant him a tacit pardon, and he had answered with a silly sarcasm the question that was to have led to peace. He could not help seeing that throughout the whole Carnival adventure she had yielded her cherished reluctances to please him, to show him that she was not stiff or prudish, to convince him that she would not be a killjoy through her devotion to conventionalities which she thought he despised. He could not help seeing that he had abused her delicate generosity, insulted her subtle concessions. He strolled along down the Arno, feeling flat and mean, as a man always does after a contest with a woman in which he has got the victory; our sex can preserve its self-respect only through defeat in such a case. It gave him no pleasure to remember that the glamour of the night before seemed still to rest on Imogene unbroken; that, indeed, was rather an added pain. He surprised himself in the midst of his poignant reflections by a yawn. Clearly the time was past when these ideal troubles could keep him awake, and there was, after all, a sort of brutal consolation in the fact. He was forty-one years old, and he was sleepy, whatever capacity for suffering remained to him. He went to his hotel to catch a little nap before lunch. When he woke it was dinner-time. The mists of slumber still hung about him, and the events of the last forty-eight hours showed vast and shapelessly threatening through them.

When the drama of the *table d'hôte* reached its climax of roast chestnuts and butter, he determined to walk over to San Marco and pay a visit to Mrs. Waters. He found the old minister from Haddam East Village, Massachusetts, Italianate outwardly in almost ludicrous degree. He wore a fur-lined overcoat indoors; his feet, cased in thick woollen shoes, rested on a strip of carpet laid before his table; a man who had lived for forty years in the pungent atmosphere of an air-tight stove, succeeding a quarter of a century of roaring hearth fires, contented himself with the spare heat of a scaldino, which he held his clasped hands over in the very Italian manner; the lamp that cast its light on the book open before him was the classic *lucerna*,* with three beaks, fed with olive oil. He looked up at his visitor over his spectacles, without recognising him, till Colville spoke. Then, after their greeting, "Is it snowing heavily?" he asked.

"It isn't snowing at all. What made you think that?"

"Perhaps I was drowsing over my book and dreamed it. We become very strange and interesting studies to ourselves as we live along."

He took up the metaphysical consideration with the promptness of a man who has no small-talk, and who speaks of the mind and soul as if they were the gossip of the neighbourhood.

"At times the forty winters that I passed in Haddam East Village seem like an alien experience, and I find myself pitying the life I lived there quite as if it were the life of some one else. It seems incredible that men should still inhabit such climates."

"Then you're not homesick for Haddam East Village?"

"Ah! for the good and striving souls there, yes; especially the souls of some women there. They used to think that it was I who gave them consolation and spiritual purpose, but it was they who really imparted it. Women souls—how beautiful they sometimes are. They seem truly like angelic essences. I trust that I shall meet them somewhere some time, but it will never be in Haddam East Village. Yes, I must have been dreaming when you came in. I thought that

I was by my fire there, and all round over the hills and in the streets the snow was deep and falling still. How distinctly," he said, closing his eyes, as artists do in looking at a picture, "I can see the black wavering lines of the walls in the fields sinking into the drifts! the snow billowed over the graves by the church where I preached! the banks of snow around the houses! the white desolation everywhere! I ask myself at times if the people are still there. Yes, I feel as blessedly remote from that terrible winter as if I had died away from it, and were in the weather of heaven."

"Then you have no reproach for feeble-spirited fellow-citizens who abandon their native climate and come to live in Italy?"

The old man drew his fur coat closer about him and shrugged his shoulders in true Florentine fashion. "There may be something to say against those who do so in the hey-day of life, but I shall not be the one to say it. The race must yet revert in its decrepitude, as I have in mine, to the climates of the South. Since I have been in Italy I have realised what used to occur to me dimly at home—the cruel disproportion between the end gained and the means expended in reclaiming the savage North. Half the human endeavour, half the human suffering, would have made the whole South Protestant and the whole East Christian, and our civilisation would now be there. No, I shall never go back to New England. New England? New Ireland—New Canada! Half the farms in Haddam are in the hands of our Irish friends, and the labour on the rest is half done by French Canadians. That is all right and well. New England must come to me here, by way of the great middle West and the Pacific coast."

Colville smiled at the Emersonian touch, but he said gravely, "I can never quite reconcile myself to the thought of dying out of my own country."

"Why not? It is very unimportant where one dies. A moment after your breath is gone you are in exile for ever—or at home for ever."

Colville sat musing upon this phase of Americanism, as he had upon many others. At last he broke the silence they had both let fall, far away from the topic they had touched.

"Well," he asked, "how did you enjoy the veglione?"

"Oh, I'm too old to go to such places for pleasure," said the minister simply. "But it was very interesting, and certainly very striking: especially when I went back, toward daylight, after seeing Mrs. Bowen home."

"Did you go back?" demanded Colville, in some amaze.

"Oh yes. I felt that my experience was incomplete without some knowledge of how the Carnival ended at such a place."

"Oh! And do you still feel that Savonarola was mistaken?"

"There seemed to be rather more boisterousness toward the close, and, if I might judge, the excitement grew a little unwholesome. But I really don't feel myself very well qualified to decide. My own life had been passed in circumstances so widely different that I am at a certain disadvantage."

"Yes," said Colville, and with a smile; "I dare say the Carnival at Haddam East Village was quite another thing."

The old man smiled responsively. "I suppose that some of my former parishioners might have been scandalised at my presence at a Carnival ball, had they known the fact merely in the abstract; but in my letters home I shall try to set it before them in an instructive light. I should say that the worst thing about such a scene of revelry would be that it took us too much out of our inner quiet. But I suppose the same remark might apply to almost any form of social entertainment."

"Yes."

"But human nature is so constituted that some means of expansion must be provided, or a violent explosion takes place. The only question is what means are most innocent. I have been looking about," added the old man quietly, "at the theatres lately."

"Have you?" asked Colville, opening his eyes, in suppressed surprise.

"Yes; with a view to determining the degree of harmless amusement that may be derived from them. It's rather a difficult question. I should be inclined to say, however, that I don't think the ballet can ever be instrumental for good.''

Colville could not deny himself the pleasure of saying, ''Well, not the highest, I suppose.''

''No,'' said Mr. Waters, in apparent unconsciousness of the irony. ''But I think the Church has made a mistake in condemning the theatre *in toto*. It appears to me that it might always have countenanced a certain order of comedy, which the motive and plot are unobjectionable. Though I don't deny that there are moods when all laughter seems low and unworthy and incompatible with the most advanced state of being. And I confess,'' he went on, with a dreamy thoughtfulness, ''that I have very great misgivings in regard to tragedy. The glare that it throws upon the play of the passions—jealousy in its anguish, revenge glutting itself, envy eating its heart, hopeless love—their nakedness is terrible. The terror may be salutary; it may be very mischievous. I am afraid that I have left some of my inquiries till it is too late. I seem to have no longer the materials of judgment left in me. If I were still a young man like you——''

''Am I still a young man?'' interrupted Colville sadly.

''You are young enough to respond to the appeals that sometimes find me silent. If I were of your age I should certainly investigate some of these interesting problems.''

''Ah, but if you become personally interested in the problems, it's as bad as if you hadn't the materials of judgment left; you're prejudiced. Besides, I doubt my youthfulness very much.''

''You are fifty, I presume?'' suggested Mr. Waters, in a leading way.

''Not very near—only too near,'' laughed Colville. ''I'm forty-one.''

''You are younger than I supposed. But I remember now that at your age I had the same feeling which you intimate. It seemed to me then that I had really passed the bound which separates us from the further possibility of youth. But I've lived long enough since to know that I was mistaken. At forty, one has still a great part of youth before him—

perhaps the richest and sweetest part. By that time the turmoil of ideas and sensations is over; we see clearly and feel
consciously. We are in a sort of quiet in which we peacefully
enjoy. We have enlarged our perspective sufficiently to
perceive things in their true proportion and relation; we are
no longer tormented with the lurking fear of death, which
darkens and embitters our earlier years; we have got into the
habit of life; we have often been ailing and we have not died.
Then we have time enough behind us to supply us with the
materials of reverie and reminiscence; the terrible solitude of
inexperience is broken; we have learned to smile at many
things besides the fear of death. We ought also to have
learned pity and patience. Yes,'' the old man concluded,
in cheerful self-corroboration, ''it is a beautiful age.''

''But it doesn't look so beautiful as it is,'' Colville protested. ''People in that rosy prime don't produce the effect
of garlanded striplings upon the world at large. The women
laugh at us; they think we are fat old fellows; they don't
recognise the slender and elegant youth that resides in our
unwieldy bulk.''

''You take my meaning a little awry. Besides, I doubt if
even the ground you assume is tenable. If a woman has lived
long enough to be truly young herself, she won't find a man
at forty either decrepit or grotesque. He can even make
himself youthful to a girl of thought and imagination.''

''Yes,'' Colville assented, with a certain discomfort.

''But to be truly young at forty,'' resumed Mr. Waters,
''a man should be already married.''

''Yes?''

''I sometimes feel,'' continued the old man, ''that I made
a mistake in yielding to a disappointment that I met with
early in life, and in not permitting myself the chance of
retrieval. I have missed a beautiful and consoling experience
in my devotion to a barren regret.''

Colville said nothing, but he experienced a mixed feeling
of amusement, of repulsion, and of curiosity at this.

''We are put into the world to be of it. I am more and
more convinced of that. We have scarcely a right to separate
ourselves from the common lot in any way. I justify myself

for having lived alone only as a widower might. I—lost her.
It was a great while ago.''

"Yes," said Colville, after the pause which ensued; "I
agree with you that one has no right to isolate himself, to
refuse his portion of the common lot; but the effects of even
a rebuff may last so long that one has no heart to put out his
hand a second time—for a second rap over the knuckles.
Oh, I know how trivial it is in the retrospect, and how what
is called a disappointment is something to be humbly
grateful for in most cases; but for a while it certainly makes
you doubtful whether you were ever really intended to share
the common lot.'' He was aware of an insincerity in his
words; he hoped that it might not be perceptible, but he did
not greatly care.

Mr. Waters took no notice of what he had been saying.
He resumed from another point. "But I should say that it
would be unwise for a man of mature life to seek his happiness with one much younger than himself. I don't deny
that there are cases in which the disparity of years counts for
little or nothing, but generally speaking, people ought to be
as equally mated in age as possible. They ought to start with
the same advantages of ignorance. A young girl can only live
her life through a community of feeling, an equality of inexperience in the man she gives her heart to. If he is tired of
things that still delight her, the chances of unhappiness are
increased.''

"Yes, that's true," answered Colville gravely. "It's apt
to be a mistake and a wrong.''

"Oh, not always—not always," said the old minister.
"We mustn't look at it in that way quite. Wrongs are of the
will." He seemed to lapse into a greater intimacy of feeling
with Colville. "Have you seen Mrs. Bowen to-day? Or—ah!
true! I think you told me.''

"No," said Colville. "Have we spoken of her? But I have
seen her.''

"And was the little one well?''

"Very much better.''

"Pretty creatures, both of them," said the minister, with
as fresh a pleasure in his recognition of the fact as if he had

not said nearly the same thing once before. "You've noticed the very remarkable resemblance between mother and daughter?"

"Oh yes."

"There is a gentleness in Mrs. Bowen which seems to me the last refinement of a gracious spirit," suggested Mr. Waters. "I have never met any lady who reconciled more exquisitely what is charming in society with what is lovely in nature."

"Yes," said Colville. "Mrs. Bowen always had that gentle manner. I used to know her here as a girl a great while ago."

"Did you? I wonder you allowed her to become Mrs. Bowen."

This sprightliness of Mr. Waters amused Colville greatly. "At that time I was preoccupied with my great mistake, and I had no eyes for Mrs. Bowen."

"It isn't too late yet," said Mr. Waters, with open insinuation.

A bachelor of forty is always flattered by any suggestion of marriage; the suggestion that a beautiful and charming woman would marry him is too much for whatever reserves of modesty and wisdom he may have stored up. Colville took leave of the old minister in better humour with himself than he had been for forty-eight hours, or than he had any very good reason for being now.

Mr. Waters came with him to the head of the stairs and held up the lamp for him to see. The light fell upon the white locks thinly straggling from beneath his velvet skull-cap, and he looked like some mediæval scholar of those who lived and died for learning in Florence when letters were a passion there almost as strong as love.

The next day Colville would have liked to go at once and ask about Effie, but upon the whole he thought he would not go till after he had been at the reception where he was going in the afternoon. It was an artist who was giving the reception; he had a number of pictures to show, and there was to be tea. There are artists and artists. This painter was one who had a distinct social importance. It was felt to be rather a nice thing to be asked to his reception; one was sure at least to meet the nicest people.

This reason prevailed with Colville so far as it related to Mrs. Bowen, whom he felt that he would like to tell he had been there. He would speak to her of this person and that— very respected and recognised social figures,—so that she might see he was not the outlaw, the Bohemian, he must sometimes have appeared to her. It would not be going too far to say that something like an obscure intention to show himself the next Sunday at the English chapel, where Mrs. Bowen went, was not forming itself in his mind. As he went along it began to seem not impossible that she would be at the reception. If Effie's indisposition was no more serious than it appeared yesterday, very probably Mrs. Bowen would be there. He even believed that he recognised her carriage among those which were drawn up in front of the old palace, under the painter's studio windows.

There were a great number of people of the four nationalities that mostly consort in Italy. There were English and Americans and Russians and the sort of Italians resulting from the native intermarriages with them; here and there were Italians of pure blood, borderers upon the foreign life through a literary interest, or an artistic relation, or a matrimonial intention; here and there, also, the large stomach of a German advanced the bounds of the new empire and the new ideal of duty. There were no Frenchmen; one may meet them in more strictly Italian assemblages, but it is as if the sorrows and uncertainties of France in these times discouraged them from the international society in which they were always an infrequent element. It is not, of course, imaginable that as Frenchmen they have doubts of their merits, but that they have their misgivings as to the intelligence of others. The language that prevailed was English—in fact, one heard no other,—and the tea which our civilisation carries everywhere with it steamed from the cups in all hands. This beverage, in fact, becomes a formidable factor in the life of a Florentine winter. One finds it at all houses, and more or less mechanically drinks it.

"I am turning out a terrible tea toper," said Colville,

stirring his cup in front of the old lady whom his relations to the ladies at Palazzo Pinti had interested so much. "I don't think I drink less than ten cups a day; seventy cups a week is a low average for me. I'm really beginning to look down at my boots a little anxiously."

Mrs. Amsden laughed. She had not been in America for forty years, but she liked the American way of talking better than any other. "Oh, didn't you hear about Inglehart when he was here? He was so good-natured that he used to drink all the tea people offered him, and then the young ladies made tea for him in his studio when they went to look at his pictures. It almost killed him. By the time spring came he trembled so that the brush flew out of his hands when he took it up. He had to hurry off to Venice to save his life. It's just as bad at the Italian houses; they've learned to like tea."

"When I was here before, they never offered you anything but coffee," said Colville. "They took tea for medicine, and there was an old joke that I thought I should die of, I heard it so often about the Italian that said to the English woman when she offered him tea, '*Grazie; sto bene.*' "*

"Oh, that's all changed now."

"Yes; I've seen the tea, and I haven't heard the joke."

The flavour of Colville's talk apparently encouraged his companion to believe that he would like to make fun of their host's paintings with her; but whether he liked them, or whether he was principled against that sort of return for hospitality, he chose to reply seriously to some ironical lures she threw out.

"Oh, if you're going to be good," she exclaimed, "I shall have nothing more to say to you. Here comes Mr. Thurston; I can make *him* abuse the pictures. There! You had better go away to a young lady I see alone over yonder, though I don't know what you will do with *one* alone." She laughed and shook her head in a way that had once been arch and lively, but that was now puckery and infirm—it is affecting to see these things in women—and welcomed the old gentleman who came up and superseded Colville.

The latter turned, with his cup still in his hand, and

wandered about through the company, hoping he might see
Mrs. Bowen among the groups peering at the pictures or
solidly blocking the view in front of them. He did not find
her, but he found Imogene Graham standing somewhat
apart near a window. He saw her face light up at sight of
him, and then darken again as he approached.

"Isn't this rather an unnatural state of things?" he asked
when he had come up. "I ought to be obliged to fight my
way to you through successive phalanxes of young men
crowding round with cups of tea outstretched in their
imploring hands. Have you *had* some tea?"

"Thank you, no; I don't wish any," said the young girl,
so coldly that he could not help noticing, though commonly
he was man enough to notice very few things.

"How is Effie to-day?" he asked quickly.

"Oh, quite well," said Imogene.

"I don't see Mrs. Bowen," he ventured further.

"No," answered the girl, still very lifelessly; "I came with
Mrs. Fleming." She looked about the room as if not to look
at him.

He now perceived a distinct intention to snub him. He
smiled. "Have you seen the pictures? There are two or three
really lovely ones."

"Mrs. Fleming will be here in a moment, I suppose,"
said Imogene evasively, but not with all her first coldness.

"Let us steal a march on her," said Colville briskly.
"When she comes you can tell her that I showed you the pictures."

"I don't know," faltered the girl.

"Perhaps it isn't necessary you should," he suggested.

She glanced at him with questioning trepidation.

"The respective duties of chaperone and *protégée* are rather
undefined. Where the chaperone isn't there to command,
the *protégée* isn't there to obey. I suppose you'd know if you
were at home?"

"Oh yes!"

"Let me imagine myself at a loan exhibition in Buffalo.
Ah! that appeal is irresistible. You'll come, I see."

She hesitated; she looked at the nearest picture, then

followed him to another. He now did what he had refused to do for the old lady who tempted him to it; he made fun of the pictures a little, but so amiably and with so much justice to their good points that the painter himself would not have minded his jesting. From time to time he made Imogene smile, but in her eyes lurked a look of uneasiness, and her manner expressed a struggle against his will which might have had its pathos for him in different circumstances, but now it only incited him to make her forget herself more and more; he treated her as one does a child that is out of sorts—coaxingly, ironically.

When they had made the round of the rooms Mrs. Fleming was not at the window where she had left Imogene; the girl detected the top of her bonnet still in the next room.

"The chaperone is never there when you come back with the *protégée*," said Colville. "It seems to be the nature of the chaperone."

Imogene turned very grave. "I think I ought to go to her," she murmured.

"Oh no; she ought to come to you; I stand out for *protégée*'s rights."

"I suppose she will come directly."

"She sees me with you; she knows you are safe."

"Oh, of course," said the girl. After a constraint which she marked by rather a long silence, she added, "How strange a roomful of talking sounds, doesn't it? Just like a great caldron boiling up and bubbling over. Wouldn't you like to know what they're all saying?"

"Oh, it's quite bad enough to see them," replied Colville frivolously.

"I think a company of gentlemen with their hats off look very queer, don't you?" she asked, after another interval.

"Well, really," said Colville, laughing, "I don't know that the spectacle ever suggested any metaphysical speculations to me. I rather think they look queerer with their hats on."

"Oh yes."

"Though there is not very much to choose. We're a queer-looking set, anyway."

He got himself another cup of tea, and coming back to her, allowed her to make the efforts to keep up the conversation, and was not without a malicious pleasure in her struggles. They interested him as social exercises which, however abrupt and undexterous now, were destined, with time and practice, to become the *finesse* of a woman of society, and to be accepted, even while they were still abrupt and undexterous, as touches of character. He had broken up that coldness with which she had met him at first, and now he let her adjust the fragments as she could to the new situation. He wore that air of a gentleman who has been talking a long time to a lady, and who will not dispute her possession with a new-comer.

But no one came, though, as he cast his eyes carelessly over the company, he found that it had been increased by the accession of eight or ten young fellows, with a refreshing light of originality in their faces, and little touches of difference from the other men in their dress.

"Oh, there are the Inglehart boys!" cried the girl, with a flash of excitement.

There was a sensation of interest and friendliness in the company as these young fellows, after their moment of social intimidation, began to gather round the pictures, and to fling their praise and blame about, and talk the delightful shop of the studio.

The sight of their fresh young faces, the sound of their voices, struck a pang of regret that was almost envy to Colville's heart.

Imogene followed them with eager eyes. "Oh," she sighed, "shouldn't you like to be an artist?"

"I should, very much."

"Oh, I beg your pardon; I forgot. I knew you were an architect."

"I should say I used to be, if you hadn't objected to my perfects and preterits."

What came next seemed almost an accident.

"I didn't suppose you cared for my objections, so long as I amused you." She suddenly glanced at him, as if terrified at her own words.

"Have you been trying to amuse me?" he asked.

"Oh no. I thought——"

"Oh, then," said Colville sharply, "you meant that I was amusing myself with you?" She glanced at him in terror of his divination, but could not protest. "Has any one told you that?" he pursued, with sudden angry suspicion.

"No, *no* one," began Imogene. She glanced about her, frightened. They stood quite alone where they were; the people had mostly wandered off into the other rooms. "Oh, don't—I didn't mean—I didn't intend to say anything——"

"But you *have* said something—something that surprises me from *you*, and hurts me. I wish to know whether you say it from yourself."

"I don't know—yes. That is, not—— Oh, I wish Mrs. Fleming——"

She looked as if another word of pursuit would put it beyond her power to control herself.

"Let me take you to Mrs. Fleming," said Colville, with freezing *hauteur;* and led the way where the top of Mrs. Fleming's bonnet still showed itself. He took leave at once, and hastily parting with his host, found himself in the street, whirled in many emotions. The girl had not said that from herself, but iₜ was from some woman; he knew that by the directness of the phrase and its excess, for he had noticed that women who liked to beat about the bush in small matters have a prodigious straightforwardness in more vital affairs, and will even call grey black in order clearly to establish the presence of the black in that colour. He could hardly keep himself from going to Palazzo Pinti.

But he contrived to go to his hotel instead, where he ate a moody dinner, and then, after an hour's solitary bitterness in his room, went out and passed the evening at the theatre. The play was one of those fleering comedies which render contemptible for the time all honest and earnest intention, and which surely are a whiff from the bottomless pit itself. It made him laugh at the serious strain of self-question that had mingled with his resentment; it made him laugh even at his resentment, and with its humour in his thoughts, sent him off to sleep in a sottish acceptance of whatever was trivial in himself as the only thing that was real and lasting.

He slept late, and when Paolo brought up his breakfast, he brought with it a letter which he said had been left with the porter an hour before. A faint appealing perfume of violet exhaled from the note, and mingled with the steaming odours of the coffee and boiled milk, when Colville, after a glance at the unfamiliar handwriting of the superscription, broke the seal.

"DEAR MR. COLVILLE,—I don't know what you will think of my writing to you, but perhaps you can't think worse of me than you do already, and anything will be better than the misery that I am in. I have not been asleep all night. I hate myself for telling you, but I do want you to understand how I have felt. I would give worlds if I could take back the words that you say wounded you. I didn't mean to wound you. Nobody is to blame for them but me; nobody ever breathed a word about you that was meant in unkindness.

"I am not ashamed of writing this, *whatever* you think, and I will sign my name in full.   IMOGENE GRAHAM."

Colville had commonly a good appetite for his breakfast, but now he let his coffee stand long untasted. There were several things about this note that touched him—the childlike simplicity and directness, the generous courage, even the imperfection and crudity of the literature. However he saw it afterward, he saw it then in its true intention. He respected that intention; through all the sophistications in which life had wrapped him, it awed him a little. He realised that if he had been younger he would have gone to Imogene herself with her letter. He felt for the moment a rush of the emotion which he would once not have stopped to examine, which he would not have been capable of examining. But now his duty was clear; he must go to Mrs. Bowen. In the noblest human purpose there is always some admixture, however slight, of less noble motive, and Colville was not without the willingness to see whatever embarrassment she might feel when he showed her the letter, and to invoke her finest tact to aid him in re-assuring the child.

She was alone in her drawing-room, and she told him in response to his inquiry for their health that Imogene and Effie had gone out to drive. She looked so pretty in the quiet house dress in which she rose from the sofa and stood, letting him come the whole way to greet her, that he did not think of any other look in her, but afterward he remembered an evidence of inner tumult in her brightened eyes.

He said, smiling, "I'm so glad to see you alone," and this brought still another look into her face, which also he afterward remembered. She did not reply, but made a sound in her throat like a bird when it stirs itself for flight or song. It was a strange, indefinite little note, in which Colville thought he detected trepidation at the time, and recalled for the sort of expectation suggested in it. She stood waiting for him to go on.

"I have come to get you to help me out of trouble."

"Yes?" said Mrs. Bowen, with a vague smile. "I always supposed you would be able to help yourself out of trouble. Or perhaps wouldn't mind it if you were in it."

"Oh yes, I mind it very much," returned Colville, refusing her banter, if it were banter. "Especially this sort of trouble, which involves some one else in the discomfort." He went on abruptly: "I have been held up to a young lady as a person who was amusing himself with her, and I was so absurd as to be angry when she told me, and demanded the name of my friend, whoever it was. My behaviour seems to have given the young lady a bad night, and this morning she writes to tell me so, and to take all the blame on herself, and to assure me that no harm was meant me by any one. Of course I don't want her to be distressed about it. Perhaps you can guess who has been writing to me."

Colville said all this looking down, in a fashion he had. When he looked up he saw a severity in Mrs. Bowen's pretty face, such as he had not seen there before.

"I didn't know she had been writing to you, but I know that you are talking of Imogene. She told me what she had said to you yesterday, and I blamed her for it, but I'm not sure that it wasn't best."

"Oh, indeed!" said Colville. "Perhaps you can tell me who put the idea into her head?"

"Yes; I did."

A dead silence ensued, in which the fragments of the situation broken by these words revolved before Colville's thought with kaleidoscopic variety, and he passed through all the phases of anger, resentment, wounded self-love, and accusing shame.

At last, "I suppose you had your reasons," he said simply.

"I am in her mother's place here," she replied, tightening the grip of one little hand upon another, where she held them laid against the side of her waist.

"Yes, I know that," said Colville; "but what reason had you to warn her against me as a person who was amusing himself with her? I don't like the phrase; but she seems to have got it from you; I use it at third hand."

"I don't like the phrase either; I didn't invent it."

"You used it."

"No; it wasn't I who used it. I should have been glad to use another, if I could," said Mrs. Bowen, with perfect steadiness.

"Then you mean to say that you believe I've been trifling with the feelings of this child?"

"I mean to say nothing. You are very much older; and she is a romantic girl, very extravagant. You have tried to make her like you."

"I certainly have. I have tried to make Effie Bowen like me too."

Mrs. Bowen passed this over in serenity that he felt was not far from contempt.

He gave a laugh that did not express enjoyment.

"You have no right to laugh!" she cried, losing herself a little, and so making her first gain upon him.

"It appears not. Perhaps you will tell me what I am to do about this letter?"

"That is for you to decide." She recovered herself, and lost ground with him in proportion.

"I thought perhaps that since you were able to judge my motives so clearly, you might be able to advise me."

"I don't judge your motives," Mrs. Bowen began. She added suddenly, as if by an after-thought, "I don't think you had any."

"I'm obliged to you."

"But you are as much to blame as if you had."

"And perhaps I'm as much to blame as if I had really wronged somebody?"

"Yes."

"It's rather paradoxical. You don't wish me to see her any more?"

"I haven't any wish about it; you must not *say* that I have," said Mrs. Bowen, with dignity.

Colville smiled. "May I *ask* if you have?"

"Not for myself."

"You put me on very short allowance of conjecture."

"I will not let you trifle with the matter!" she cried. "You have made me speak, when a word, a look, ought to have been enough. Oh, I didn't think you had the miserable vanity to wish it!"

Colville stood thinking a long time and she waiting. "I see that everything is at an end. I am going away from Florence. Good-bye, Mrs. Bowen." He approached her, holding out his hand. But if he expected to be rewarded for this, nothing of the kind happened. She shrank swiftly back.

"No, no. You shall not touch me."

He paused a moment, gazing keenly at her face, in which, whatever other feeling showed, there was certainly no fear of him. Then with a slight bow he left the room.

Mrs. Bowen ran from it by another door, and shut herself into her own room. When she returned to the salotto, Imogene and Effie were just coming in. The child went to lay aside her hat and sacque; the girl, after a glance at Mrs. Bowen's face, lingered inquiringly.

"Mr. Colville came here with your letter, Imogene."

"Yes," said Imogene faintly. "Do you think I oughtn't to have written it?"

"Oh, it makes no difference now. He is going away from Florence."

"Yes?" breathed the girl.

"I spoke openly with him."

"Yes?"

"I didn't spare him. I made him think I hated and despised him."

Imogene was silent. Then she said, "I know that whatever you have done, you have acted for the best."

"Yes, I have a right that you should say that—I have a right that you should always say it. I think he has behaved very foolishly, but I don't blame him——"

"No! I was to blame."

"I don't *know* that he was to blame, and I won't let you think he was."

"Oh, he is the best man in the world!"

"He gave up at once; he didn't try to defend himself. It's nothing for you to lose a friend at your age; but at mine——"

"I *know* it, Mrs. Bowen."

"And I wouldn't even shake hands with him when he was going; I——"

"Oh, I don't see how you could be so hard!" cried Imogene. She put up her hands to her face, and broke into tears. Mrs. Bowen watched her, dry eyed, with her lips parted, and an intensity of question in her face.

"Imogene," she said at last, "I wish you to promise me one thing."

"Yes."

"Not to write to Mr. Colville again."

"No, no; indeed I won't, Mrs. Bowen!" The girl came up to kiss her; Mrs. Bowen turned her cheek.

Imogene was going from the room, when Mrs. Bowen spoke again. "But I wish you to promise me this only because you don't feel sure of yourself about him. If you care for him—if you think you care for him—then I leave you perfectly free."

The girl looked up, scared. "No, no. I'd rather you wouldn't leave me free—you mustn't; I shouldn't know what to do."

"Very well, then," said Mrs. Bowen.

They both waited a moment, as if each were staying for the other to speak. Then Imogene asked. "Is he—going soon?"

"I don't know," said Mrs. Bowen. "Why should he want to delay? He had better go at once. And I hope he will go home—as far from Florence as he can. I should think he would *hate* the place.''

''Yes,'' said the girl, with a quivering sigh; ''it must be hateful to him.'' She paused, and then she rushed on with bitter self-reproach. ''And I—*I* have helped to make it so! O Mrs. Bowen, perhaps it's *I* who have been trifling with *him?* Trying to make him believe—no, not trying to do that, but letting him see that I sympathised—— Oh, do you think I have?''

''You know what you have been doing, Imogene,'' said Mrs. Bowen, with the hardness it surprises men to know women use with each other, they seem such tender creatures in the abstract. ''You have no need to ask me.''

''No, no.''

''As you say, I warned you from the first.''

''Oh yes; you did.''

''I couldn't do more than hint; it was too much to expect——''

''Oh, yes, yes.''

''And if you couldn't take my hints, I was helpless.''

''Yes; I see it.''

''I was only afraid of saying too much, and all through that miserable veglione business I was trying to please you and him, because I was afraid I *had* said too much—gone too far. I wanted to show you that I disdained to be suspicious, that I was ashamed to suppose that a girl of your age could care for the admiration of a man of his.''

''Oh, I didn't care for his admiration. I admired *him*—and pitied him.''

Mrs. Bowen apparently would not be kept now from saying all that had been rankling in her breast. ''I didn't approve of going to the veglione. A great many people would be shocked if they knew I went; I wouldn't at all like to have it known. But I was not going to have him thinking that I was severe with you, and wanted to deny you any really harmless pleasure.''

''Oh, who could think that? You're only too good to me. You see,'' said the girl, ''what a return I have made for your trust. I knew you didn't want to go to the veglione. If I hadn't been the most selfish girl in the world I wouldn't have let you. But I did. I *forced* you to go, and then after we got there, I seized every advantage, and abused your kindness till I wonder I didn't sink through the floor. Yes; I ought to have refused to dance—if I'd had a spark of generosity or gratitude I would have done it; and I ought to have come straight back to you the instant the waltz was done. And now see what has come of it! I've made you think he was trifling with me, and I've made him think that I'm a false and hollow-hearted thing.''

''You know best what you have done, Imogene,'' said Mrs. Bowen, with a smiling tearfulness that was somehow very bitter. She rose from the sofa, as if to indicate that there was no more to be said, and Imogene, with a fresh burst of grief, rushed away to her own room.

She dropped on her knees beside her bed, and stretched out her arms upon it, an image of that desolation of soul which, when we are young, seems limitless, but which in later life we know has comparatively narrow bounds beyond the clouds that rest so blackly around us.

XII

In his room Colville was devouring as best he might the chagrin with which he had come away from Palazzo Pinti, while he packed his trunk for departure. Now that the thing was over, the worst was past. Again he observed that his emotions had no longer the continuity that the emotions of his youth possessed. As he remembered, a painful or pleasant impression used to last indefinitely; but here he was with this humiliating affair hot in his mind, shrugging his shoulders with a sense of relief, almost a sense of escape. Does the soul really wear out with the body? The question flitted across his mind as he took down a pair of trousers, and noticed that they were considerably frayed about the feet; he determined to give them to Paolo, and this reminded him to ring for Paolo, and send word to the office that he was going to take the evening train for Rome.

He went on packing, and putting away with the different garments the unpleasant thoughts that he knew he should be su.₃ to unpack with them in Rome; but they would then have less poignancy. For the present he was doing the best he could, and he was not making any sort of pretences. When his trunk was locked he kindled himself a fire, and sat down before it to think of Imogene. He began with her, but presently it seemed to be Mrs. Bowen that he was thinking of; then he knew he was dropping off to sleep by the manner in which their two ideas mixed. The fatigues and excitements of the week had been great, but he would not give way; it was too disgraceful.

Some one rapped at his door. He called out "*Avanti!*"* and he would have been less surprised to see either of those ladies than Paolo with the account he had ordered to be made out. It was a long, pendulous, minutely itemed affair, such as the traveller's recklessness in candles and firewood comes to in the books of the Continental landlord, and it almost swept the floor when its volume was unrolled. But it was not the sum-total that dismayed Colville when he glanced at the final figure; that, indeed, was not so very great, with all the items; it was the conviction, suddenly flashing upon him, that he had not money enough by him to pay it. His watch, held close to the fire, told him that it was five o'clock; the banks had been closed an hour, and this was Saturday afternoon.

The squalid accident had all the effect of intention, as he viewed it from without himself, and considered that the money ought to have been the first thing in his thoughts after he determined to go away. He must get the money somehow, and be off to Rome by the seven o'clock train. A whimsical suggestion, which was so good a bit of irony that it made him smile, flashed across him: he might borrow it of Mrs. Bowen. She was, in fact, the only person in Florence with whom he was at all on borrowing terms, and a sad sense of the sweetness of her lost friendship followed upon the antic notion. No; for once he could not go to Mrs. Bowen. He recollected now the many pleasant talks they had had together, confidential in virtue of their old acquaintance, and harmlessly intimate in many things. He recalled how, when he was feeling dull from the Florentine air, she had told him to take a little quinine, and he had found immediate advantage in it. These memories did strike him as grotesque or ludicrous; he only felt their pathos. He was ashamed even to seem in anywise recreant further. If she should ever hear that he had lingered for thirty-six hours in Florence after he had told her he was going away, what could she think but that he had repented his decision? He determined to go down to the office of the hotel, and see if he could not make some arrangement with the landlord. It would be extremely distasteful, but his ample letter of credit would be at least a voucher of his final ability to pay. As a desperate resort he could go and try to get the money of Mr. Waters.

He put on his coat and hat, and opened the door to some one who was just in act to knock at it, and whom he struck against in the obscurity.

"I beg your pardon," said the visitor.

"Mr. Waters! Is it possible?" cried Colville, feeling something fateful in the chance. "I was just going to see you."

"I'm fortunate in meeting you, then. Shall we go to my room?" he asked, at a hesitation in Colville's manner.

"No, no," said the latter; "come in here." He led the way back into his room, and struck a match to light the candles on his chimney. Their dim rays fell upon the disorder his packing had left. "You must excuse the look of things," he said. "The fact is, I'm just going away. I'm going to Rome at seven o'clock."

"Isn't this rather sudden?" asked the minister, with less excitement than the fact might perhaps have been expected to create in a friend. "I thought you intended to pass the winter in Florence."

"Yes, I did—sit down, please—but I find myself obliged to cut my stay short. Won't you take off your coat?" he asked, taking off his own.

"Thank you; I've formed the habit of keeping it on indoors," said Mr. Waters. "And I oughtn't to stay long, if you're to be off so soon."

Colville gave a very uncomfortable laugh. "Why, the fact is, I'm not off so very soon unless you help me."

"Ah?" returned the old gentleman, with polite interest.

"Yes, I find myself in the absurd position of a man who had reckoned without his host. I have made all my plans for going, and have had my hotel bill sent to me in pursuance of that idea, and now I discover that I not only haven't money enough to pay it and get to Rome, but I haven't much more than half enough to pay it. I have credit galore," he said, trying to give the situation a touch of liveliness, "but the bank is shut."

Mr. Waters listened to the statement with a silence concerning which Colville was obliged to form his conjectures. "That is unfortunate," he said sympathetically, but not encouragingly.

Colville pushed on desperately. "It is, unless you can help me, Mr. Waters. I want you to lend me fifty dollars for as many hours."

Mr. Waters shook his head with a compassionate smile. "I haven't fifty francs in cash. You are welcome to what there is. I'm very forgetful about money matters, and haven't been to the bankers."

"Oh, don't excuse yourself to me, unless you wish to embitter my shame. I'm obliged to you for offering to share your destitution with me. I must try to run my face with the landlord,'' said Colville.

"Oh no,'' said Mr. Waters gently. "Is there such haste as all that?''

"Yes, I must go at once.''

"I don't like to have you apply to a stranger,'' said the old man, with fatherly kindness. "Can't you remain over till Monday? I had a little excursion to propose.''

"No, I can't possibly stay; I must go to-night,'' cried Colville.

The minister rose. "Then I really mustn't detain you, I suppose. Good-bye.'' He offered his hand. Colville took it, but could not let it go at once. "I would like extremely to tell you why I'm leaving Florence in such haste. But I don't see what good it would do, for I don't want you to persuade me to stay.''

The old gentleman looked at him with friendly interest.

"The fact is,'' Colville proceeded, as if he had been encouraged to do so, "I have had the misfortune—yes, I'm afraid I've had the fault—to make myself very displeasing to Mrs. Bowen, and in such a way that the very least I can do is to take myself off as far and as soon as I conveniently can.''

"Yes?'' said Mr. Waters, with the cheerful note of incredulity in his voice with which one is apt to respond to others' confession of extremity. "Is it so bad as that? I've just seen Mrs. Bowen, and she told me you were going.''

"Oh,'' said Colville, with disagreeable sensation, "perhaps she told you why I was going.''

"No,'' answered Mr. Waters; "she didn't do that.'' Colville imagined a consciousness in him, which perhaps did not exist. "She didn't allude to the subject further than to state the fact, when I mentioned that I was coming to see you.''

Colville had dropped his hand. "She was very forbearing,'' he said, with bitterness that might well have been incomprehensible to Mr. Waters upon any theory but one.

"Perhaps,'' he suggested, "you are precipitate; perhaps you have mistaken; perhaps you have been hasty. These things are often the result of impulse in women. I have often wondered how they could make up their minds; I believe they certainly ought to be allowed to change them at least once.''

Colville turned very red. "What in the world do you mean? Do you imagine that I have been offering myself to Mrs. Bowen?"

"Wasn't it that which you wished to—which you said you would like to tell me?"

Colville was suddenly silent, on the verge of a self-derisive laugh. When he spoke, he said gently: "No; it wasn't that. I never thought of offering myself to her. We have always been very good friends. But now I'm afraid we can't be friends any more—at least we can't be acquaintances."

"Oh!" exclaimed Mr. Waters. He waited a while as if for Colville to say more, but the latter remained silent, and the old man gave his hand again in farewell. "I must really be going. I hope you won't think me intrusive in my mistaken conjecture?"

"Oh no."

"It was what I supposed you had been telling me——"

"I understand. You mustn't be troubled," said Colville, though he had to own to himself that it seemed superfluous to make this request of Mr. Waters, who was taking the affair with all the serenity of age concerning matters of senti-ment. "I wish you were going to Rome with me," he added, to disembarrass the moment of parting.

"Thank you. But I shall not go to Rome for some years. Shall you come back on your way in the spring?"

"No, I shall not come to Florence again," said Colville sadly.

"Ah, I'm sorry. Good-bye, my dear young friend. It's been a great pleasure to know you." Colville walked down to the door of the hotel with his visitor and parted with him there. As he turned back he met the landlord, who asked him if he would have the omnibus for the station. The landlord bowed smil-ingly, after his kind, and rubbed his hands. He said he hoped Colville was pleased with his hotel, and ran to his desk in the little office to get some cards for him, so that he might recom-mend it accurately to American families.

Colville looked absently at the cards. "The fact is," he said, to the little bowing, smiling man; "I don't know but I shall be obliged to postpone my going till Monday." He smiled too, trying to give the fact a jocose effect, and added, "I find myself out of money, and I've no means of paying your bill till I can see my bankers."

After all his heroic intention, this was as near as he could come to asking the landlord to let him send the money from Rome.

The little man set his head on one side.

"Oh, well, occupy the room until Monday, then," he cried hospitably. "It is quite at your disposition. You will not want the omnibus?"

"No, I shall not want the omnibus," said Colville, with a laugh, doubtless not perfectly intelligible to the landlord, who respectfully joined him in it.

He did not mean to stop that night without writing to Mrs. Bowen, and assuring her that though an accident had kept him in Florence till Monday, she need not be afraid of seeing him again. But he could not go back to his room yet; he wandered about the town, trying to pick himself up from the ruin into which he had fallen again, and wondering with a sort of alien compassion what was to become of his aimless, empty existence. As he passed through the Piazza San Marco he had half a mind to pick a pebble from the gardened margin of the fountain there and toss it against the Rev. Mr. Waters's window, and when he put his skull-cap out, to ask that optimistic agnostic what a man had best do with a life that had ceased to interest him. But, for the time being, he got rid of himself as he best could by going to the opera. They professed to give *Rigoletto*,* but it was all Mrs. Bowen and Imogene Graham to Colville.

It was so late when he got back to his hotel that the outer gate was shut, and he had to wake up the poor little porter, as on that night when he returned from Madame Uccelli's. The porter was again equal to his duty, and contrived to light a new candle to show him the way to his room. The repetition, almost mechanical, of this small chicane made Colville smile, and this apparently encouraged the porter to ask, as if he supposed him to have been in society somewhere—

"You have amused yourself this evening?"

"Oh, very much."

"I am glad. There is a letter for you."

"A letter! Where?"

"I sent it to your room. It came just before midnight."

XIII

MRS. BOWEN sat before the hearth in her *salon*, with her hands fallen in her lap. At thirty-eight the emotions engrave themselves more deeply in the face than they do in our first youth, or than they will when we have really aged, and the pretty woman looked haggard.

Imogene came in, wearing a long blue robe, flung on as if with desperate haste; her thick hair fell crazily out of a careless knot, down her back. "I couldn't sleep," she said, with quivering lips, at the sight of which Mrs. Bowen's involuntary smile hardened. "Isn't it eleven yet?" she added, with a glance at the clock. "It seems years since I went to bed."

"It's been a long day," Mrs. Bowen admitted. She did not ask Imogene why she could not sleep, perhaps because she knew already, and was too honest to affect ignorance.

The girl dropped into a chair opposite her, and began to pull her fingers through the long tangle of her hair, while she drew her breath in sighs that broke at times on her lips; some tears fell down her cheeks unheeded. "Mrs Bowen," she said, at length, "I should like to know what right we have to drive any one from Florence? I should think people would call it rather a high-handed proceeding if it were known."

Mrs. Bowen met this feebleness promptly. "It isn't likely to be known. But we are not driving Mr. Colville away."

"He is going."

"Yes; he said he would go."

"Don't you believe he will go?"

"I believe he will do what he says."

"He has been very kind to us all; he has been as *good!*"

"No one feels that more than I," said Mrs. Bowen, with a slight tremor in her voice. She faltered a moment. "I can't let you say those things to me, Imogene."

"No; I know it's wrong. I didn't know what I was saying. Oh, I wish I could tell what I ought to do! I wish I could make up my mind. Oh, I can't let him go—*so*. I—I don't know what to think any more. Once it was clear, but now I'm not sure; no, I'm not sure."

"Not sure about what?"

"I think I am the one to go away, if any one."

"You know you can't go away," said Mrs. Bowen, with weary patience.

"No, of course not. Well, I shall never see any one like him."

Mrs. Bowen made a start in her chair, as if she had no longer the power to remain quiet, but only placed herself a little more rigidly in it.

"No," the girl went on, as if uttering a hopeless reverie. "He made every moment interesting. He was always thinking of us—he never thought of himself. He did as much for Effie as for any one; he tried just as hard to make himself interesting to her. He was unselfish. I have seen him at places being kind to the stupidest people. You never caught him choosing out the stylish or attractive ones, or trying to shine at anybody's expense. Oh, he's a true gentleman—I shall always say it. How delicate he was, never catching you up, or if you said a foolish thing, trying to turn it against you. No, never, never, never! Oh dear! And now, what can he think of me? Oh, how frivolous and fickle and selfish he must think me!"

"Imogene!" Mrs. Bowen cried out, but quelled herself again.

"Yes," pursued the girl, in the same dreary monotone, "he thinks I couldn't appreciate him because he was old. He thinks that I cared for his not being handsome! Perhaps—perhaps——" She began to catch her breath in the effort to keep back the sobs that were coming. "Oh, I can't bear it! I would rather die than let him think it—such a thing as that!" She bent her head aside, and cried upon the two hands with which she clutched the top of her chair.

Mrs. Bowen sat looking at her distractedly. From time to time she seemed to silence a word upon her lips, and in fact she did not speak.

Imogene lifted her head at last, and softly dried her

eyes. Then, as she pushed her handkerchief back into the pocket of her robe, "What sort of looking girl was that other one?"

"That other one?"

"Yes; you know what I mean: the one who behaved so badly to him before."

"Imogene!" said Mrs. Bowen severely, "this is nonsense, and I can't let you go on so. I might pretend not to know what you mean; but I won't do that; and I tell you that there is no sort of likeness—of comparison——"

"No, no," wailed the girl, "there *is* none. I feel that. She had nothing to warn her—he hadn't suffered then; he was young; he was able to bear it—you said it yourself, Mrs. Bowen. But now—*now*, what will he do? He could make fun of that, and not hate her so much, because she didn't know how much harm she was doing. But I did; and what can he think of me?"

Mrs. Bowen looked across the barrier between them, that kept her from taking Imogene into her arms, and laughing and kissing away her craze, with cold dislike, and only said, "You know whether you've really anything to accuse yourself of, Imogene. I can't and won't consider Mr. Colville in the matter; I *didn't* consider him in what I said today. And I tell you again that I will not interfere with you in the slightest degree beyond appearances and the responsibility I feel to your mother. And it's for you to know your own mind. You are old enough. I will do what you say. It's for you to be sure that you wish what you say."

"Yes," said Imogene huskily, and she let an interval that was long to them both elapse before she said anything more. "Have I always done what you thought best, Mrs. Bowen?"

"Yes, I have never complained of you."

"Then why can't you tell me now what you think best?"

"Because there is nothing to be done. It is all over."

"But if it were not, would you tell me?"

"No."

"Why?"

"Because I—couldn't."

"Then I take back my promise not to write to Mr. Colville. I am going to ask him to stay."

"Have you made up your mind to that, Imogene?" asked Mrs. Bowen, showing no sign of excitement, except to take a faster hold of her own wrists with the slim hands in which she had caught them.

"Yes."

"You know the position it places you in?"

"What position?"

"Has he offered himself to you?"

"No!" the girl's face blazed.

"Then, after what's passed, this is the same as offering yourself to him."

Imogene turned white. "I must write to him, unless you forbid me."

"Certainly I shall not forbid you." Mrs. Bowen rose and went to her writing-desk. "But if you have fully made up your mind to this step, and are ready for the consequences, whatever they are——" She stopped, before sitting down, and looked back over her shoulder at Imogene.

"Yes," said the girl, who had also risen.

"Then I will write to Mr. Colville for you, and render the proceeding as little objectionable as possible."

Imogene made no reply. She stood motionless while Mrs. Bowen wrote.

"Is this what you wished?" asked the latter, offering the sheet:—

"DEAR MR. COLVILLE,—I have reasons for wishing to recall my consent to your going away. Will you not come and lunch with us to-morrow, and try to forget everything that has passed during a few days?

"Yours very sincerely,
"EVALINA BOWEN."

"Yes, that will do," gasped Imogene.

Mrs Bowen rang the bell for the porter, and stood with her back to the girl, waiting for him at the salon door. He came after a delay that sufficiently intimated the lateness of the hour. "This letter must go at once to the Hotel d'Atene," said Mrs. Bowen peremptorily.

"You shall be served," said the porter, with fortitude.

As Mrs. Bowen turned, Imogene ran toward her with clasped hands. "Oh, how merciful—how good——"

Mrs. Bowen shrank back. "Don't touch me, Imogene, please!"

It was her letter which Colville found on his table and read by the struggling light of his newly acquired candle. Then he sat down and replied to it.

"DEAR MRS. BOWEN,—I know that you mean some sort of kindness by me, and I hope you will not think me prompted by any poor resentment in declining to-morrow's lunch. I am satisfied that it is best for me to go; and I am ashamed not to be gone already. But a ridiculous accident has kept me, and when I came in and found your note I was just going to write and ask your patience with my presence in Florence till Monday morning.

            "Yours sincerely,
                    "THEODORE COLVILLE."

He took his note down to the porter, who had lain down again in his little booth, but sprang up with a cheerful request to be commanded. Colville consulted him upon the propriety of sending the note to Palazzo Pinti at once, and the porter, with his head laid in deprecation upon one of his lifted shoulders, owned that it was perhaps the very least little bit in the world late.

"Send it the first thing in the morning, then," said Colville.

Mrs. Bowen received it by the servant who brought her coffee to the room, and she sent it without any word to Imogene. The girl came instantly back with it. She was fully dressed, as if she had been up a long time, and she wore a very plain, dull dress, in which one of her own sex might have read the expression of a potential self-devotion.

"It's just as I wish it, Mrs. Bowen," she said, in a low key of impassioned resolution. "*Now*, my conscience is at

rest. And you have done this for me, Mrs. Bowen!'' She
stood timidly with the door in her hand, watching Mrs.
Bowen's slight smile; then, as if at some sign in it, she flew
to the bed and kissed her, and so fled out of the room again.

Colville slept late, and awoke with a vague sense of self-
reproach, which faded afterward to such poor satisfaction as
comes to us from the concsiousness of having made the best
of a bad business; some pangs of softer regret mixed with
this. At first he felt a stupid obligation to keep indoors, and
he really did not go out till after lunch. The sunshine had
looked cold from his window, and with the bright fire which
he found necessary in his room, he fancied a bitterness in the
gusts that caught up the dust in the piazza, and blew it
against the line of cabs on the other side; but when he got
out into the weather he found the breeze mild and the sun
warm. The streets were thronged with people, and at all the
corners there were groups of cloaked and overcoated talkers,
soaking themselves full of the sunshine. The air throbbed, as
always, with the sound of bells, but it was a mellower and
opener sound than before, and looking at the purple bulk of
one of those hills which seem to rest like clouds at the end
of each avenue in Florence, Colville saw that it was clear of
snow. He was going up through Via Cavour to find Mr.
Waters and propose a walk, but he met him before he had
got half-way to San Marco.

The old man was at a momentary stand-still, looking up
at the Riccardi Palace, and he received Colville with
apparent forgetfulness of anything odd in his being still in
Florence. ''Upon the whole,'' he said, without preliminary
of any sort, as Colville turned and joined him in walking on,
''I don't know any homicide that more distinctly proves the
futility of assassination as a political measure than that over
yonder.'' He nodded his head sidewise toward Colville's
elbow.

''You might say that the moment when Lorenzino killed
Alessandro* was the most auspicious for a deed of that kind.
The Medici had only recently been restored; Alessandro was
the first ruler in Florence, who had worn a title; no more
reckless, brutal, and insolent tyrant ever lived, and his right,

even such as the Medici might have, to play the despot was
involved in the doubt of his origin; the heroism of the great
siege* ought still to have survived in the people who
withstood the forces of the whole German Empire for fifteen
months; it seems as if the taking off of that single wretch
should have ended the whole Medicean domination; but
there was not a voice raised to second the homicide's appeal
to the old love of liberty in Florence. The Medici party were
able to impose a boy of eighteen upon the most fiery
democracy that ever existed, and to hunt down and destroy
Alessandro's murderer at their leisure. No," added the old
man thoughtfully, "I think that the friends of progress must
abandon assassination as invariably useless. The trouble was
not that Alessandro was alive, but that Florence was dead.
Assassination always comes too early or too late in any
popular movement. It may be," said Mr. Waters, with a
carefulness to do justice to assassination which made Colville
smile, "that the modern scientific spirits may be able to
evolve something useful from the principle, but considering
the enormous abuses and perversions to which it is liable, I
am very doubtful of it—very doubtful."

Colville laughed. "I like your way of bringing a fresh
mind to all these questions in history and morals, whether
they are conventionally settled or not. Don't you think the
modern scientific spirit could evolve something useful out of
the old classic idea of suicide?"

"Perhaps," said Mr. Waters; "I haven't yet thought it
over. The worst thing about suicide—and this must always
rank it below political assassination—is that its interest is
purely personal. No man ever kills himself for the good of
others."

"That's certainly against it. We oughtn't to countenance
such an abominably selfish practice. But you can't bring that
charge against euthanasy. What have you to say of that?"

"I have heard one of the most benevolent and tender-
hearted men I ever knew defend it in cases of hopeless suffering. But I don't know that I should be prepared to take his
ground. There appears to be something so sacred about

human life that we must respect it even in spite of the prayers of the sufferer who asks us to end his irremediable misery."

"Well," said Colville, "I suspect we must at least class murder with the ballet as a means of good. One might say there was still some virtue in the primal, eldest curse against bloodshed."

"Oh, I don't by any means deny those things," said the old man, with the air of wishing to be scrupulously just. "Which way are you walking?"

"Your way, if you will let me," replied Colville. "I was going to your house to ask you to take a walk with me."

"Ah, that's good. I was reading of the great siege last night, and I thought of taking a look at Michelangelo's bastions.* Let us go together, if you don't think you'll find it too fatiguing."

"I shall be ashamed to complain if I do."

"And you didn't go to Rome after all?" said Mr. Waters.

"No; I couldn't face the landlord with a petition so preposterous as mine. I told him that I found I had no money to pay his bill till I had seen my banker, and as he didn't propose that I should send him the amount back from Rome, I stayed. Landlords have their limitations; they are not imaginative, as a class."

"Well, a day more will make no great difference to you, I suppose," said the old man, "and a day less would have been a loss to me. I shall miss you."

"Shall you, indeed?" asked Colville, with a grateful stir of the heart. "It's very nice of you to say that."

"Oh no. I meet few people who are willing to look at life objectively with me, and I have fancied some such willingness in you. What I chiefly miss over here is a philosophic lift in the human mind, but probably that is because my opportunities of meeting the best minds are few, and my means of conversing with them are small. If I had not the whole past with me, I should feel lonely at times."

"And is the past such good company always?"

"Yes, in a sense it is. The past is humanity set free from circumstance, and history studied where it was once life is the past rehumanised."

As if he found this rarefied air too thin for his lungs, Colville made some ineffectual gasps at response, and the old man continued: "What I mean is that I meet here the characters I read of, and commune with them before their errors were committed, before they had condemned themselves to failure, while they were still wise and sane, and still active and vital forces."

"Did they all fail? I thought some of the bad fellows had a pretty fair worldly success?"

"The blossom of decay."

"Oh! what black pessimism!"

"Not at all! Men fail, but man succeeds. I don't know what it all means, or any part of it; but I have had moods in which it seemed as if the whole secret of the mystery were about to flash upon me. Walking along in the full sun, in the midst of men, or sometimes in the solitude of midnight, poring over a book, and thinking of quite other things, I have felt that I had almost surprised it."

"But never quite?"

"Oh, it isn't too late yet."

"I hope you won't have your revelation before I get away from Florence, or I shall see them burning you here like the great *frate*."*

They had been walking down the Via Calzioli from the Duomo, and now they came out into the Piazza della Signoria, suddenly, as one always seems to do, upon the rise of the old palace and the leap of its tower into the blue air. The history of all Florence is there, with memories of every great time in bronze or marble, but the supreme presence is the martyr who hangs for ever from the gibbet over the quenchless fire in the midst.

"Ah, they *had* to kill him!" sighed the old man. "It has always been so with the benefactors. They have always meant mankind more good than any one generation can bear, and it must turn upon them and destroy them."

"How will it be with you, then, when you have read us 'the riddle of the painful earth'?"*

"That will be so simple that every one will accept it willingly and gladly, and wonder that no one happened to think of it before. And, perhaps, the world is now grown old enough and docile enough to receive the truth without resentment.''

"I take back my charge of pessimism," said Colville. "You are an optimist of the deepest dye.''

They walked out of the Piazza and down to the Lung' Arno, through the corridor of the Uffizzi, where the illustrious Florentines stand in marble under the arches, all reconciled and peaceful and equal at last. Colville shivered a little as he passed between the silent ranks of the statues.

"I can't stand those fellows, to-day. They seem to feel such a smirk satisfaction at having got out of it all.''

They issued upon the river, and he went to the parapet and looked down on the water. "I wonder," he mused aloud, "if it has the same Sunday look to these Sabbathless Italians as it has to us.''

"No; Nature isn't puritan," replied the old minister.

"Not at Haddam East Village?''

"No; there less than here; for she's had to make a harder fight for her life there.''

"Ah, then you believe in Nature—you're a friend of Nature?" asked Colville, following the lines of an oily swirl in the current with indolent eye.

"Only up to a certain point." Mr. Waters seemed to be patient of any direction which the other might be giving the talk. "Nature is a savage. She has good impulses, but you can't trust her altogether.''

"Do you know," said Colville, "I don't think there's very much of her left in us after we reach a certain point in life? She drives us on at a great pace for a while, and then some fine morning we wake up and find that Nature has got tired of us and has left us to taste and conscience. And taste and conscience are by no means so certain of what they want you to do as Nature was.''

"Yes," said the minister, "I see what you mean." He joined Colville in leaning on the parapet, and he looked out on the river as if he saw his meaning there. "But by the time we reach that point in life most of us have got the direction which Nature meant us to take, and there's no longer any need of her driving us on.''

"And what about the unlucky fellows who haven't got the direction, or haven't kept it?"

"They had better go back to it."

"But if Nature herself seemed to change her mind about you?"

"Ah, you mean persons of weak will. They are a great curse to themselves and to everybody else."

"I'm not so sure of that," said Colville. "I've seen cases in which a strong will looked very much more like the devil."

"Yes, a perverted will. But there can be no good without a strong will. A weak will means inconstancy. It means, even in good, good attempted and relinquished, which is always a terrible thing, because it is sure to betray some one who relied upon its accomplishment."

"And in evil? Perhaps the evil, attempted and relinquished, turns into good."

"Oh, never!" replied the minister fervently. "There is something very mysterious in what we call evil. Apparently it has infinitely greater force and persistence than good. I don't know why it should be so. But so it appears."

"You'll have the reason of that along with the rest of the secret when your revelation comes," said Colville, with a smile. He lifted his eyes from the river, and looked up over the clustering roofs beyond it to the hills beyond them, flecked to the crest of their purple slopes with the white of villas and villages. As if something in the beauty of the wonderful prospect had suggested the vision of its opposite, he said, dreamily, "I don't think I shall go to Rome to-morrow, after all. I will go to Des Vaches! Where did you say you were walking, Mr. Waters? Oh yes! You told me. I will cross the bridge with you. But I couldn't stand anything quite so vigorous as the associations of the siege this afternoon. I'm going to the Boboli Gardens, to debauch myself with a final sense of nerveless despotism, as it expressed itself in marble allegory and formal alleys. The fact is that if I stay with you any longer I shall tell you something that I'm too old to tell and you're too old to hear." The old man smiled, but offered no urgence or comment, and at the thither end of the bridge Colville said hastily, "Good-bye. If you ever come to Des Vaches, look me up."

"Good-bye," said the minister. "Perhaps we shall meet in Florence again."

"No, no. Whatever happens, that won't."

They shook hands and parted. Colville stood a moment, watching the slight bent figure of the old man as he moved briskly up the Via de' Bardi, turning his head from side to side, to look at the palaces as he passed, and so losing himself in the dim, cavernous curve of the street. As soon as he was out of sight, Colville had an impulse to hurry after him and rejoin him; then he felt like turning about and going back to his hotel.

But he shook himself together into the shape of resolution, however slight and transient. "I must do *something* I intended to do," he said, between his set teeth, and pushed on up through the Via Guicciardini. "I will go to the Boboli because I *said* I would."

As he walked along, he seemed to himself to be merely crumbling away in this impulse and that, in one abortive intent and another. What did it all mean? Had he been his whole life one of these weak wills which are a curse to themselves and others, and most a curse when they mean the best? Was that the secret of his failure in life? But for many years he had seemed to succeed, to be as other men were, hard, practical men; he had once made a good newspaper, which was certainly not a dream of romance. Had he given that up at last because he was a weak will? And now was he running away from Florence because his will was weak? He could look back to that squalid tragedy of his youth, and see that a more violent, a more determined man could have possessed himself of the girl whom he had lost. And now would it not be more manly, if more brutal, to stay here, where a hope, however fleeting, however fitful, of what might have been, had revisited him in the love of this young girl? He felt sure, if anything were sure, that something in him, in spite of their wide disparity of years, had captured her fancy, and now, in his abasement, he felt again the charm of his own power over her. They were no farther apart in years than many a husband and wife; they would grow more and more together; there was youth enough in his heart yet; and who was pushing him away from her, forbidding him this treasure that he had but to put out his hand and make his own? Some one whom through all his thoughts of another he was trying to please, but whom he had made finally inexorably his enemy. Better stay, then, something said to him; and when he answered, "I will," something else reminded him that this also was not willing but unwilling.

XIV

W HEN he entered the beautiful old garden, its benison of peace fell upon his tumult, and he began to breathe a freer air, reverting to his purpose to be gone in the morning and resting in it, as he strolled up the broad curve of its alley from the gate. He had not been there since he walked there with one now more like a ghost to him than any of the dead who had since died. It was there that she had refused him; he recalled with a grim smile the awkwardness of getting back with her to the gate from the point, far within the garden, where he had spoken. Except that this had happened in the fall, and now it was early spring, there seemed no change since then; the long years that had elapsed were like a winter between.

He met people in groups and singly loitering through the paths, and chiefly speaking English; but no one spoke to him, and no one invaded the solitude in which he walked. But the garden itself seemed to know him, and to give him a tacit recognition; the great, foolish grotto before the gate, with its statues by Bandinelli,* and the fantastic effects of drapery and flesh in party-coloured statues lifted high on either side of the avenue; the vast shoulder of wall, covered thick with ivy and myrtle, which he passed on his way to the amphitheatre behind the palace; the alternate figures and urns on their pedestals in the hemicycle, as if the urns were placed there to receive the ashes of the figures when they became extinct; the white statues or the colossal busts set at the ends of the long alleys against black curtains of foliage; the big fountain, with its group in the centre of the little lake, and the meadow, quiet and sad, that stretched away on one side from this; the keen light under the levels of the dense pines and ilexes; the paths striking straight on either hand from the avenue through which he sauntered, and the walk that coiled itself through the depths of the plantations; all knew him, and from them and from the winter neglect which was upon the place distilled a subtle influence, a charm, an appeal belonging to that combination of artifice and nature which is perfect only in an Italian garden under an Italian sky. He was right in the name which he mockingly gave the effect before he felt it; it was a debauch, delicate, refined, of unserious pensiveness, a smiling melancholy, in which he walked emancipated from his harassing hopes, and keeping only his shadowy regrets.

Colville did not care to scale the easy height from which you have the magnificent view, conscious of many photographs, of Florence. He wandered about the skirt of the silent meadow, and seeing himself unseen, he invaded its borders far enough to pluck one of those large scarlet anemones, such as he had given his gentle enemy. It was tilting there in the breeze above the unkempt grass, and the grass was beginning to feel the spring, and to stir and stretch itself after its winter sleep; it was sprinkled with violets, but these he did not molest. He came back to a stained and mossy stone bench on the avenue, fronting a pair of rustic youths carved in stone, who had not yet finished some game in which he remembered seeing them engaged when he was there before. He had not walked fast, but he had walked far, and was warm enough to like the whiffs of soft wind on his uncovered head. The spring was coming; that was its breath, which you know unmistakably in Italy after all the kisses that winter gives. Some birds were singing in the trees; down an alley into which he could look, between the high walls of green, he could see two people in flirtation: he waited patiently till the young man should put his arm round the girl's waist, for the fleeting embrace from which she pushed it and fled further down the path.

"Yes, it's spring," thought Colville; and then, with the selfishness of the troubled soul, he wished that it might be winter still and indefinitely. It occurred to him now that he should not go back to Des Vaches, for he did not know what he should do there. He would go to New York; though he did not know what he should do in New York, either.

He became tired of looking at the people who passed, and of speculating about them through the second consciousness which enveloped the sad substance of his misgivings like an atmosphere; and he let his eyelids fall, as he leaned his head back against the tree behind his bench. Then their voices pursued him through the twilight that he had made himself, and forced him to the same weary conjecture as if he had seen their faces. He heard gay laughter, and laughter that affected gaiety; the tones of young men in earnest disquisition reached him through the veil, and the talk, falling to whisper, of girls, with the names of men in it; sums of money, a hundred francs, forty thousand francs, came in high tones; a husband and wife went by quarrelling in the false security of English, and snapping at each other as confidingly as if in the sanctuary of home. The man bade the woman not be a fool, and she asked him how she was to endure his company if she was not a fool.

Colville opened his eyes to look after them, when a voice that he knew called out, "Why, it *is* Mr. Colville!"

It was Mrs. Amsden, and pausing with her, as if they had passed him in doubt, and arrested themselves when they had got a little way by, were Effie Bowen and Imogene Graham. The old lady had the child by the hand, and the girl stood a few paces apart from them. She was one of those beauties who have the property of looking very plain at times, and Colville, who had seen her in more than one transformation, now beheld her somehow clumsy of feature, and with the youth gone from her aspect. She seemed a woman of thirty, and she wore an unbecoming walking dress of a fashion that contributed to this effect of age. Colville was aware afterward of having wished that she was really as old and plain as she looked.

He had to come forward, and put on the conventional delight of a gentleman meeting lady friends.

"It's remarkable how your having your eyes shut estranged you," said Mrs. Amsden. "Now, if you had let me see you oftener in church, where people close their eyes a good deal for one purpose or another, I should have known you at once."

"I hope you haven't lost a great deal of time, as it is, Mrs. Amsden," said Colville. "Of course I should have had my eyes open if I had known you were going by."

"Oh, don't apologise!" cried the old thing, with ready enjoyment of his tone.

"I don't apologise for not being recognisable; I apologise for being visible," said Colville, with some shapeless impression that he ought to excuse his continued presence in Florence to Imogene, but keeping his eyes upon Mrs. Amsden, to whom what he said could not be intelligible. "I ought to be in Turin to-day."

"In Turin! Are you going away from Florence?"

"I'm going home."

"Why, did *you* know that?" asked the old lady of Imogene, who slightly nodded, and then of Effie, who also assented. "Really, the silence of the Bowen family in regard to the affairs of others is extraordinary. There never was a family more eminently qualified to live in Florence. I dare say that if I saw a little more of them, I might hope to reach the years of discretion myself some day. *Why* are you going away? (You see I haven't reached them yet!) Are you tired of Florence already?"

"No," said Colville passively; "Florence is tired of me."

"You're quite sure?"

"Yes; there's no mistaking one of her sex on such a point."

Mrs. Amsden laughed. "Ah, a great many people mistake us, both ways. And you're really going back to America. What in the world for?"

"I haven't the least idea."

"Is America fonder of you than Florence?"

"She's never told her love. I suspect it's merely that she's more used to me."

They were walking, without any volition of his, down the slope of the broad avenue to the fountain, where he had already been.

"Is your mother well?" he asked of the little girl. It seemed to him that he had better not speak to Imogene, who still kept that little distance from the rest, and get away as soon as he decently could.

"She has a headache," said Effie.

"Oh, I'm sorry," returned Colville.

"Yes, she deputed me to take her young people out for an airing," said Mrs. Amsden; "and Miss Graham decided us for the Boboli, where she hadn't been yet. I've done what I could to make the place attractive. But what is an old woman to do for a girl in a garden? We ought to have brought some other young people—some of the Inglehart boys. But we're respectable, we Americans abroad; we're decorous, above all things; and I don't know about meeting *you* here, Mr. Colville. It has a very bad appearance. Are you sure that you didn't know I was to go by here at exactly half-past four?"

"I was living from breath to breath in the expectation of seeing you. You must have noticed how eagerly I was looking out for you."

"Yes, and with a single red anemone in your hand, so that I should know you without being obliged to put on my spectacles."

"You divine everything, Mrs. Amsden," he said, giving her the flower.

"I shall make my brags to Mrs. Bowen when I see her," said the old lady. "How far into the country did you walk for this?"

"As far as the meadow yonder."

They had got down to the sheet of water from which the sea-horses of the fountain sprang, and the old lady sank upon a bench near it. Colville held out his hand toward Effie. "I saw a lot of violets over there in the grass."

"Did you?" She put her hand eagerly into his, and they strolled off together. After a first motion to accompany them, Imogene sat down beside Mrs. Amsden, answering quietly the talk of the old lady, and seeming in nowise concerned about the expedition for violets. Except for a dull first glance, she did not look that way. Colville stood in the border of the grass, and the child ran quickly hither and thither in it, stooping from time to time upon the flowers. Then she came out to where he stood, and showed her bunch of violets, looking up into the face which he bent upon her, while he trifled with his cane. He had a very fatherly air with her.

"I think I'll go and see what they've found," said Imogene irrelevantly, to a remark of Mrs. Amsden's about the expensiveness of Madame Bossi's bonnets.

"Well," said the old lady. Imogene started, and the little girl ran to meet her. She detained Effie with her admiration of the violets till Colville lounged reluctantly up. "Go and show them to Mrs. Amsden," she said, giving back the violets, which she had been smelling. The child ran on. "Mr. Colville, I want to speak with you."

"Yes," said Colville helplessly.

"Why are you going away?"

"Why? Oh, I've accomplished the objects—or no-objects—I came for," he said, with dreary triviality, "and I must hurry away to other fields of activity." He kept his eyes on her face, which he saw full of a passionate intensity, working to some sort of overflow.

"That is not true, and you needn't say it to spare me. You are going away because Mrs. Bowen said something to you about me."

"Not quite that," returned Colville gently.

"No; it was something that she said to me about you. But it's the same thing. It makes no difference. I ask you not to go for that."

"Do you know what you are saying, Imogene?"

"Yes."

Colville waited a long moment. "Then, I thank you, you dear girl, and I am going to-morrow, all the same. But I shan't forget this; whatever my life is to be, this will make it less unworthy and less unhappy. If it could buy anything to give you joy, to add some little grace to the good that must come to you, I would give it. Some day you'll meet the young fellow whom you're to make immortal, and you must tell of an old fellow who knew you afar off, and understood how to worship you for an angel of pity and unselfishness. Ah, I hope he'll understand, too! Good-bye." If he was to fly, that was the sole instant. He took her hand, and said again, "Good-bye." And then he suddenly cried, "Imogene, do you wish me to stay?"

"Yes!" said the girl, pouring all the intensity of her face into that whisper.

"Even if there had been nothing said to make me go away—should you still wish me to stay?"

"Yes."

He looked her in the starry, lucid eyes, where a divine fervour deepened. He sighed in nerveless perplexity; it was she who had the courage.

"It's a mistake! You mustn't! I am too old for you! It would be a wrong and a cruelty! Yes, you must let me go, and forget me. I have been to blame. If Mrs. Bowen has blamed me, she was right—I deserved it; I deserved all she could say against me."

"She never said anything against you. Do you think I would have let her? No; it was I that said it, and I blamed you. It was because I thought that you were—you were——"

"Trifling with you? How could you think that?"

"Yes, I know now how it was, and it makes you seem all the grander to me. Did you think I cared for your being older than I was? I never cared for it—I never hardly thought of it after the very first. I tried to make you understand that, and how it hurt me to have you speak of it. Don't you think that I could see how good you were? Do you suppose that all I want is to be happy? I don't care for that—I despise it, and I always hate myself for seeking my own pleasure, if I find myself doing it. I have seen enough of life to know what *that* comes to! And what hurt me worst of all was that you seemed to believe that I cared for nothing but amusing myself, when I wished to be something better, higher! It's nothing whether you are of my age or not, if—if—you care for me."

"Imogene!"

"All that I ask is to be with you, and try to make you forget what's been sad in your life, and try to be of use to you in whatever you are doing, and I shall be prouder and gladder of that than anything that people *call* happiness."

Colville stood holding her hand, while she uttered these ideas and incoherent repetitions of them, with a deep sense of powerlessness. "If I believed that I could keep you from regretting this——"

"What should I regret? I won't let you depreciate yourself—make yourself out not good enough for the best. Oh, I know how it happened! But now you shall never think of it again. No; I will not let you. That is the only way you could make me regret anything."

"I am going to stay," said Colville. "But on my own terms. I will be bound to you, but you shall not be bound to me."

"You doubt me! I would rather have you go! No; stay. And let me prove to you how wrong you are. I mustn't ask more than that. Only give me the chance to show you how different I am from what you think—how different you are, too."

"Yes. But you must be free."

"Well."

"What are they doing so long there?" asked Mrs. Amsden of Effie, putting her glasses to her eyes. "I can't see."

"They are just holding hands," said the child, with an easy satisfaction in the explanation, which perhaps the old lady did not share. "He always holds my hand when he is with me."

"Does he, indeed?" exclaimed Mrs. Amsden, with a cackle. She added, "That's very polite of him, isn't it? You must be a great favourite with Mr. Colville. You will miss him when he's gone."

"Yes. He's very nice."

Colville and Imogene returned, coming slowly across the loose, neglected grass toward the old woman's seat. She rose as they came up.

"You don't seem to have succeeded so well in getting flowers for Miss Graham as for the other ladies. But perhaps you didn't find her favourite over there. What is your favourite flower, Miss Graham? Don't say you have none! I didn't know that I preferred scarlet anemones. Were there no forget-me-nots over there in the grass?"

"There was no occasion for them," answered Colville.

"You always did make such pretty speeches!" said the old lady. "And they have such an orphic character, too; you can interpret them in so many different ways. Should you mind saying just what you meant by that one?''

"Yes, very much," replied Colville.

The old lady laughed with cheerful resignation. She would as lief report that reply of his as another. Even more than a man whom she could entangle in his speech she liked a man who could slip through the toils with unfailing ease. Her talk with such a man was the last consolation which remained to her from a life of harmless coquetries.

"I will refer it to Mrs. Bowen," she said. "She is a very wise woman, and she used to know you a great while ago."

"If you like, I will do it for you, Mrs. Amsden. I'm going to see her."

"To renew your adieux? Well, why not? Parting is such sweet sorrow! And if I were a young man I would go to say good-bye to Mrs. Bowen as often as she would let me. Now tell me honestly, Mr. Colville, did you ever see such an exquisite, perfect *creature*?''

"Oh, that's asking a good deal."

"What?''

"To tell you a thing honestly. How did you come here, Mrs. Amsden?''

"In Mrs. Bowen's carriage. I sent it round from the Pitti entrance to the Porta Romana. It's waiting there now, I suppose.''

"I thought you had been corrupted, somehow. Your zeal is carriage-bought. It *is* a delightful vehicle. Do you think you could give me a lift home in it?''

"Yes, indeed. I've always a seat for you in my carriage. To Hotel d'Atene?''

"No, to Palazzo Pinti.''

"This is deliciously mysterious," said Mrs. Amsden, drawing her shawl up about her shoulders, which, if no longer rounded, had still a charming droop. One realises in looking at such old ladies that there are women who could manage their own skeletons winningly. She put her glasses, which were an old-fashioned sort, held to the nose by a handle, and perused the different persons of the group. "Mr. Colville concealing an inward trepidation under a bold front; Miss Graham agitated but firm; the child as much puzzled as the old woman. I feel that we are a very interesting group—almost dramatic.''

"Oh, call us a passage from a modern novel,'' suggested Colville, ''if you're in the romantic mood. One of Mr. James's.''

"Don't you think we ought to be rather more of the great world for that? I hardly feel up to Mr. James. I should have said Howells.* Only nothing happens in that case!''

"Oh, very well; that's the most comfortable way. If it's only Howells, there's no reason why I shouldn't go with Miss Graham to show her the view of Florence from the cypress grove up yonder.''

"No; he's very particular when he's on Italian ground,'' said Mrs. Amsden, rising. ''You must come another time with Miss Graham, and bring Mrs. Bowen. It's quite time we were going home.''

The light under the limbs of the trees had begun to grow more liquid. The currents of warm breeze streaming through the cooler body of the air had ceased to ruffle the lakelet round the fountain, and the naiads rode their sea-horses through a perfect calm. A damp, pierced with fresh odour of the water and of the springing grass, descended upon them. The saunterers through the different paths and alleys were issuing upon the main avenues, and tending in gathering force toward the gate.

They found Mrs. Bowen's carriage there, and drove first to her house, beyond which Mrs. Amsden lived in a direct line. On the way Colville kept up with her the bantering talk that they always carried on together, and found in it a respite from the formless future pressing close upon him. He sat with Effie on the front seat, and he would not look at Imogene's face, which, nevertheless, was present to some inner vision. When the porter opened the iron gate below and rang Mrs. Bowen's bell, and Effie sprang up the stairs before them to give her mother the news of Mr. Colville's coming, the girl stole her hand into his.

"Shall you—tell her?''

"Of course. She must know without an instant's delay."

"Yes, yes; that is right. Oh!— Shall I go with you?"

"Yes; come!"

XV

MRS. BOWEN came in to them, looking pale and pain-worn, as she did that evening when she would not let Colville go away with the other tea-taking callers to whom she had made her headache an excuse. The eyelids which she had always a little difficulty in lifting were heavy with suffering, and her pretty smile had an effect of very great remoteness. But there was no consciousness of anything unusual or unexpected in his presence expressed in her looks or manner. Colville had meant to take Imogene by the hand and confront Mrs. Bowen with an immediate declaration of what had happened; but he found this impossible, at least in the form of his intention; he took, instead, the hand of conventional welcome which she gave him, and he obeyed her in taking provisionally the seat to which she invited him. At the same time the order of his words was dispersed in that wonder, whether she suspected anything, with which he listened to her placid talk about the weather; she said she had thought it was a chilly day outdoors; but her headaches always made her very sensitive.

"Yes," said Colville, "I supposed it was cold myself till I went out, for I woke with a tinge of rheumatism." He felt a strong desire to excuse, to justify what had happened, and he went on, with a painful sense of Imogene's eyes bent in bewildered deference upon him. "I started out for a walk with Mr. Waters, but I left him after we got across the Ponte Vecchio; he went up to look at the Michelangelo bastions, and I strolled over to the Boboli Gardens—where I found your young people."

He had certainly brought himself to the point, but he seemed actually further from it than at first, and he made a desperate plunge, trying at the same time to keep something of his habitual nonchalance. "But that doesn't account for my being here. Imogene accounts for that. She has allowed me to stay in Florence."

Mrs. Bowen could not turn paler than her headache had left her, and she now underwent no change of complexion. But her throat was not clear enough to say to the end, "Allowed you to stay in——" The trouble in her throat arrested her again.

Colville became very red. He put out his hand and took Imogene's, and now his eyes and Mrs. Bowen's met in the kind of glance in which people intercept and turn each other aside before they have reached a resting-place in each other's souls. But at the girl's touch his courage revived—in some physical sort. "Yes, and if she will let me stay with her, we are not going to part again."

Mrs. Bowen did not answer at once, and in the hush Colville heard the breathing of all three.

"Of course," he said, "we wished you to know at once, and I came in with Imogene to tell you."

"What do you wish me," asked Mrs. Bowen, "to do?"

Colville forced a nervous laugh. "Really, I'm so little used to this sort of affair that I don't know whether I have any wish. Imogene is here with you, and I suppose I supposed you would wish to do something."

"I will do whatever you think best."

"Thank you: that's very kind of you." He fell into a silence, in which he was able only to wish that he knew what was best, and from which he came to the surface with, "Imogene's family ought to know, of course."

"Yes; they put her in my charge. They will have to know. Shall I write to them?"

"Why, if you will."

"Oh, certainly."

"Thank you."

He had taken to stroking with his right hand the hand of Imogene which he held in his left, and now he looked round at her with a glance which it was a relief not to have her meet. "And till we can hear from them, I suppose you will let me come to see her?"

"You know you have always been welcome here."

"Thank you very much." It seemed as if there ought to be something else to say, but Colville could not think of

anything except: 'We wish to act in every way with your
approval, Mrs. Bowen. And I know that you are very particular in some things"—the words, now that they were
said, struck him as unfortunate, and even vulgar—"and I
shouldn't wish to annoy you——"

"Oh, I understand. I think it will be—I have no doubt
you will know how to manage all that. It isn't as if you were
both——"

"Young?" Colville. "No; one of us is quite old enough
to be thoroughly up in the *convenances*.* We are qualified, I'm
afraid, as far as that goes," he added bitterly, "to set all
Florence an example of correct behaviour."

He knew there must be pain in the face which he would
not look at; he kept looking at Mrs. Bowen's face, in which
certainly there was not much pleasure, either.

There was another silence, which became very oppressive
before it ended in a question from Mrs. Bowen, who stirred
slightly in her chair, and bent forward as if about to rise in
asking it. "Shall you wish to consider it an engagement?"

Colville felt Imogene's hand tremble in his, but he received
no definite prompting from the tremor. "I don't believe I
know what you mean."

"I mean, till you have heard from Imogene's mother."

"I hadn't thought of that. Perhaps under the circumstances——" The tremor died out of the hand he held; it lay
lax between his. "What do you say, Imogene?"

"I can't say anything. Whatever you think will be
right—for me."

"I wish to do what will seem right and fair to your
mother."

"Yes."

Colville heaved a hopeless sigh. Then with a deep inward
humiliaton, he said, "Perhaps if you know Imogene's
mother, Mrs. Bowen, you can suggest—advise——
You——"

"You must excuse me; I can't suggest or advise anything.
I must leave you perfectly free." She rose from her chair,
and they both rose too from the sofa on which he had seated
himself at Imogene's side. "I shall have to leave you, I'm

afraid; my head aches still a little. Imogene!'' She advanced toward the girl, who stood passively letting her come the whole distance. As if sensible of the rebuff expressed in this attitude, she halted a very little. Then she added, ''I hope you will be very happy,'' and suddenly cast her arms round the girl, and stood long pressing her face into her neck. When she released her, Colville trembled lest she should be going to give him her hand in congratulation. But she only bowed slightly to him, with a sidelong, aversive glance, and walked out of the room with a slow, rigid pace, like one that controls a tendency to giddiness.

Imogene threw herself on Colville's breast. It gave him a shock, as if he were letting her do herself some wrong. But she gripped him fast, and began to sob and to cry. ''Oh! oh! oh!''

''What is it?—what is it, my poor girl?'' he murmured. ''Are you unhappy? Are you sorry? Let it all end, then!''

''No, no; it isn't that! But I am very unhappy—yes, very, very unhappy! Oh, I didn't suppose I should ever feel so toward any one. I hate her!''

''You hate her?'' gasped Colville.

''Yes, I hate her. And she—she is so good to me! It must be that I've done her some deadly wrong, without knowing it, or I couldn't hate her as I know I do.''

''Oh no,'' said Colville soothingly; ''that's just your fancy. You haven't harmed her, and you don't hate her.''

''Yes, yes, I do! You can't understand how I feel toward her.''

''But you can't feel so toward her long,'' he urged, dealing as he might with what was wholly a mystery to him. She is so good——''

''It only makes my badness worse, and makes me hate her more.''

''I don't understand. But you're excited now. When you're calmer you'll feel differently, of course. I've kept you restless and nervous a long time, poor child; but now our peace begins, and everything will be bright and——'' He stopped: the words had such a very hollow sound.

She pushed herself from him, and dried her eyes. ''Oh yes.''

"And, Imogene—perhaps—perhaps—— Or, no; never mind, now. I must go away——" She looked at him, frightened but submissive. But I will be back to-night, or perhaps to-morrow morning. I want to think—to give you time to think. I don't want to be selfish about you—I want to consider you, all the more because you won't consider yourself. Good-bye." He stooped over and kissed her hair. Even in this he felt like a thief; he could not look at the face she lifted to his.

Mrs. Bowen sent word from her room that she was not coming to dinner, and Imogene did not come till the dessert was put on. Then she found Effie Bowen sitting alone at the table, and served in serious formality by the man, whom she had apparently felt it right to repress, for they were both silent. The little girl had not known how to deny herself an excess of the less wholesome dishes, and she was perhaps anticipating the regret which this indulgence was to bring, for she was very pensive.

"Isn't mamma coming at *all*?" she asked plaintively, when Imogene sat down, and refused everything but a cup of coffee. "Well," she went on, "I can't make out what is coming to this family. You were all crying last night because Mr. Colville was going away, and now, when he's going to stay, it's just as bad. I don't think you make it very pleasant for *him*. I should think he would be perfectly puzzled by it, after he's done so much to please you all. I don't believe he think it's very polite. I suppose it *is* polite, but it doesn't seem so. And he's always so cheerful and nice. I should think he would want to visit in some family where there was more amusement. There used to be plenty in this family, but now it's as dismal! The first of the winter you and mamma used to be so pleasant when he came, and would try everything to amuse him, and would let me come in to get some of the good of it; but now you seem to fly every way as soon as he comes in sight of the house, and I'm poked off in holes and corners before he can open his lips. And I've borne it about as long as I can. I would rather be back in Vevay. Or anywhere." At this point her own pathos overwhelmed her, and the tears rolling down her cheeks moistened the crumbs of pastry at the corners of her pretty mouth. "What was so strange, I should like to know, about his staying, that mamma should pop up like a ghost, when I told her he had come home with us, and grab me by the wrist, and twitch me about, and ask me all sorts of questions I couldn't answer, and frighten me almost to death? I haven't got over it yet. And I don't think it's very nice. It used to be a very polite family, and pleasant with each other, and always having something agreeable going on in it; but if it keeps on *very* much longer in this way, I shall think the Bowens are beginning to lose their good-breeding. I suppose that if Mr. Colville were to go down on his knees to mamma and ask her to let him take me somewhere now, she wouldn't do it." She pulled her handkerchief out of her pocket, and dried her eyes on a ball of it. "I don't see what *you've* been crying about, Imogene. *You've* got nothing to worry you."

"I'm not very well, Effie," returned the girl gently. "I haven't been well all day."

"It seems to me that nobody is well any more. I don't believe Florence is a very healthy place. Or at least this house isn't. *I* think it must be the drainage. If we keep on, I suppose we shall all have diphtheria. Don't you, Imogene?"

"Yes," asserted the girl distractedly.

"The girls had it at Vevay frightfully. And none of them were as strong afterward. Some of the parents came and took them away; but Madame Schebres never let mamma know. Do you think that was right?"

"No; it was very wrong."

"I suppose Mr. Colville will have it if we do. That is, if he keeps coming here. Is he coming any more?"

"Yes; he's coming to-morrow morning."

"*Is* he?" A smile flickered over the rueful face. "What time is he coming?"

"I don't know exactly," said Imogene, listlessly stirring her coffee. "Some time in the forenoon."

"Do you suppose he's going to take us anywhere?"

"Yes—I think so. I can't tell exactly."

"If he asks me to go somewhere, will you tease mamma?

She always lets you, Imogene, and it seems sometimes as if she just took a pleasure in denying me.''

"You mustn't talk so of your mother, Effie.''

"No; I wouldn't to *every*body. I know that she means for the best; but I don't believe she understands how much I suffer when she won't let me go with Mr. Colville. Don't you think he's about the nicest gentleman we know, Imogene?''

"Yes, he's very kind.''

"And I think he's handsome. A good many people would consider him old-looking, and of course he isn't so young as Mr. Morton was, or the Inglehart boys; but that makes him all the easier to get along with. And his being just a little fat, that way, seems to suit so well with his character.'' The smiles were now playing across the child's face, and her eyes, sparkling. "*I* think Mr. Colville would make a good Saint Nicholas—the kind they have going down chimneys in America. I'm going to tell him, for the next veglione. It would be such a nice surprise.''

"No, better not tell him that,'' suggested Imogene.

"Do you think he wouldn't like it?''

"Yes.''

"Well, it would become him. How old do you suppose he is, Imogene? Seventy-five?''

"What an idea!'' cried the girl fiercely. "He's forty-one.''

"I didn't know they had those little jiggering lines at the corners of their eyes so quick. But forty-one is pretty old, isn't it? Is Mr. Waters——''

"Effie,'' said her mother's voice at the door behind her, "will you ring for Giovanni, and tell him to bring me a cup of coffee in here?'' She spoke from the *portière* of the *salotto*.*

"Yes, mamma. I'll bring it to you myself.''

"Thank you, dear,'' Mrs. Bowen called from within.

The little girl softly pressed her hands together. "I *hope* she'll let me stay up! I feel so excited, and I hate to lie and think so long before I get to sleep. Couldn't you just hint a little to her that I might stay up? It's Sunday night.''

"I can't, Effie,'' said Imogene. "I oughtn't to interfere with any of your mother's rules.''

The child sighed submissively and took the coffee that Giovanni brought to her. She and Imogene went into the *salotto* together. Mrs. Bowen was at her writing-desk. "You can bring the coffee here, Effie," she said.

"Must I go to bed at once, mamma?" asked the child, setting the cup carefully down.

The mother looked distractedly up from her writing. "No; you may sit up a while," she said, looking back to her writing.

"How long, mamma?' pleaded the little girl.

"Oh, till you're sleepy. It doesn't matter *now*."

She went on writing; from time to time she tore up what she had written.

Effie softly took a book from the table, and perching herself on a stiff, high chair, bent over it and began to read.

Imogene sat by the hearth, where a small fire was pleasant in the indoor chill of an Italian house, even after so warm a day as that had been. She took some large beads of the strand she wore about her neck into her mouth, and pulled at the strand listlessly with her hand while she watched the fire. Her eyes wandered once to the child.

"What made you take such an uncomfortable chair, Effie?"

Effie shut her book over her hand. "It keeps me wakeful longer," she whispered, with a glance at her mother from the corner of her eye.

"I don't see why any one should wish to be wakeful," sighed the girl.

When Mrs. Bowen tore up one of her half-written pages Imogene started nervously forward, and then relapsed again into her chair. At last Mrs. Bowen seemed to find the right phrases throughout, and she finished rather a long letter, and read it over to herself. Then she said, without leaving her desk, "Imogene, I've been trying to write to your mother. Will you look at this?"

She held the sheet over her shoulder, and Imogene came languidly and took it; Mrs. Bowen dropped her face forward on the desk, into her hands, while Imogene was reading.

"FLORENCE, *March* 10, 18 –

"DEAR MRS. GRAHAM,—I have some very important news to give you in regard to Imogene, and as there is no way of preparing you for it, I will tell you at once that it relates to her marriage.

"She has met at my house a gentleman whom I knew in Florence when I was here before, and of whom I never knew anything but good. We have seen him very often, and I have seen nothing in him that I could not approve. He is Mr. Theodore Colville, of Prairie des Vaches, Indiana, where he was for many years a newspaper editor; but he was born somewhere in New England. He is a very cultivated, interesting man; and though not exactly a society man, he is very agreeable and refined in his manners. I am sure his character is irreproachable, though he is not a member of any church. In regard to his means I know nothing whatever, and can only infer from his way of life that he is in easy circumstances.

"The whole matter has been a surprise to me, for Mr. Colville is some twenty-one or two years older than Imogene, who is very young in her feelings for a girl of her age. If I could have realised anything like a serious attachment between them sooner, I would have written before. Even now I do not know whether I am to consider them engaged or not. No doubt Imogene will write you more fully.

"Of course I would rather not have had anything of the kind happen while Imogene was under my charge, though I am sure that you will not think I have been careless or imprudent about her. I interfered as far as I could, at the first moment I could, but it appears that it was then too late to prevent what has followed—

"Yours sincerely,

"EVALINA BOWEN."

Imogene read the letter twice over, and then she said, "Why isn't he a society man?"

Probably Mrs. Bowen expected this sort of approach. "I don't think a society man would have undertaken to dance the Lancers as he did at Madam Uccelli's," she answered patiently, without lifting her head.

Imogene winced, but "I should depise him if he were merely a society man," she said. "I have seen enough of them. I think it's better to be intellectual and good."

Mrs. Bowen made no reply, and the girl went on. "And

as to his being older, I don't see what difference it makes.
If people are in sympathy, then they are of the same
age, no difference how much older than one the other is. I
have always heard that." She urged this as if it were a
question.

"Yes," said Mrs. Bowen.

"And how should his having been a newspaper editor be
anything against him?"

Mrs. Bowen lifted her face and stared at the girl in
astonishment. "Who said it was against him?"

"You hint as much. The whole letter is against him."

"Imogene!"

"Yes! Every word! You make him out perfectly
detestable. I don't know why you should hate *him*. He's
done everything he could to satisfy you."

Mrs. Bowen rose from her desk, putting her hand to her
forehead, as if to soften a shock of headache that her change
of posture had sent there. "I will leave the letter with you,
and you can send it or not as you think best. It's merely a
formality, my writing to your mother. Perhaps you'll see it
differently in the morning. Effie!" she called to the child,
who with her book shut upon her hand had been staring
at them and listening intently. "It's time to go to bed
now."

When Effie stood before the glass in her mother's room,
and Mrs. Bowen was braiding her hair and tying it up for
the night, she asked ruefully, "What's the matter with
Imogene, mamma?"

"She isn't very happy to-night."

"*You* don't seem very happy either," said the child,
watching her own face as it quivered in the mirror. "I
should think that now Mr. Colville's concluded to stay, we
would all be happy again. But we don't seem to. We're—
we're perfectly demoralised!" It was one of the words she
had picked up from Colville.

The quivering face in the glass broke in a passion of tears,
and Effie sobbed herself to sleep.

Imogene sat down at Mrs. Bowen's desk, and pushing her
letter away, began to write.

"Florence, *March* 10, 18—.

"Dear Mother,— I inclose a letter from Mrs. Bowen which will tell you better than I can what I wish to tell. I do not see how I can add anything that would give you more of an idea of him, or less, either. No person can be put down in cold black and white, and not seem like a mere inventory. I do not suppose you expected me to become engaged when you sent me out to Florence, and, as Mrs. Bowen says, I don't know whether I am engaged or not. I will leave it entirely to Mr. Colville; if he says we are engaged, we are. I am sure he will do what is best. I only know that he was going away from Florence because he thought I supposed he was not in earnest, and I asked him to stay.

"I am a good deal excited to-night, and cannot write very clearly. But I will write soon again, and more at length.

"Perhaps something will be decided by that time. With much love to father,

                    "Your affectionate daughter,
                                    "Imogene."

She put this letter into an envelope with Mrs. Bowen's, and leaving it unsealed to show her in the morning, she began to write again. This time she wrote to a girl with whom she had been on terms so intimate that when they left school they had agreed to know each other by names expressive of their extremely confidential friendship, and to address each other respectively as Diary and Journal. They were going to write every day, if only a line or two; and at the end of a year they were to meet and read over together the records of their lives as set down in these letters. They had never met since, though it was now three years since they parted, and they had not written since Imogene came abroad; that is, Imogene had not answered the only letter she had received from her friend in Florence. This friend was a very serious girl, and had wished to be a minister, but her family would not consent, or even accept the compromise of studying medicine, which she proposed, and she was still living at home in a small city of central New York. Imogene now addressed her—

"Dear Diary,— You cannot think how far away the events of this day have pushed the feelings and ideas of the time when I agreed to write to you under this name. Till now it seems to me as if I had not changed in the least thing since we parted, and now I can hardly know myself for the same person. O dear Di! something very wonderful has come into my life, and I feel that it rests with me to make it the greatest blessing to myself and others, or the greatest misery. If I prove unworthy of it or unequal to it, then I am sure that nothing but wretchedness will come of it.

"I am engaged—yes!—and to a man more than twice my own age. It is so easy to tell *you* this, for I know that your large-mindedness will receive it very differently from most people, and that you will see it as I do. He is the noblest of men, though he tries to conceal it under the light, ironical manner with which he has been faithful to a cruel disappointment. It was here in Florence, twenty years ago, that a girl—I am ashamed to call her a girl— trifled with the priceless treasure that has fallen to me, and flung it away. *You*, Di, will understand how I was first fascinated with the idea of trying to atone to him here fore all the wrong he had suf- fered. At first it was only the vaguest suggestion—something like what I had read in a poem or a novel—that had nothing to do with me personally, but it grew upon me more and more the more I saw of him, and felt the witchery of his light, indifferent manner, which I learned to see was tense with the anguish he had suffered. She had killed his youth; she had spoiled his life: if I could revive them, restore them! It came upon me like a great flash of light at last, and as soon as this thought took possession of me, I felt my whole being elevated and purified by it, and I was enabled to put aside with con- tempt the selfish considerations that had occurred to me at first. At first the difference between our ages was very shocking to me; for I had always imagined it would be some one young; but when this light broke upon me, I saw that *he* was young, younger even than I, as a man is at the same age with a girl. Sometimes with my ex- periences, the fancies and flirtations that every one has and must have, however one despises them, I felt so *old* beside him; for he had been true to one love all his life, and he had not wavered for a moment. If I could make him forget it, if I could lift every feather's weight of sorrow from his breast, if I could help him to complete the destiny, grand and beautiful as it would have been, which another had arrested, broken off—don't you see, Di dear, how rich my reward would be?

"And he, how forbearing, how considerate, how anxious for me, how full of generous warning he has been! always putting me in mind, at every step, of the difference in years between us; never thinking of himself, and shrinking so much from even seeming to control me or sway me, that I don't know really whether I have not made all the advances!

"I cannot write his name yet, and you must not ask it till I can; and I cannot tell you anything about his looks or his life without seeming to degrade him, somehow, and make him a common man like others.

"How can I make myself his companion in everything? How can I convince him that there is no sacrifice for me, and that he alone is giving up? These are the thoughts that keep whirling through my mind. I hope I shall be helped, and I hope that I shall be tried, for that is the only way for me to be helped. I feel strong enough for anything that people can say. I should *welcome* criticism and opposition from any quarter. But I can see that *he* is very sensitive—it comes from his keen sense of the ridiculous—and if I suffer, it will be on account of this grand unselfish nature, and I shall be glad of that.

"I know you will understand me, Di, and I am not afraid of your laughing at these ravings. But if you did I should not care. It is such a comfort to say these things about him, to exalt him, and get him in the true light at last.

"Your faithful

JOURNAL.

"I shall tell him about you, one of the first things, and perhaps he can suggest some way out of your trouble, he has had so much experience of every kind. You will worship him, as I do, when you see him; for you will feel at once that he understands you, and that is such a *rest*.

"J."

Before Imogene fell asleep, Mrs. Bowen came to her in the dark, and softly closed the door that opened from the girl's room into Effie's. She sat down on the bed, and began to speak at once, as if she knew Imogene must be awake. "I thought you would come to *me*, Imogene; but as you didn't, I have come to you, for if you can go to sleep with hard thoughts of me to-night, I can't let you. You need me for your friend, and I wish to be your friend; it would be wicked in me to be anything else; I would give the world if your mother were here; but I tried to make my letter to her everything that it should be. If you don't think it is, I will write it over in the morning.''

''No,'' said the girl coldly; ''it will do very well. I don't wish to trouble you so much.''

''Oh, how can you speak so to me? Do you think that I blame Mr. Colville? Is that it? I don't ask you—I shall never ask you—how he came to remain, but I know that he has acted truthfully and delicately. I knew him long before you did, and no one need take his part with me.'' This was not perhaps what Mrs. Bowen meant to say when she began. ''I have told you all along what I thought, but if you imagine that I am not satisfied with Mr. Colville, you are very much mistaken. I can't burst out into praises of him to your mother: that would be very patronising and very bad taste. Can't you see that it would?''

''Oh yes.''

Mrs. Bowen lingered, as if she expected Imogene to say something more, but she did not, and Mrs. Bowen rose. ''Then I hope we understand each other,'' she said, and went out of the room.

XVI

WHEN Colville came in the morning, Mrs. Bowen received him. They shook hands, and their eyes met in the intercepting glance of the night before.

"Imogene will be here in a moment," she said, with a naturalness that made him awkward and conscious.

"Oh, there is no haste," he answered uncouthly. "That is, I am very glad of the chance to speak a moment with you, and to ask your—to profit by what you think best. I know you are not very well pleased with me, and I don't know that I can ever put myself in a better light with you—the true light. It seems that there are some things we must not do even for the truth's sake. But that's neither here nor there. What I am most anxious for is not to take a shadow of advantage of this child's—of Imogene's inexperience, and her remoteness from her family. I feel that I must in some sort protect her from herself. Yes—that is my idea. But I have to do this in so many ways that I hardly know how to begin. I should be very willing, if you thought best, to go away and stay away till she has heard from her people, and let her have that time to think it all over again. She is very young—so much younger than I! Or, if you thought it better, I would stay, and let her remain free while I held myself bound to any decision of hers. I am anxious to do what is right. At the same time"—he smiled ruefully—"there is such a thing as being so *dis*interested that one may seem *un*interested. I may leave her so very free that she may begin to suspect that I want a little freedom myself. What shall I do? I wish to act with your approval."

Mrs. Bowen had listened with acquiescence and intelligence that might well have looked like sympathy, as she sat fingering the top of her hand-screen, with her eyelids fallen. She lifted them to say, "I have told you that I will not advise you in any way. I cannot. I have no longer any wish in this matter. I must still remain in the place of Imogene's mother; but I will do only what you wish. Please understand that, and don't ask me for advice any more. It is painful." She drew her lower lip in a little, and let the screen fall into her lap.

"I'm sorry, Mrs. Bowen, to do anything—say anything —that is painful to you," Colville began. "You know that I would give the world to please you——" The words escaped him and left him staring at her.

"What are you saying to me, Theodore Colville?" she exclaimed, flashing a full-eyed glance upon him, and then breaking into a laugh, as unnatural for her. "Really, I don't believe you know!"

"Heaven knows I meant nothing but what I said," he answered, struggling stupidly with a confusion of desires which every man but no woman will understand. After eighteen hundred years, the man is still imperfectly monogamous. "Is there anything wrong in it?"

"Oh no! Not for you," she said scornfully.

"I am very much in earnest," he went on hopelessly, "in asking your opinion, your help, in regard to how I shall treat this affair."

"And I am still more in earnest in telling you that I will give you no opinion, no help. I forbid you to recur to the subject." He was silent, unable to drop his eyes from hers. "But for her," continued Mrs. Bowen, "I will do anything in my power. If she asks my advice I will give it, and I will give her all the help I can."

"Thank you," said Colville vaguely.

"I will not have your thanks," promptly retorted Mrs. Bowen, "for I mean you no kindness. I am trying to do my duty to Imogene, and when that is ended, all is ended. There is no way now for you to please me—as you call it— except to keep her from regretting what she had done."

"Do you think I shall fail in that?" he demanded indignantly.

"I can offer you no opinion. I can't tell what you will do."

"There are two ways of keeping her from regretting what she has done; and perhaps the simplest and best way would be to free her from the consequences, as far as they're involved in me," said Colville.

Mrs. Bowen dropped herself back in her armchair. "If you choose to force these things upon me, I am a woman, and can't help myself. Especially, I can't help myself against a guest."

"Oh, I will relieve you of my presence," said Colville. "I've no wish to force anything upon you—least of all myself." He rose, and moved toward the door.

She hastily intercepted him. "Do you think I will let you go without seeing Imogene? Do you understand me so little as that? It's *too late* for you to go! You know what I think of all this, and I know, better than you, what you think. I shall play my part, and you shall play yours. I have refused to give you advice or help, and I never shall do it. But I know what my duty to her is, and I will fulfil it. No matter how distasteful it is to either of us, you must come here as before. The house is as free to you as ever—freer. And we are to be as good friends as ever—better. You can see Imogene alone or in my presence and, as far as I am concerned, you shall consider yourself engaged or not, as you choose. Do you understand?"

"Not in the least," Colville, in the ghost of his old bantering manner. "But don't explain, or I shall make still less of it."

"I mean simply that I do it for Imogene and not for you."

"Oh, I understand that you don't do it for me."

At this moment Imogene appeared between the folds of the *portière*, and her timid, embarrassed glance from Mrs. Bowen to Colville was the first gleam of consolation that had visited him since he parted with her the night before. A thrill of inexplicable pride and fondness passed through his heart, and even the compunction that followed could not spoil its sweetness. But if Mrs. Bowen discreetly turned her head aside that she need not witness a tender greeting between them, the precaution was unnecessary. He merely went forward and took the girl's hand, with a sigh of relief. "Good morning, Imogene," he said, with a kind of compassionate admiration.

"Good morning," she returned half-inquiringly.

She did not take a seat near him, and turned, as if for instruction, to Mrs. Bowen. It was probably the force of habit. In any case, Mrs. Bowen's eyes gave no response. She bowed slightly to Colville, and began, "I must leave Imogene to entertain you for the present, Mr.——"

"No!" cried the girl impetuously; "don't go." Mrs. Bowen stopped. "I wish to speak with you—with you and Mr. Colville together. I wish to say—I don't know how to say it exactly; but I wish to know—— You asked him last night, Mrs. Bowen, whether he wished to consider it an engagement?"

"I thought perhaps you would rather hear from your mother——"

"Yes, I would be glad to know that my mother approved; but if she didn't, I couldn't help it. Mr. Colville said he was bound, but I was not. That can't be. I *wish* to be bound, if he is."

"I don't quite know what you expect me to say."

"Nothing," said Imogene. "I merely wished you to know. And I don't wish you to sacrifice anything to us. If you think best, Mr. Colville will not see me till I hear from home; though it won't make any difference with me *what* I hear."

"There's no reason why you shouldn't meet," said Mrs. Bowen absently.

"If you wish it to have the same appearance as an Italian engagement——"

"No," said Mrs. Bowen, putting her hand to her head with a gesture she had; "that would be quite unnecessary. It would be ridiculous under the circumstances. I have thought of it, and I have decided that the American way is the best."

"Very well, then," said Imogene, with the air of summing up; "then the only question is whether we shall make it known or not to other people."

This point seemed to give Mrs. Bowen greater pause than any. She was a long time silent, and Colville saw that Imogene was beginning to chafe at her indecision. Yet he did not see the moment to intervene in a debate in which he found himself somewhat ludicrously ignored, as if the affair were solely the concern of these two women, and none of his.

"Of course, Mrs. Bowen," said the girl haughtily, "if it will be disagreeable to you to have it known——"

Mrs. Bowen blushed delicately—a blush of protest and of generous surprise, or so it seemed to Colville. "I was not thinking of myself, Imogene, I only wish to consider you. And I was thinking whether, at this distance from home, you wouldn't prefer to have your family's approval before you made it known."

"I am sure of their approval. Father will do what mother says, and she has always said that she would never interfere with me in—in—such a thing."

"Perhaps you would like all the more, then, to show her the deference of waiting for her consent."

Imogene started as if stopped short in swift career; it was not hard for Colville to perceive that she saw for the first time the reverse side of a magnanimous impulse. She suddenly turned to him.

"I think Mrs. Bowen is right," he said gravely, in answer to the eyes of Imogene. He continued, with a flicker of his wonted mood: "You must consider me a little in the matter. I have some small shreds of self-respect about me somewhere, and I would rather not be put in the attitude of defying your family, or ignoring them."

"No," said Imogene, in the same effect of arrest.

"When it isn't absolutely necessary," continued Colville. "Especially as you say there will be no opposition."

"Of course," Imogene assented; and in fact what he said was very just, and he knew it; but he could perceive that he had suffered loss with her. A furtive glance at Mrs. Bowen did not assure him that he had made a compensating gain in that direction, where, indeed, he had no right to wish for any.

"Well then," the girl went on, "it shall be so. We will wait. It will only be waiting. I ought to have thought of you before; I make a bad beginning," she said tremulously. "I suppose I *was* thinking of you; but I see that I was only thinking of myself." The tears stood in her eyes. Mrs. Bowen, quite overlooked in this apology, slipped from the room.

"Imogene!" said Colville, coming toward her.

She dropped herself upon his shoulder. "Oh, why, why, *why* am I so miserable?"

"Miserable, Imogene!" he murmured, stroking her beautiful hair.

"Yes, yes! Utterly miserable! It must be because I'm unworthy of you—unequal every way. If you think so, cast me off at once. Don't be weakly merciful!"

The words pierced his heart. "I would give the world to make you happy, my child!" he said, with perfidious truth, and a sigh that came from the bottom of his soul. "Sit down here by me," he said, moving to the sofa; and with whatever obscure sense of duty to her innocent self-abandon, he made a space between them, and reduced her embrace to a clasp of the hand she left with him. "Now tell me," he said, "what is it makes you unhappy?"

"Oh, I don't know," she answered, drying her averted eyes. "I suppose I am overwrought from not sleeping, and from thinking how we should arrange it all."

"And now that it's all arranged, can't you be cheerful again?"

"Yes."

"You're satisfied with the way we've arranged it? Because if——"

"Oh, perfectly—perfectly!" She hastily interrupted. "I wouldn't have it otherwise. Of course," she added, "it wasn't very pleasant having some one else suggest what I ought to have thought of myself, and seem more delicate about you than I was."

"Some one else?"

"You know! Mrs. Bowen."

"Oh! But I couldn't see that she was anxious to spare me. It occurred to me that she was concerned about your family."

"It led up to the other! It's all the same thing."

"Well, even in that case, I don't see why you should mind

it. It was certainly very friendly of her, and I know that she
has your interest at heart entirely."

"Yes; she knows how to make it seem so."

Colville hesitated in bewilderment. "Imogene!" he cried
at last, "I don't understand this. Don't you think Mrs.
Bowen likes you?"

"She detests me."

"Oh, no, no, no! That's too cruel an error. You mustn't
think that. I can't let you. It's morbid. I'm sure that she's
devotedly kind and good to you."

"Being kind and good isn't liking. I know what she
thinks. But of course I can't expect to convince you of it; no
one else could see it."

"No!" said Colville, with generous fervour. "Because it
doesn't exist and you mustn't imagine it. You are as sincerely and unselfishly regarded in this house as you could be
in your own home. I'm sure of that. I know Mrs. Bowen.
She has her little worldlinesses and unrealities of manner, but
she is truth and loyalty itself. She would rather die than be
false, or even unfair. I knew her long ago——"

"Yes," cried the girl, "long before you knew me!"

"And I know her to be the soul of honour," said Colville,
ignoring the childish outburst. "Honour—like a man's," he
added. "And, Imogene, I want you to promise me that
you'll not think of her any more in that way. I want you to
think of her as faithful and loving to you, for she is so. Will
you do it?"

Imogene did not answer him at once. Then she turned
upon him a face of radiant self-abnegation. "I will do
anything you tell me. Only tell me things to do."

The next time he came he again saw Mrs. Bowen alone
before Imogene appeared. The conversation was confined to
two sentences.

"Mr Colville," she said, with perfectly tranquil point,
while she tilted a shut book to and fro on her knee, "I will
thank you not to defend me."

Had she overheard? Had Imogene told her? He
answered, in a fury of resentment for her ingratitude that
stupefied him. "I will never speak of you again."

Now they were enemies; he did not know how or why, but
he said to himself, in the bitterness of his heart, that it was
better so; and when Imogene appeared, and Mrs. Bowen
vanished, as she did without another word to him, he folded
the girl in a vindictive embrace.

"What is the matter?" she asked, pushing away from
him.

"With me?"

"Yes; you seem so excited."

"Oh, nothing," he said, shrinking from the sharpness of
that scrutiny in a woman's eyes, which, when it begins the
perusal of a man's soul, astonishes and intimidates him; he
never perhaps becomes able to endure it with perfect self-
control. "I suppose a slight degree of excitement in meeting
you may be forgiven me." He smiled under the unrelaxed
severity of her gaze.

"Was Mrs. Bowen saying anything about me?"

"Not a word," said Colville, glad of getting back to the
firm truth again, even if it were mere literality.

"We have made it up," she said, her scrutiny changing
to a lovely appeal for his approval. "What there was to make
up."

"Yes?"

"I told her what you had said. And now it's all right between us, and you mustn't be troubled at that any more. I
did it to please you."

She seemed to ask him with the last words whether she
really had pleased him, as if something in his aspect suggested a doubt; and he hastened to reassure her. "That was
very good of you. I appreciate it highly. It's extremely
gratifying."

She broke into a laugh of fond derision. "I don't believe
you really cared about it, or else you're not thinking about
it now. Sit down here; I want to tell you of something I've
thought out." She pulled him to the sofa, and put his arm
about her waist, with a simple fearlessness and matter-of-
course promptness that made him shudder. He felt that he
ought to tell her not to do it, but he did not quite know how
without wounding her. She took hold of his hand and drew

his lax arm taut. Then she looked up into his eyes, as if some
sense of his misgiving had conveyed itself to her, but she did
not release her hold of his hand.

"Perhaps we oughtn't, if we're not engaged?" she suggested, with such utter trust in him as made his heart quake.

"Oh," he sighed, from a complexity of feeling that no explanation could wholly declare, "we're engaged enough for
that, I suppose."

"I'm glad you think so," she answered innocently. "I
knew you wouldn't let me if it were not right." Having settled the question, "Of course," she continued, "we shall all
do our best to keep our secret; but in spite of everything it
may get out. Do you see?"

"Well?"

"Well, of course it will make a great deal of remark."

"Oh yes; you must be prepared for that, Imogene," said
Colville, with as much gravity as he could make comport
with his actual position.

"I am prepared for it, and prepared to despise it,"
answered the girl. "I shall have no trouble except the fear
that you will mind it." She pressed his hand as if she expected him to say something to this.

"I shall never care for it," he said, and this was true
enough. "My only care will be to keep you from regretting.
I have tried from the first to make you see that I was very
much older than you. It would be miserable enough if you
came to see it too late."

"I have never seen it, and I never shall see it, because
there's no such difference between us. It isn't the years that
make us young or old—who is it says that? No matter, it's
true. And I want you to believe it. I want you to feel that
I am your youth—the youth you were robbed of—given
back to you. Will you do it? Oh, if you could, I should be
the happiest girl in the world." Tears of fervour dimmed the
beautiful eyes which looked into his. "Don't speak!" she
hurried on. "I won't let you till I have said it all. It's been
this idea, this hope, with me always—ever since I knew what
happened to you here long ago—that you might go back in
my life and take up yours where it was broken off; that I

might make your life what it would have been—complete your destiny—"

Colville wrenched himself loose from the hold that had been growing more tenderly close and clinging. "And do you think I could be such a vampire as to let you? Yes, yes; I have had my dreams of such a thing; but I see now how hideous they were. You shall make no such sacrifice to me. You must put away the fancies that could never be fulfilled, or if by some infernal magic they could, would only bring sorrow to you and shame to me. God forbid! And God forgive me, if I have done or said anything to put this in your head! And thank God it isn't too late yet for you to take yourself back."

"Oh," she murmured. "Do you think it is self-sacrifice for me to give myself to *you*? It's self-glorification! You don't understand—I haven't told you what I mean, or else I've told it in such a way that I've made it hateful to you. Do you think I don't care for you except to be something to you? I'm not so generous as that. You are all the world to me. If I take myself back from you, as you say, what shall I do with myself?"

"Has it come to that?" asked Colville. He sat down again with her, and this time he put his arm around her and drew her to him, but it seemed to him he did it as if she were his child. "I was going to tell you just now that each of us lived to himself in this world, and that no one could hope to enter into the life of another and complete it. But now I see that I was partly wrong. We two are bound together, Imogene, and whether we become all in all or nothing to each other, we can have no separate fate."

The girl's eyes kindled with rapture. "Then let us never speak of it again. I was going to say something, but now I won't say it."

"Yes, say it."

"No; it will make you think that I am anxious on my own account about appearances before people."

"You poor child, I shall never think you are anxious on your own account about anything. What were you going to say?"

"Oh, nothing! It was only—are you invited to the Phillipses' fancy ball?"

"Yes," said Colville, silently making what he could of the diversion, "I believe so."

"And are you going—did you mean to go?" she asked timidly.

"Good heavens, no! What in the world should I do at another fancy ball? I walked about with the airy grace of a bull in a china shop at the last one."

Imogene did not smile. She faintly sighed. "Well, then, I won't go either."

"Did you intend to go?"

"Oh no!"

"Why, of course you did, and it's very right you should. Did you want me to go?"

"It would bore you."

"Not if you're there." She gave his hand a grateful pressure. "Come, I'll go, of course, Imogene. A fancy ball to please you is a very different thing from a fancy ball in the abstract."

"Oh, what nice things you say! Do you know, I always admired your compliments? I think they're the most charming compliments in the world."

"I don't think they're half so pretty as yours; but they're more sincere."

"No, honestly. They flatter, and at the same time they make fun of the flattery a little; they make a person feel that you like them, even while you laugh at them."

"They appear to be rather an intricate kind of compliment—sort of *salsa agradolce** affair—tutti frutti style—species of moral mayonnaise."

"No—be quiet! You know what I mean. What were we talking about? Oh! I was going to say that the most fascinating thing about you always was that ironical way of yours."

"Have I an ironical way? You were going to tell me something more about the fancy ball."

"I don't care for it. I would rather talk about you."

"And I prefer the ball. It's a fresher topic—to me."

"Very well, then. But this I *will* say. No matter how happy you should be, I should always want you to keep that tone of persiflage. You've no idea how perfectly intoxicating it is."

"Oh yes, I have. It seems to have turned the loveliest and wisest head in the world."

"Oh, do you really think so? I would give anything if you did."

"What?"

"Think I was pretty," she pleaded, with full eyes. "Do you?"

"No, but I think you are wise. Fifty per cent. of truth—it's a large average in compliments. What are you going to wear?"

"Wear? Oh! At the ball! Something Egyptian, I suppose. It's to be an Egyptian ball. Didn't you understand that?"

"Oh yes. But I supposed you could go in any sort of dress."

"You can't. You must go in some Egyptian character."

"How would Moses do? In the bulrushes, you know. You could be Pharaoh's daughter, and recognise me by my three hats. And toward the end of the evening when I became very much bored, I could go round killing Egyptians."

"No, no. Be serious. Though I like you to joke, too. I shall always want you to joke. Shall you, always?"

"There may be emergencies when I shall fail—like family prayers, and grace before meat, and dangerous sickness."

"Why, of course. But I mean when we're together, and there's no reason why you shouldn't?"

"Oh, at such times I shall certainly joke."

"And before people, too! I won't have them saying that it's sobered you—that you used to be very gay, and now you're cross, and never say anything."

"I will try to keep it up sufficiently to meet the public demand."

"And I shall want you to joke *me, too*. You must satirise me. It does more to show me my faults than anything else, and it will show other people how perfectly submissive I am, and how I think everything you do is just right."

"If I were to beat you a little in company, don't you think it would serve the same purpose?"

"No, no; be serious."

"About joking?"

"No, about me. I know that I'm very intense, and you must try to correct that tendency in me."

"I will, with pleasure. Which of my tendencies are you going to correct?"

"You have none."

"Well, then, neither have you. I'm not going to be out-done in civilities."

"Oh, if people could only hear you talk in this light way, and then know what *I* know!"

Colville broke out into a laugh at the deep sigh which accompanied these words. As a whole, the thing was grotesque and terrible to him, but after a habit of his, he was finding a strange pleasure in its details.

"No, no," she pleaded. "Don't laugh. There are girls that would give their eyes for it."

"As pretty eyes as yours?"

"Do you think they're nice?"

"Yes, if they were not so mysterious."

"Mysterious?"

"Yes, I feel that your eyes can't really be as honest as they look. That was what puzzled me about them the first night I saw you."

"No—did it, really?"

"I went home saying to myself that no girl could be so sincere as that Miss Graham seemed."

"Did you say that?"

"Words to that effect."

"And what do you think now?"

"Ah, I don't know. You had better go as the Sphinx."

Imogene laughed in simple gaiety of heart. "How far we've got from the ball!" she said, as if the remote excursion were a triumph. "What shall we really go as?"

"Isis and Osiris."*

"Weren't they gods of some kind?"

"Little one-horse deities—not very much."

"It won't do to go as gods of any kind. They're always failures. People expect too much of them."

"Yes," said Colville. "That's human nature under all circumstances. But why go to an Egyptian ball at all?"

"Oh, we *must* go. If we both stayed away it would make talk at once, and my object is to keep people in the dark till the very last moment. Of course it's unfortunate your having told Mrs. Amsden that you were going away, and then telling her just after you came back with me that you were going to stay. But it can't be helped now. And I don't really care for it. But don't you see why I want you to go to all these things?"

"*All* these things?"

"Yes, everything you're invited to after this. It's not merely for a blind as regards ourselves now, but if they see that you're very fond of all sorts of gaieties, they will see that you are—they will understand——"

There was no need for her to complete the sentence. Colville rose. "Come, come, my dear child," he said, "why don't you end all this at once? I don't blame you. Heaven knows I blame no one but myself? I ought to have the strength to break away from this mistake, but I haven't. I couldn't bear to see you suffer from pain that I should give you even for your good. But do it yourself, Imogene, and for pity's sake don't forbear from any notion of sparing me. I have no wish except for your happiness, and now I tell you clearly that no appearance we can put on before the world will deceive the world. At the end of all our trouble I shall still be forty——"

She sprang to him and put her hand over his mouth. "I know what you're going to say, and I won't let you say it, for you've promised over and over again not to speak of that any more. Oh, do you think I care for the world, or what it will think or say?"

"Yes, very much."

"That shows how little you understand me. It's because I wish to *defy* the world——"

"Imogene! Be as honest with yourself as you are with me."

"I *am* honest."

"Look me in the eyes, then."

She did so for an instant, and then hid her face on his shoulder.

"You silly girl," he said. "What is it you really do wish?"

"I wish there was no one in the world but you and me."

"Ah, you'd find it very crowded at times," said Colville sadly. 'Well, well," he added, "I'll go to your fandangoes, because you want me to go."

"That's all I wished you to say," she replied, lifting her head, and looking him radiantly in the face. "I don't want you to go at all! I only want you to promise that you'll come here every night that you're invited out, and read to Mrs. Bowen and me."

"Oh, I can't do that," said Colville; "I'm too fond of society. For example, I've been invited to an Egyptian fancy ball, and I couldn't think of giving that up."

"Oh, how delightful you are! They couldn't any of them talk like you."

He had learned to follow the processes of her thought now. "Perhaps they can when they come to my age."

"There!" she exclaimed, putting her hand on his mouth again, to remind him of another broken promise. "Why can't you give up the Egyptian ball?"

"Because I expect to meet a young lady there—a very beautiful young lady."

"But how shall you know her if she's disguised?"

"Why, I shall be disguised too, you know."

"Oh, what delicious nonsense you *do* talk! Sit down here and tell me what you are going to wear."

She tried to pull him back to the sofa. "What character shall you go in?"

"No, no," he said, resisting the gentle traction. "I can't; I have urgent business down-town."

"Oh! Business in *Florence!*"

"Well, if I stayed, I should tell you what disguise I'm going to the ball in."

"I knew it was that. What do you think would be a good character for me?"

"I don't know. The serpent of old Nile would be pretty good for you."

"Oh, I know you don't think it!" she cried fondly. She had now let him take her hand, and he stood holding it at arm's-length. Effie Bowen came into the room. "Good-bye," said Imogene, with an instant assumption of society manner.

"Good-bye," said Colville, and went out.

"Oh, Mr. Colville!" she called, before he got to the outer door.

"Yes," he said, staring back.

She met him midway of the dim corridor. "Only to——" She put her arms about his neck and sweetly kissed him.

Colville went out into the sunlight feeling like some strange, newly invented kind of scoundrel—a rascal of such recent origin and introduction that he had not yet had time to classify himself and ascertain the exact degree of his turpitude. The task employed his thoughts all that day, and kept him vibrating between an instinctive conviction of monstrous wickedness and a logical and well-reasoned perception that he had all the facts and materials for a perfectly good conscience. He was the betrothed lover of this poor child, whose affection he could not check without a degree of brutality for which only a better man would have the courage. When he thought of perhaps refusing her caresses, he imagined the shock it would give her, and the look of grief and mystification that would come into her eyes, and he found himself incapable of that cruel rectitude. He knew that these were the impulses of a white and loving soul; but at the end of all his argument they remained a terror to him, so that he lacked nothing but the will to fly from Florence and shun her altogether till she had heard from her family. This, he recalled, with bitter self-reproach was what had been his first inspiraton; he had spoken of it to Mrs. Bowen, and it had still everything in its favour except that it was impossible.

Imogene returned to the *salotto*, where the little girl was standing with her face to the window, drearily looking out; her back expressed an inner desolation which revealed itself in her eyes when Imogene caught her head between her hands, and tilted up her face to kiss it.

"What is the matter, Effie?" she demanded gaily.

"Nothing."

"Oh yes, there is."

"Nothing that you will care for. As long as he's pleasant to you, you don't care what he does to me."

"What has he done to you?"

"He didn't take the slightest notice of me when I came into the room. He didn't speak to me, or even look at me."

Imogene caught the little grieving, quivering face to her breast. "He is a wicked, wicked wretch! And I will give him the awfulest scolding he ever had when he comes here again. I will teach him to neglect my pet. I will let him understand that if he doesn't notice you, he needn't notice me. I will tell you, Effie—I've just thought of a way. The next time he comes we will both receive him. We will sit up very stiffly on the sofa together, and just answer Yes, No, Yes, No, to everything he says, till he begins to take the hint, and learns how to behave himself. Will you?"

A smile glittered through the little girl's tears; but she asked, "Do you think it would be very polite?"

"No matter, polite or not, it's what he deserves. Of course, as soon as he begins to take the hint, we will be just as we always are."

Imogene despatched a note, which Colville got the next morning, to tell him of his crime, and apprise him of his punishment, and of the sweet compunction that had pleaded for him in the breast of the child. If he did not think he could help play the comedy through, he must come prepared to offer Effie some sort of atonement.

It was easy to do this: to come with his pockets full of presents, and take the little girl on his lap, and pour out all his troubled heart in the caresses and tendernesses which would bring him no remorse. He humbled himself to her thoroughly, and with a strange sincerity in the harmless duplicity, and promised, if she would take him back into favour, that he would never offend again. Mrs. Bowen had sent word that she was not well enough to see him; she had another of her headaches; and he sent back a sympathetic and respectful message by Effie, who stood thoughtfully at her mother's pillow after she had delivered it, fingering the bouquet Colville had brought her, and putting her head first on this side, and then on that to admire it.

"I think Mr. Colville and Imogene are much more affectionate than they used to be," she said.

Mrs. Bowen started up on her elbow. "What do you mean, Effie?"

"Oh, they're both so good to me."

"Yes," said her mother, dropping back to her pillow. "Both?"

"Yes; he's the *most* affectionate."

The mother turned her face the other way. "Then he must be," she murmured.

"What?" asked the child.

"Nothing. I didn't know I spoke."

The little girl stood a while still playing with her flowers. "*I* think Mr. Colville is about the pleasantest gentleman that comes here. Don't you, mamma?"

"Yes."

"He's so interesting, and says such nice things. I don't know whether children ought to think of such things, but I wish I was going to marry some one like Mr. Colville. Of course I should want to be tolerably old if I did. How old do you think a person ought to be to marry him?"

"You mustn't talk of such things, Effie," said her mother.

"No; I suppose it isn't very nice." She picked out a bud in her bouquet, and kissed it; then she held the nosegay at arm's-length before her, and danced away with it.

XVII

In the ensuing fortnight a great many gaieties besides the Egyptian ball took place, and Colville went wherever he and Imogene were both invited. He declined the quiet dinners which he liked, and which his hearty appetite and his habit of talk fitted him to enjoy, and accepted invitations to all sorts of evenings and At Homes, where dancing occupied a modest corner of the card, and usurped the chief place in the pleasures. At these places it was mainly his business to see Imogene danced with by others, but sometimes he waltzed with her himself, and then he was complimented by people of his own age, who had left off dancing, upon his vigour. They said they could not stand that sort of thing, though they supposed, if you kept yourself in practice, it did not come so hard. One of his hostesses, who had made a party for her daughters, told him that he was an example to everybody, and that if middle-aged people at home mingled more in the amusements of the young, American society would not be the silly, insipid, boy-and-girl affair that it was now. He went to these places in the character of a young man, but he was not readily accepted or recognised in that character. They gave him frumps to take out to supper, mothers and maiden aunts, and if the mothers were young-ish, they threw off on him, and did not care for his talk.

At one of the parties Imogene seemed to become aware for the first time that the lapels of his dress-coat were not faced with silk.

"Why don't you have them so?" she asked. "All the *other* young men have. And you ought to wear a *boutonnière.*"

"Oh, I think a man looks rather silly in silk lapels at my——" He arrested himself, and then continued: "I'll see what the tailor can do for me. In the meantime, give me a bud out of your bouquet."

"How sweet you are!" she sighed. "You do the least

thing so that it is ten times as good as if any one else did it.''

The same evening, as he stood leaning against a doorway, behind Imogene and a young fellow with whom she was beginning a quadrille, he heard her taking him to task.

''Why do you say 'Sir' to Mr. Colville?''

''Well, I know the English laugh at us for doing it, and say it's like servants; but I never feel quite right answering just 'Yes' and 'No' to a man of his age.''

This was one of the Inglehart boys, whom he met at nearly all of these parties, and not all of whom were so respectful. Some of them treated him upon an old-boy theory, joking him as freely as if he were one of themselves, laughing his antiquated notions of art to scorn, but condoning them because he was good-natured, and because a man could not help being of his own epoch anyway. They put a caricature of him among the rest on the walls of their *trattoria*, where he once dined with them.

Mrs. Bowen did not often see him when he went to call upon Imogene, and she was not at more than two or three of the parties. Mrs. Amsden came to chaperon the girl, and apparently suffered an increase of unrequited curiosity in regard to his relations to the Bowen household, and the extraordinary development of his social activity. Colville not only went to all those evening parties, but he was in continual movement during the afternoon at receptions and at ''days,'' of which he began to think each lady had two or three. Here he drank tea, cup after cup, in reckless excitement, and at night when he came home from the dancing parties, dropping with fatigue, he could not sleep till toward morning. He woke at the usual breakfast-hour, and then went about drowsing throughout the day till the tea began again in the afternoon. He fell asleep whenever he sat down, not only in the reading-room at Viesseux's, where he disturbed the people over their newspapers by his demonstrations of somnolence, but even at church, whither he went one Sunday to please Imogene, and started awake during the service with the impression that the clergyman had been making a joke. Everybody but Imogene was smiling. At the café he slept without scruple, selecting a corner seat for the purpose, and proportioning his *buonnamano* to the indulgence of the *giovane*.* He could not tell how long he slept at these places, but sometimes it seemed to him hours.

One day he went to see Imogene, and while Effie Bowen stood prattling to him as he sat waiting for Imogene to come in, he faded light-headedly away from himself on the sofa, as if he had been in his corner at the café. Then he was aware of some one saying " 'Sh!" and he saw Effie Bowen, with her finger on her lip, turned toward Imogene, a figure of beautiful despair in the doorway. He was all tucked up with sofa pillows, and made very comfortable, by the child, no doubt. She slipped out, seeing him awake so as to leave him and Imogene alone as she had apparently been generally instructed to do, and Imogene came forward.

"What is the matter, Theodore?" she asked patiently. She had taken to calling him Theodore when they were alone. She owned that she did not like the name, but she said it was right she should call him by it, since it was his. She came and sat down beside him, where he had raised himself to a sitting posture, but she did not offer him any caress.

"Nothing," he answered. "But this climate is making me insupportably drowsy; or else the spring weather."

"Oh no; it isn't that," she said, with a slight sigh. He had left her in the middle of a german at three o'clock in the morning, but she now looked as fresh and lambent as a star. "It's the late hours. They're killing you."

Colville tried to deny it; his incoherencies dissolved themselves in a yawn, which he did not succeed in passing for a careless laugh.

"It won't do," she said, as if speaking to herself; "no, it won't do."

"Oh yes, it will," Colville protested. "I don't mind being up. I've been used to it all my life on the paper. It's just some temporary thing. It'll come all right."

"Well, no matter," said Imogene. "It makes you ridiculous, going to all those silly places, and I'd rather give it up."

The tears began to steal down her cheeks, and Colville sighed. It seemed to him that somebody or other was always crying. A man never quite gets used to the tearfulness of women.

"Oh, don't mind it," he said. "If you wish me to go, I will go! Or die in the attempt," he added, with a smile.

Imogene did not smile with him. "I don't wish you to go any more. It was a mistake in the first place, and from this out I will adapt myself to you."

"And give up all your pleasures? Do you think I would let you do that? No, indeed? Neither in this nor in anything else. I will not cut off your young life in any way, Imogene—not shorten it or diminish it. If I thought I should do that, or you would try to do it for me, I should wish I had never seen you."

"It isn't that. I know how good you are, and that you would do anything for me."

"Well, then, why don't you go to these fandangoes alone? I can see that you have me on your mind all the time, when I'm with you."

"Oughtn't I?"

"Yes, up to a certain point, but not up to the point of spoiling your fun. I will drop in now and then, but I won't try to come to all of them, after this; you'll get along perfectly well with Mrs. Amsden, and I shall be safe from her for a while. That old lady has marked me for her prey: I can see it in her glittering eyeglass. I shall fall asleep some evening between dances, and then she will get it all out of me."

Imogene still refused to smile. "No; I shall give it up. I don't think it's well, going so much without Mrs. Bowen. People will begin to talk."

"Talk?"

"Yes; they will begin to say that I had better stay with her a little more, if she isn't well."

"Why, isn't Mrs. Bowen well?" asked Colville, with trepidation.

"No; she's miserable. Haven't you noticed?"

"She sees me so seldom now. I thought it was only her headaches——"

"It's much more than that. She seems to be failing every way. The doctor has told her she ought to get away from Florence." Colville could not speak; Imogene went on. "She's always delicate, you know. And I feel that all that's keeping her here now is the news from home that I—we're waiting for."

Colville got up. "This is ghastly! She mustn't do it!"

"How can you help her doing it? If she thinks anything is right, she can't help doing it. Who could?"

Colville thought to himself that he could have said; but he was silent. At the moment he was not equal to so much joke or so much truth; and Imogene went on—

"She'd be all the more strenuous about it if it were disagreeable, and rather than accept any relief from *me* she would die."

"Is she—unkind to you?" faltered Colville.

"She is only *too* kind. You can feel that she's determined to be so—that she's said she will have nothing to reproach herself with, and she won't. You don't suppose Mrs. Bowen would be unkind to any one she disliked?"

"Ah, I didn't know," sighed Colville.

"The more she disliked them, the better she would use them. It's because our engagement is so distasteful to her that she's determined to feel that she did nothing to oppose it."

"But how can you tell that it's distasteful, then?"

"She lets you feel it by—not saying anything about it."

"I can't see how——"

"She never speaks of you. I don't believe she ever mentions your name. She asks me about the places where I've been, and about the people—every one but you. It's very uncomfortable."

"Yes," Colville, "it's uncomfortable."

"And if I allude to letters from home, she merely presses her lips together. It's perfectly wretched."

"I see. It's I whom she dislikes, and I would do anything to please her. She must know that," mused Colville aloud. "Imogene!" he exclaimed, with a sudden inspiration. "Why shouldn't I go away?"

"Go away?" she palpitated. "What should *I* do?"

The colours faded from his brilliant proposal. "Oh, I only meant till something was settled—determined—concluded; till this terrible suspense was over." He added hopelessly, "But nothing can be done!"

"I proposed," said Imogene, "that we should *all* go away. "I suggested Via Reggio—the doctor said she ought to have sea air—or Venice; but she wouldn't hear of it. No; we must wait."

"Yes, we must wait," repeated Colville hollowly. "Then nothing can be done?"

"Why, haven't you said it?"

"Oh yes—yes. I can't go away, and you can't. But couldn't we do something—get up something?"

"I don't know what you mean."

"I mean, couldn't we—amuse her somehow? help her to take her mind off herself?"

Imogene stared at him rather a long time. Then, as if she had satisfied herself in her own mind, she shook her head. "She wouldn't submit to it."

"No; she seems to take everything amiss that I do," said Colville.

"She has no right to do that," cried Imogene. "I'm sure that you're always considering her, and proposing to do things for her. I won't let you humble yourself, as if you had wronged her."

"Oh, I don't call it humbling. I—I should only be too happy if I could do *anything* that was agreeable to her."

"Very well, I will tell her," said the girl haughtily. "Shall you object to my joining you in your amusements, whatever they are? I assure you I will be very unobtrusive."

"I don't understand all this," replied Colville. "Who has proposed to exclude you? Why did you tell me anything about Mrs. Bowen if you didn't want me to say or do something? I suppose you did; but I'll withdraw the offensive proposition, whatever it was."

"There was nothing offensive. But if you pity her so much, why can't you pity me a little?"

"I didn't know anything was the matter with you. I thought you were enjoying yourself——"

"Enjoying? Keeping you up at dances till you drop asleep whenever you sit down? And then coming home and talking to a person who won't mention your name? Do you call that enjoying? I can't speak of you to any one; and no one speaks to me——"

"If you like, I will talk to you on the subject," Colville essayed, in dreary jest.

"Oh, don't joke about it! This perpetual joking, I believe it's that that's wearing me out. When I come to you for a little comfort in circumstances that drive me almost distracted, you want to amuse Mrs. Bowen, and when I ask to be allowed to share in the amusement, you laugh at me! If you don't understand it all, I'm sure *I* don't."

"Imogene!"

"No! It's very strange. There's only one explanation. You don't care for me."

"Not care for you!" cried Colville, thinking of his sufferings in the past fortnight.

"And I would have made any—*any* sacrifice for you. At least I wouldn't have made you show yourelf a mean and grudging person if you had come to me for a little sympathy."

"O poor child!" he cried, and his heart ached with the sense that she really was nothing but an unhappy child. "I do sympathise with you, and I see how hard it is for you to manage with Mrs. Bowen's dislike for me. But you mustn't think of it. I dare say it will be different; I've no doubt we can get her to look at me in some brighter light. I——" He did not know what he should urge next; but he goaded his invention, and was able to declare that if they loved each other they need not regard any one else. This flight, when accomplished, did not strike him as of very original effect, and it was with a dull surprise that he saw it sufficed for her.

"No; no one!" she exclaimed, accepting the platitude as if it were now uttered for the first time. She dried her eyes and smile. "I will tell Mrs. Bowen how you feel and what you've said, and I know she will appreciate your generosity."

"Yes," said Colville pensively; "there's nothing I won't *propose* doing for people."

She suddenly clung to him, and would not let him go. "Oh, what is the matter?" she moaned afresh. "I show out the worst that is in me, and only the worst. Do you think I shall always be so narrow-minded with you? I thought I loved you enough to be magnanimous. *You* are. It seemed to me that our lives together would be grand and large; and here I am grovelling in the lowest selfishness! I am worrying and scolding you because you wish to please some one that has been as good as my own mother to me. Do you call that noble?"

Colville did not venture any reply to a demand evidently addressed to her own conscience.

But when she asked if he really thought he had better go away, he said, "Oh no; that was a mistake."

"Because, if you do, you shall—to punish me."

"My dearest girl, why should I wish to punish you?"

"Because I've been low and mean. Now I want you to do something for Mrs. Bowen—something to amuse her; to show that we appreciate her. And I don't want you to sympathise with me at all. When I ask for your sympathy, it's a sign that I don't deserve it."

"Is that so?"

"Oh, be serious with me. I mean it. And I want to beg your pardon for something."

"Yes; what's that?"

"Can't you guess?"

"No.'

"You needn't have your lapels silk-lined. You needn't wear *boutonnières*."

"Oh, but I've had the coat changed."

"No matter! Change it back! It isn't for me to make you over. I must make myself over. It's my right it's my sacred privilege to conform to you in every way, and I humble myself in the dust for having forgotten it at the very start. Oh, *do* you think I can ever be worthy of you? I *will* try; indeed I will! I shall not wear my light dresses another time! From this out, I shall dress more in keeping with you. I boasted that I should live to comfort and console you, to recompense you for the past, and what have I been doing? Wearying and degrading you!"

"Oh no," pleaded Colville. "I am very comfortable. I don't need any compensation for the past. I need—sleep. I'm going to bed to-night at eight o'clock, and I am going to sleep twenty-four hours. Then I shall be fresh for Mrs. Fleming's ball."

"I'm not going," said Imogene briefly.

"Oh yes, you are. I'll come round to-morrow evening and see."

"No. There are to be no more parties."

"Why?"

"I can't endure them."

She was looking at him and talking at him, but she seemed far aloof in the abstraction of a sublime regret; he seemed puzzled, bewildered at herself.

Colville got away. He felt the pathos of the confusion and question to which he left her, but he felt himself powerless against it. There was but one solution to it all, and that was impossible. He could only grieve over her trouble, and wait; grieve for the irrevocable loss which made her trouble remote and impersonal to him, and submit.

XVIII

THE young clergyman whom Colville saw talking to Imogene on his first evening at Mrs. Bowen's had come back from Rome, where he had been spending a month or two, and they began to meet at Palazzo Pinti again. If they got on well enough together, they did not get on very far. The suave house-priest manners of the young clergyman offended Colville; he could hardly keep from sneering at his taste in art and books, which in fact was rather conventional; and no doubt Mr. Morton had his own reserves, under which he was perfectly civil, and only too deferential to Colville, as to an older man. Since his return, Mrs. Bowen had come back to her *salon*. She looked haggard; but she did what she could to look otherwise. She was always polite to Colville, and she was politely cordial with the clergyman. Sometimes Colville saw her driving out with him and Effie; they appeared to make excursions, and he had an impression, very obscure, that Mrs. Bowen lent the young clergyman money; that he was a superstition of hers, and she a patron of his; he must have been ten years younger than she; not more than twenty-five.

The first Sunday after his return, Colville walked home with Mr. Waters from hearing a sermon of Mr. Morton's which they agreed was rather well judged, and simply and fitly expressed.

"And he spoke with the authority of the priest," said the old minister. "His Church alone of all the Protestant Churches has preserved that to its ministers. Sometimes I have thought it was a great thing."

"Not always?" asked Colville, with a smile.

"These things are matters of mood rather than conviction with me," returned Mr. Waters. "Once they affected me very deeply; but now I shall so soon know all about it that they don't move me. But at times I think that if I were to live my life over again, I would prefer to be of some formal,

some inflexibly ritualised, religion. At solemnities—
weddings and funerals—I have been impressed with the advantage of the Anglican rite: it is the Church speaking to and
for humanity—or seems so," he added, with cheerful indifference. "Something in its favour," he continued, after a
while, "is the influence that every ritualised faith has with
women. If they apprehend those mysteries more subtly than
we, such a preference of theirs must mean a good deal. Yes;
the other Protestant systems are men's systems. Women
must have form. They don't care for freedom."

"They appear to like the formalist too, as well as the
form," said Colville, with scorn not obviously necessary.

"Oh yes; they must have everything in the concrete,"
said the old gentleman cheerfully.

"I wonder where Mr. Morton met Mrs. Bowen first,"
said Colville.

"Here, I think. I believe he had letters to her. Before you
came I used often to meet him at her house. I think she has
helped him with money at times."

"Isn't that rather an unpleasant idea?"

"Yes; it's disagreeable. And it places the ministry in a
dependent attitude. But under our system it's unavoidable.
Young men devoting themselves to the ministry frequently
receive gifts of money."

"I don't like it," cried Colville.

"They don't feel it as others would. I didn't myself. Even
at present I may be said to be living on charity. But
sometimes I have fancied that in Mr. Morton's case there
might be peculiarly mitigating circumstances."

"What do you mean?"

"When I met him first at Mrs. Bowen's I used to think
that it was Miss Graham in whom he was interested——"

"I can assure you," interrupted Colville, "that she was
never interested in him."

"Oh no; I didn't suppose that," returned the old man
tranquilly. "And I've since had reason to revise my opinion.
I think he is interested in Mrs. Bowen."

"Mrs. Bowen! And you think that would be a mitigating
circumstance in his acceptance of money from her? If he

had the spirit of a man at all, it would make it all the more revolting."

"Oh no, oh no," softly pleaded Mr. Waters. "We must not look at these things too romantically. He probably reasons that she would give him all her money if they were married."

"But he has no right to reason in that way," retorted Colville, with heat. "They are not married; it's ignoble and unmanly for him to count upon it. It's preposterous. She must be ten years older than he."

"Oh, I don't say that they're to be married," Mr. Waters replied. "But these disparities of age frequently occur in marriage. I don't like them, though sometimes I think the evil is less when it is the wife who is the elder. We look at youth and age in a gross, material way too often. Women remain young longer than men. They keep their youthful sympathies; an old woman understands a young girl. Do you— or do I—understand a young man?"

Colville laughed harshly. "It isn't *quite* the same thing, Mr. Waters. But yes; I'll admit, for the sake of argument, that I don't understand young men. I'll go further, and say that I don't like them; I'm afraid of them. And you wouldn't think," he added abruptly, "that it would be well for me to marry a girl twenty years younger than myself."

The old man glanced up at him with innocent slyness. "I prefer always to discuss these things in an impersonal way."

"But you can't discuss them impersonally with me; I'm engaged to Miss Graham. Ever since you first found me here after I told you I was going away I have wished to tell you this, and this seems as good a time as any—or as bad." The defiance faded from his voice, which dropped to a note of weary sadness. "Yes, we're engaged—or shall be, as soon as she can hear from her family. I wanted to tell you because it seemed somehow your due, and because I fancied you had a friendly interest in us both."

"Yes, that is true," returned Mr. Waters. "I wish you joy." He went through the form of offering his hand to Colville, who pressed it with anxious fervour.

"I confess," he said, "that I feel the risks of the affair. It's not that I have any dread for my own part; I have lived my life, such as it is. But the child is full of fancies about me that can't be fulfilled. She dreams of restoring my youth somehow, of retrieving the past for me, of avenging me at her own cost for an unlucky love affair that I had here twenty years ago. It's pretty of her, but it's terribly pathetic—it's tragic. I know very well that I'm a middle-aged man, and that there's no more youth for me. I'm getting grey, and I'm getting fat; I wouldn't be young if I could; it's a bore. I suppose I could keep up an illusion of youthfulness for five or six years more; and then if I could be quietly chloroformed out of the way, perhaps it wouldn't have been so very bad.''

"I have always thought,'' said Mr. Waters dreamily, "that a good deal might be said for abbreviating hopeless suffering. I have known some very good people advocate its practice by science.''

"Yes,'' answered Colville. "Perhaps I've presented that point too prominently. What I wished you to understand was that I don't care for myself; that I consider only the happiness of this young girl that's somehow—I hardly know how—been put in my keeping. I haven't forgotten the talks that we've had heretofore on this subject, and it would be affectation and bad taste in me to ignore them. Don't be troubled at anything you've said; it was probably true, and I'm sure it was sincere. Sometimes I think that the kindest—the least cruel—thing I could do would be to break with her, to leave her. But I know that I shall do nothing of the kind; I shall drift. The child is very dear to me. She has great and noble qualities; she's supremely unselfish; she loves me through her mistaken pity, and because she thinks she can sacrifice herself to me. But she can't. Everything is against that; she doesn't know how, and there is no reason why. I don't express it very well. I think nobody clearly understands it but Mrs. Bowen, and I've somehow alienated her.''

He became aware that his self-abnegation was taking the character of self-pity, and he stopped.

Mr. Waters seemed to be giving the subject serious attention in the silence that ensued. "There is this to be remembered," he began, "which we don't consider in our mere speculations upon any phase of human affairs; and that is the wonderful degree of amelioration that any given difficulty finds in the realisation. It is the anticipation, not the experience, that is the trial. In a case of this kind, facts of temperament, of mere association, of union, work unexpected mitigations; they not only alleviate, they allay. You say that she cherishes an illusion concerning you: well, with women, nothing is so indestructible as an illusion. Give them any chance at all, and all the forces of their nature combine to preserve it. And if, as you say, she is so dear to you, that in itself is almost sufficient. I can well understand your misgivings, springing as they do from a sensitive conscience; but we may reasonably hope that they are exaggerated. Very probably there will not be the rapture for her that there would be if—if you were younger; but the chances of final happiness are great—yes, very considerable. She will learn to appreciate what is really best in you, and you already understand her. Your love for her is the key to the future. Without that, of course——"

"Oh, of course," interrupted Colville hastily. Every touch of this comforter's hand had been a sting; and he parted with him in that feeling of utter friendlessness involving a man who has taken counsel upon the confession of half his trouble.

Something in Mrs. Bowen's manner when he met her next made him think that perhaps Imogene had been telling her of the sympathy he had expressed for her ill-health. It was in the evening, and Imogene and Mr. Morton were looking over a copy of *The Marble Faun*,* which he had illustrated with photographs at Rome. Imogene asked Colville to look at it too, but he said he would examine it later; he had his opinion of people who illustrated *The Marble Faun* with photographs; it surprised him that she seemed to find something novel and brilliant in the idea.

Effie Bowen looked round where she was kneeling on a chair beside the couple with the book, and seeing Colville wandering neglectedly about before he placed himself, she jumped down and ran and caught his hand.

"Well, what now?" he asked, with a dim smile, as she began to pull him toward the sofa. When he should be expelled from Palazzo Pinti he would really miss the worship of that little thing. He knew that her impulse had been to console him for his exclusion from the pleasures that Imogene and Mr. Morton were enjoying.

"Nothing. Just talk," she said, making him fast in a corner of the sofa by crouching tight against him.

"What about? About which is the pleasantest season?"

"Oh no; we've talked about that so often. Besides, of course you'd say spring, now that it's coming on so nicely."

"Do you think I'm so changeable as that? Haven't I always said winter when this question of the seasons was up? And I say it now. Shan't you be awfully sorry when you can't have a pleasant little fire on the hearth like this any more?"

"Yes; I know. But it's very nice having the flowers, too. The grass was all full of daisies to-day—perfectly powdered with them."

"To-day? Where?"

"At the Cascine. And in under the trees there were millions of violets and crow's-feet. Mr. Morton helped me to get them for mamma and Imogene. And we stayed so long that when we drove home the daisies had all shut up, and the little pink leaves outside made it look like a field of red clover. Are you never going there any more?"

Mrs. Bowen came in. From the fact that there was no greeting between her and Mr. Morton, Colville inferred that she was returning to the room after having already been there. She stood a moment, with a little uncertainty, when she had shaken hands with him, and then dropped upon the sofa beyond Effie. The little girl ran one hand through Colville's arm, and the other through her mother's, and gripped them fast. "Now I have got you both," she triumphed, and smiled first into her face, and then into his.

"Be quiet, Effie," said her mother, but she submitted.

"I hope you're better for your drive to-day, Mrs. Bowen. Effie has been telling me about it."

"We stayed out a long time. Yes, I think the air did me good; but I'm not an invalid, you know."

"Oh no."

"I'm feeling a little fagged. And the weather was tempting. I suppose you've been taking one of your long walks."

"No, I've scarcely stirred out. I usually feel like going to meet the spring a little more than half-way; but this year I don't, somehow."

"A good many people are feeling rather languid, I believe," said Mrs. Bowen.

"I hope you'll get away from Florence," said Colville.

"Oh," she returned, with a faint flush, "I'm afraid Imogene exaggerated that a little." She added, "You are very good."

She was treating him more kindly than she had ever done since that Sunday afternoon when he came in with Imogene to say that he was going to stay. It might be merely because she had worn out her mood of severity, as people do, returning in good-humour to those with whom they were offended, merely through the reconciling force of time. She did not look at him, but this was better than meeting his eye with that interceptive glance. A strange peace touched his heart. Imogene and the young clergyman at the table across the room were intent on the book still; he was explaining and expatiating, and she listening. Colville saw that he had a fine head, and an intelligent, handsome, gentle face. When he turned again to Mrs. Bowen it was with the illusion that she had been saying something; but she was, in fact, sitting mute, and her face, with its bright colour, showed pathetically thin.

"I should imagine that Venice would be good for you," he said.

"It's still very harsh there, I hear. No; when we leave Florence, I think we will go to Switzerland."

"Oh, not to Madame Schebres's," pleaded the child, turning upon her.

"No, not to Madame Schebres," consented the mother. She continued, addressing Colville: "I was thinking of Lausanne. Do you know Lausanne at all?"

"Only from Gibbon's report.* It's hardly up to date."

"I thought of taking a house there for the summer," said

Mrs. Bowen, playing with Effie's fingers. "It's pleasant by the lake, I suppose."

"It's lovely by the lake!" cried the child. "Oh, do go, mamma! I could get a boat and learn to row. Here you can't row, the Arno's so swift."

"The air would bring you up," said Colville to Mrs. Bowen. "Switzerland's the only country where you're perfectly sure of waking new every morning."

This idea interested the child. "Waking new!" she repeated.

"Yes; perfectly made over. You wake up another person. Shouldn't you think that would be nice!"

"No."

"Well, I shouldn't, in your place. But in mine, I much prefer to wake up another person. Only it's pretty hard on the other person."

"How queer you are!" The child set her teeth for fondness of him, and seizing his cheeks between her hands, squeezed them hard, admiring the effect upon his features, which in some respects was not advantageous.

"Effie!" cried her mother sternly; and she dropped to her place again, and laid hold of Colville's arm for protection. "You are really very rude. I shall send you to bed."

"Oh no, don't, Mrs. Bowen," he begged. "I'm responsible for these violences. Effie used to be a very well behaved child before she began playing with me. It's all my fault."

They remained talking on the sofa together, while Imogene and Mr. Morton continued to interest themselves in the book. From time to time she looked over at them, and then turned again to the young clergyman, who, when he had closed the book, rested his hands on its top and began to give an animated account of something, conjecturably his sojourn in Rome.

In a low voice, and with pauses adjusted to the occasional silences of the young people across the room, Mrs. Bowen told Colville how Mr. Morton was introduced to her by an old friend who was greatly interested in him. She said, frankly, that she had been able to be of use to him, and that he was now going back to America very soon; it was as if she

were privy to the conjecture that had come to the surface in
his talk with Mr. Waters, and wished him to understand exactly how matters stood with the young clergyman and
herself. Colville, indeed, began to be more tolerant of him;
he succeeded in praising the sermon he had heard him
preach.

"Oh, he has talent." said Mrs. Bowen.

They fell into the old, almost domestic strain, from which
she broke at times with an effort, but returning as if helplessly to it. He had the gift of knowing how not to take an
advantage with women; that sense of unconstraint in them
fought in his favour; when Effie dropped her head wearily
against his arm, her mother even laughed in sending her off
to bed; she had hitherto been serious. Imogene said she
would go to see her tucked in, and that sent the clergyman
to say good-night to Mrs. Bowen and to put an end to Colville's audience.

In these days, when Colville came every night to Palazzo
Pinti, he got back the tone he had lost in the past fortnight.
He thought that it was the complete immunity from his late
pleasures, and the regular and sufficient sleep, which had set
him firmly on his feet again, but he did not inquire very
closely. Imogene went two or three times, after she had
declared she would go no more, from the necessity women
feel of blunting the edge of comment; but Colville profited
instantly and fully by the release from the parties which she
offered him. He did not go even to afternoon tea-drinkings;
the "days" of the different ladies, which he had been so
diligent to observe, knew him no more. At the hours when
society assembled in this house or that and inquired for him,
or wondered about him, he was commonly taking a nap, and
he was punctually in bed every night at eleven, after his
return from Mrs. Bowen's.

He believed, of course, that he went there because he now
no longer met Imogene elsewhere, and he found the house
pleasanter than it had ever been since the veglione. Mrs.
Bowen's relenting was not continuous, however. There were
times that seemed to be times of question and of a struggle
with her, when she vacillated between the old cordiality and

the later alienation; when she went beyond the former, or lapsed into moods colder and more repellent than the latter. It would have been difficult to mark the moment when these struggles ceased altogether, and an evening passed in unbroken kindness between them. But afterwards Colville could remember an emotion of grateful surprise at a subtle word or action of hers in which she appeared to throw all restraint— scruple or rancour, whichever it might be—to the winds, and become perfectly his friend again. It must have been by compliance with some wish or assent to some opinion of his; what he knew was that he was not only permitted, he was invited, to feel himself the most favoured guest. The charming smile, so small and sweet, so very near to bitterness, came back to her lips, the deeply fringed eyelids were lifted to let the sunny eyes stream upon him. She did, now, whatever he asked her. She consulted his taste and judgment on many points; she consented to resume, when she should be a little stronger, their visits to the churches and galleries: it would be a shame to go away from Florence without knowing them thoroughly. It came to her asking him to drive with her and Imogene in the Cascine; and when Imogene made some excuse not to go, Mrs. Bowen did not postpone the drive, but took Colville and Effie.

They drove quite down to the end of the Cascine, and got out there to admire the gay monument, with the painted bust, of the poor young Indian prince* who died in Florence. They strolled all about, talking of the old times in the Cascine, twenty years before; and walking up the road beside the canal, while the carriage slowly followed, they stopped to enjoy the peasants lying asleep in the grass on the other bank. Colville and Effie gathered wild-flowers, and piled them in her mother's lap when she remounted to the carriage and drove along while they made excursions into the little dingles beside the road. Some people who overtook them in these sylvan pleasures reported the fact at a reception to which they were going, and Mrs. Amsden, whose mind had been gradually clearing under the simultaneous withdrawal of Imogene and Colville from society, professed herself again as thickly clouded as a weather-glass before a storm. She appealed to the sympathy of others against this hardship.

Mrs. Bowen took Colville home to dinner; Mr. Morton was coming, she said, and he must come too. At table the young clergyman made her his compliment on her look of health, and she said, Yes; she had been driving, and she believed that she needed nothing but to be in the air a little more, as she very well could, now the spring weather was really coming. She said that they had been talking all winter of going to Fiesole, where Imogene had never been yet; and upon comparison it appeared that none of them had yet been to Fiesole except herself. Then they must all go together, she said; the carriage would hold four very comfortably.

"Ah! that leaves me out," said Colville, who had caught sight of Effie's fallen countenance.

"Oh no. How is that? It leaves Effie out."

"It's the same thing. But I might ride, and Effie might give me her hand to hold over the side of the carriage; that would sustain me."

"We could take her between us, Mrs. Bowen," suggested Imogene. "The back seat is wide."

"Then the party is made up," said Colville, "and Effie hasn't demeaned herself by asking to go where she wasn't invited."

The child turned inquiringly toward her mother, who met her with an indulgent smile, which became a little flush of grateful appreciation when it reached Colville; but Mrs. Bowen ignored Imogene in the matter altogether.

The evening passed delightfully. Mr. Morton had another book which he had brought to show Imogene, and Mrs. Bowen sat a long time at the piano, striking this air and that of the songs which she used to sing when she was a girl: Colville was trying to recall them. When he and Imogene were left alone for their adieux, they approached each other in an estrangement through which each tried to break.

"Why don't you scold me?" she asked. "I have neglected you the whole evening."

"How have you neglected me?"

"How? Ah! if you don't know——"

"No. I dare say I must be very stupid. I saw you talking with Mr. Morton, and you seemed interested. I thought I'd better not intrude."

She seemed uncertain of his intention, and then satisfied of its simplicity.

"Isn't it pleasant to have Mrs. Bowen in the old mood again?" he asked.

"Is she in the old mood?"

"Why, yes. Haven't you noticed how cordial she is?"

"I thought she was rather colder than usual."

"Colder!" The chill of the idea penetrated even through the density of Colville's selfish content. A very complex emotion, which took itself for indignation, throbbed from his heart. "Is she cold with you, Imogene?"

"Oh, if you saw nothing——"

"No; and I think you must be mistaken. She never speaks of you without praising you."

"Does she speak of me?" asked the girl, with her honest eyes wide open upon him.

"Why, no," Colville acknowledged. "Come to reflect, it's I who speak of you. But how—how is she cold with you?"

"Oh, I dare say it's a delusion of mine. Perhaps I'm cold with her."

"Then don't be so, my dear! Be sure that she's your friend—true and good. Good night."

He caught the girl in his arms, and kissed her tenderly. She drew away, and stood a moment with her repellent fingers on his breast.

"Is it all for me?" she asked.

"For the whole obliging and amiable world," he answered gaily.

XIX

THE next time Colville came he found himself alone with Imogene, who asked him what he had been doing all day.

"Oh, living along till evening. What have you?"

She did not answer at once, nor praise his speech for the devotion implied in it. After a while she said: "Do you believe in courses of reading? Mr. Morton has taken up a course of reading in Italian poetry. He intends to master it."

"Does he?"

"Yes. Do you think something of the kind would be good for me?"

"Oh, if you thirst for conquest. But I should prefer to rest on my laurels if I were you."

Imogene did not smile. "Mr. Morton thinks I should enjoy a course of Kingsley.* He says he's very earnest."

"Oh, immensely. But aren't you earnest enough already, my dear?"

"Do you think I'm too earnest?"

"No; I should say you were just right."

"You know better than that. I wish you would criticise me sometimes."

"Oh, I'd rather not."

"Why? Don't you see anything to criticise in me? Are you satisfied with me in every way? You ought to think. You ought to think now. Do you think that I am doing right in all respects? Am I all that I could be to you, and to you alone? If I am wrong in the least thing, criticise me, and I will try to be better."

"Oh, you might criticise back, and I shouldn't like that."

"Then you don't approve of a course of Kingsley?" asked the girl.

"Does that follow? But if you're going in for earnestness, why don't you take up a course of Carlyle?"*

"Do you think that would be better than Kingsley?"

"Not a bit. But Carlyle's so earnest that he can't talk straight."

"I can't make out what you mean. Wouldn't you like me to improve?"

"Not much," laughed Colville. "If you did, I don't know what I should do. I should have to begin to improve too, and I'm very comfortable as I am."

"I should wish to do it to—to be more worthy of you," grieved the girl, as if deeply disappointed at his frivolous behaviour.

He could not help laughing, but he was sorry, and would have taken her hand; she kept it from him, and removed to the farthest corner of the sofa. Apparently, however, her ideal did not admire of open pique, and she went on trying to talk seriously with him.

"You think, don't you, that we oughtn't to let a day pass without storing away some thought—suggestion——"

"Oh, there's no hurry," he said lazily. "Life is rather a long affair—if you live. There appears to be plenty of time, though people say not, and I think it would be rather odious to make every day of use. Let a few of them go by without doing anything for you! And as for reading, why not read when you're hungry, just as you eat? Shouldn't you hate to take up a course of roast beef, or a course of turkey?"

"Very well, then," said Imogene. "I shall not begin Kingsley."

"Yes, do it. I dare say Mr. Morton's quite right. He will look at these things more from your own point of view. All the Kingsley novels are in the Tauchnitz. By all means do what he says."

"I will do what *you* say."

"Oh, but I say nothing."

"Then I will do nothing."

Colville laughed at this too, and soon after the clergyman appeared. Imogene met him so coldly that Colville felt obliged to make him some amends by a greater show of cordiality than he felt. But he was glad of the effort, for he began to like him as he talked to him; it was easy for him to like people; the young man showed sense and judgment, and if he was a little academic in his mind and manners, Colville tolerantly reflected that some people seemed to be born so, and that he was probably not artificial, as he had once imagined from the ecclesiastical scrupulosity of his dress.

Imogene ebbed away to the piano in the corner of the room, and struck some chords on it. At each stroke the young clergyman, whose eyes had wandered a little toward her from the first, seemed to vibrate in response. The conversation became incoherent before Mrs. Bowen joined them. Then, by a series of illogical processess, the clergyman was standing beside Imogene at the piano, and Mrs. Bowen was sitting beside Colville on the sofa.

"Isn't there to be any Effie, to-night?" he asked.

"No. She has been up too much of late. And I wished to speak with you—about Imogene."

"Yes," said Colville, not very eagerly. At that moment he could have chosen another topic.

"It is time that her mother should have got my letter. In less than a fortnight we ought to have an answer."

"Well?" said Colville, with a strange constriction of the heart.

"Her mother is a person of very strong character; her husband is absorbed in business, and defers to her in everything."

"It isn't an uncommon American situation," said Colville, relieving his tension by this excursion.

Mrs. Bowen ignored it. "I don't know how she may look at the affair. She may give her assent at once, or she may decide that nothing has taken place till—she sees you."

"I could hardly blame her for that," he answered submissively.

"It isn't a question of that," said Mrs. Bowen. "It's a question of—others. Mr. Morton was here before you came, and I know he was interested in Imogene—I am certain of it. He has come back, and he sees no reason why he should not renew his attentions."

"No—o—o," faltered Colville.

"I wish you to realise the fact."

"But what would you——"

"I told you," said Mrs. Bowen, with a full return of that severity whose recent absence Colville had found so comfortable, "that I can't advise or suggest anything at all."

He was long and miserably silent. At last, "Did you ever think," he asked, "did you ever suppose—that is to say, did you ever suspect that—she—that Imogene was—at all interested in him?"

"I think she was—at one time," said Mrs. Bowen promptly.

Colville sighed, with a wandering disposition to whistle.

"But that is nothing," she went on. "People have many passing fancies. The question is, what are you going to do now? I want to know, as Mr. Morton's friend."

"Ah, I wish you wanted to know as *my* friend, Mrs. Bowen!" A sudden thought flashed upon him. "Why shouldn't I go away from Florence till Imogene hears from her mother? That seemed to me right in the first place. There is no tie that binds her to me. I hold her to nothing. If she finds in my absence that she likes this young man better——" An expression of Mrs. Bowen's face stopped him. He perceived that he had said something very shocking to her; he perceived that the thing was shocking in itself, but it was not that which he cared for. "I don't mean that I won't hold myself true to her as long as she will. I recognise my responsibility fully. I know that I am answerable for all this, and that no one else is; and I am ready to bear any penalty. But what I can't bear is that you should misunderstand me, that you should—— I have been so wretched ever since you first began to blame me for my part in this, and so happy this past fortnight that I can't—I *won't*—go back to that state of things. No; you have no right to relent toward me, and then fling me off as you have tried to do to-night! I have some feeling too—some rights. You should receive me as a friend, or not at all! How can I live if you——"

She had been making little efforts as if to rise; now she forced herself to her feet, and ran from the room.

The young people looked up from their music; some wave of the sensation had spread to them, but seeing Colville remain seated, they went on with their playing till he rose.

Then Imogene called out, "Isn't Mrs. Bowen coming back?"

"I don't know; I think not," answered Colville stupidly, standing where he had risen.

She hastened questioning toward him. "What is the matter? Isn't she well?"

Mr. Morton's face expressed a polite share in her anxiety.

"Oh yes; quite, I believe," Colville replied.

"She heard Effie call, I suppose," suggested the girl.

"Yes, yes; I think so; that is—yes. I must be going. Good night."

He took her hand and went away, leaving the clergyman still there; but he lingered only for a report from Mrs. Bowen, which Imogene hurried to get. She sent word that she would join them presently. But Mr. Morton said that it was late already, and he would beg Miss Graham to say good-night for him. When Mrs. Bowen returned Imogene was alone.

She did not seem surprised or concerned at that. "Imogene, I have been talking to Mr. Colville about you and Mr. Morton."

The girl started and turned pale.

"It is almost time to hear from your mother, and she may consent to your engagement. Then you must be prepared to act."

"Act?"

"To make it known. Matters can't go on as they have been going. I told Mr. Colville that Mr. Morton ought to know at once."

"Why ought he to know?" asked Imogene, doubtless with that impulse to temporise which is natural to the human soul in questions of right and interest. She sank into the chair beside which she had been standing.

"If your mother consents, you will feel bound to Mr. Colville?"

"Yes," said the girl.

"And if she refuses?"

"He has my word. I will keep my word to him," replied Imogene huskily. "Nothing shall make me break it."

"Very well, then!" exclaimed Mrs. Bowen. "We need not wait for your mother's answer. Mr. Morton ought to know and he ought to know at once. Don't try to blind yourself, Imogene, to what you see as plainly as I do. He is in love with you."

"Oh," moaned the girl.

"Yes; you can't deny it. And it's cruel, it's treacherous, to let him go on thinking that you are free."

"I will never see him again."

"Ah! that isn't enough. He has a claim to know why. I will not let him be treated so."

They were both silent. Then, "What did Mr. Colville say?" asked Imogene.

"He? I don't know that he said anything. He——" Mrs. Bowen stopped.

Imogene rose from her chair.

"I will not let him tell Mr. Morton. It would be too indelicate."

"And shall you let it go on so?"

"No. I will tell him myself."

"How will you tell him?"

"I will tell him if he speaks to me."

"You will let it come to that?"

"There is no other way. I shall suffer more than he."

"But you will deserve to suffer, and your suffering will not help him."

Imogene trembled into her chair again.

"I see," said Mrs. Bowen bitterly, "how it will be at last. It will be as it has been from the first." She began to walk up and down the room, mechanically putting the chairs in place, and removing the disorder in which the occupancy of several people leaves a room at the end of an evening. She closed the piano, which Imogene had forgot to shut, with a clash that jarred the strings from their silence. "But I will do it, and I wonder——"

"You will speak to him?" faltered the girl.

"Yes!" returned Mrs. Bowen vehemently, and arresting herself in her rapid movements. "It won't do for you to tell him, and you won't let Mr. Colville."

"No, I can't." said Imogene, slowly shaking her head. "But I will discourage him; I will not see him any more." Mrs. Bowen silently confronted her. "I will not see any one now till I have heard from home."

"And how will that help? He must have some explanation, and I will have to make it. What shall it be?"

Imogene did not answer. She said: "I will not have any one know what is between me and Mr. Colville till I have heard from home. If they try to refuse, then it will be for him to take me against their will. But if he doesn't choose to do that, then he shall be free, and I won't have him humiliated a second time before the world. *This* time *he* shall be the one to reject. And I don't care who suffers. The more I prize the person, the gladder I shall be; and if I could suffer before everybody I would. If people ever find it out, I will tell them that it was he who broke it off." She rose again from her chair, and stood flushed and thrilling with the notion of her self-sacrifice. Out of the tortuous complexity of the situation she had evolved this brief triumph, in which she rejoiced as if it were enduring success. But she suddenly fell from it in the dust. "Oh, what can I do for him? How can I make him feel more and more that I would give up anything, everything, for him! It's because he asks nothing and wants nothing it's so hard! If I could see that he was unhappy, as I did once! If I could see that he was at all different since—since—— Oh, what I dread is this smooth tranquillity! If our lives could only be stormy and full of cares and anxieties and troubles that I could take on myself, then, then I shouldn't be afraid of the future! But I'm afraid they won't be so—no, I'm afraid that they will be easy and quiet, and then what shall I do? O Mrs. Bowen, do you think he cares for me?"

Mrs. Bowen turned white; she did not speak.

The girl wrung her hands. "Sometimes it seems as if he didn't—as if I had forced myself on him through a mistake, and he had taken me to save me from the shame of knowing that I had made a mistake. Do you think that is true? If you can only tell me that it isn't—— Or, no! If it is true, tell me that! *That* would be real mercy."

The other trembled, as if physically beaten upon by this appeal. But she gathered herself together rigidly. "How can I answer you such a thing as that! I mustn't listen to you; you mustn't ask me." She turned and left the girl standing still in her attitude of imploring. But in her own room, where she locked herself in, sobs mingled with the laughter which broke crazily from her lips as she removed this ribbon and that jewel, and pulled the bracelets from her wrists. A man would have plunged from the house and walked the night away; a woman must wear it out in her bed.

XX

IN the morning Mrs. Bowen received a note from her banker covering a despatch by cable from America. It was from Imogene's mother; it acknowledged the letters they had written, and announced that she sailed that day for Liverpool. It was dated at New York, and it was to be inferred that after perhaps writing in answer to their letters, she had suddenly made up her mind to come out.

"Yes, that is it," said Imogene, to whom Mrs. Bowen hastened with the despatch. "Why should she have telegraphed to *you*?" she asked coldly, but with a latent fire of resentment in her tone.

"You must ask her when she comes," returned Mrs. Bowen, with all her gentleness. "It won't be long now."

They looked as if they had neither of them slept; but the girl's vigil seemed to have made her wild and fierce, like some bird that has beat itself all night against its cage, and still from time to time feebly strikes the bars with its wings. Mrs. Bowen was simply worn to apathy.

"What shall you do about this?" she asked.

"Do about it? Oh, I will think. I will try not to trouble you."

"Imogene!"

"I shall have to tell Mr. Colville. But I don't know that I shall tell him at once. Give me the despatch, please." She possessed herself of it greedily, offensively. "I shall ask you not to speak of it."

"I will do whatever you wish."

"Thank you."

Mrs. Bowen left the room, but she turned immediately to re-open the door she had closed behind her.

"We were to have gone to Fiesole to-morrow," she said inquiringly.

"We can still go if the day is fine," returned the girl. "Nothing is changed. I wish very much to go. Couldn't we go to-day?" she added, with eager defiance.

"It's too late to-day," said Mrs. Bowen quietly. "I will write to remind the gentlemen."

"Thank you. I wish we could have gone to-day."

"You can have the carriage if you wish to drive any-where," said Mrs. Bowen.

"I will take Effie to see Mrs. Amsden." But Imogene changed her mind, and went to call upon two Misses Guic-ciardi, the result of an international marriage, whom Mrs. Bowen did not like very well. Imogene drove with them to the Cascine, where they bowed to a numerous military ac-quaintance, and they asked her if Mrs. Bowen would let her join them in a theatre that evening: they were New Yorkers by birth, and it was to be a theatre party in the New York style; they were to be chaperoned by a young married lady; two young men cousins of theirs, just out from America, had taken the box.

When Imogene returned home she told Mrs. Bowen that she had accepted this invitation. Mrs. Bowen said nothing, but when one of the young men came up to hand Imogene down to the carriage, which was waiting with the others at the gate, she could not have shown a greater tolerance of his second-rate New Yorkiness if she had been a Boston dowager offering him the scrupulous hospitalities of her city.

Imogene came in at midnight; she hummed an air of the opera as she took off her wraps and ornaments in her room, and this in the quiet of the hour had a terrible, almost pro-fane effect: it was as if some other kind of girl had whistled. She showed the same nonchalance at breakfast, where she was prompt, and answered Mrs. Bowen's inquiries about her pleasure the night before with a liveliness that ignored the polite resolution that prompted them.

Mr. Morton ws the first to arrive, and if his discourage-ment began at once, the first steps masked themselves in a reckless welcome, which seemed to fill him with joy, and Mrs. Bowen with silent perplexity. The girl ran on about her evening at the opera, and about the weather, and the excur-sion they were going to make; and after an apparently needless ado over the bouquet which he brought her, together with one for Mrs. Bowen, she put it into her belt, and made Colville notice it when he came: he had not thought to bring flowers.

He turned from her hilarity with anxious question to Mrs. Bowen, who did not meet his eye, and who snubbed Effie when the child found occasion to whisper: "*I* think Imogene is acting very strangely, for *her*; don't you, mamma? It seems as if going with those Guicciardi girls just once had spoiled her.

"Don't make remarks about people, Effie," said her mother sharply. "It isn't nice in little girls, and I don't want you to do it. You talk too much lately."

Effie turned grieving away from this rejection, and her face did not light up even at the whimsical sympathy in Colville's face, who saw that she had met a check of some sort; he had to take her on his knee and coax and kiss her before her wounded feelings were visibly healed. He put her down with a sighing wish that some one could take him up and soothe his troubled sensibilities too, and kept her hand in his while he saw waiting for the last of those last moments in which the hurrying delays of ladies preparing for an excursion seem never to end.

When they were ready to get into the carriage, the usual contest of self-sacrifice arose, which Imogene terminated by mounting to the front seat; Mr. Morton hastened to take the seat beside her, and Colville was left to sit with Effie and her mother. "You old people will be safer back there," said Imogene. It was a little joke which she addressed to the child, but a gleam from her eye as she turned to speak to the young man at her side visited Colville in desperate defiance. He wondered what she was about in that allusion to an idea which she had shrunk from so sensitively hitherto. But he found himself in a situation which he could not penetrate at any point. When he spoke with Mrs. Bowen, it was with a dark undercurrent of conjecture as to how and when she expected him to tell Mr. Morton of his relation to Imogene, or whether she still expected him to do it; when his eyes fell upon the face of the young man, he despaired as to the terms in which he should put the fact; any form in which he tacitly dramatised it remained very embarrassing, for he felt bound to say that while he held himself promised in the matter, he did not allow her to feel herself so.

A sky of American blueness and vastness, a mellow sun, and a delicate breeze did all that these things could for them, as they began the long, devious climb of the hills crowned by the ancient Etruscan city. At first they were all in the constraint of their own and one another's moods, known or imagined, and no talk began till the young clergyman turned to Imogene and asked, after a long look at the smiling landscape, "What sort of weather do you suppose they are having at Buffalo to-day?"

"At Buffalo?" she repeated, as if the place had only a dim existence in her remotest consciousness. "Oh! The ice isn't near out of the lake yet. You can't count on it before the first of May."

"And the first of May comes sooner or later, according to the season," said Colville. "I remember coming on once in the middle of the month, and the river was so full of ice between Niagara Falls and Buffalo that I had to shut the car window that I'd kept open all the way through Southern Canada. But we have very little of that local weather at home; our weather is as democratic and continental as our political constitution. Here it's March or May any time from September till June, according as there's snow on the mountains or not."

The young man smiled. "But don't you like," he asked with deference, "this slow, orderly advance of the Italian spring, where the flowers seem to come out one by one, and every blossom has its appointed time?"

"Oh yes, it's very well in its way; but I prefer the rush of the American spring; no thought of mild weather this morning; a warm, gusty rain tomorrow night; day after to-morrow a burst of blossoms and flowers and young leaves and birds. I don't know whether we were made for our climate or our climate was made for us, but its impatience and lavishness seem to answer some inner demand of our go-ahead souls. This happens to be the week of the peach blossoms here, and you see their pink everywhere to-day, and you don't see anything else in the blossom line. But

imagine the American spring abandoning a whole week of
her precious time to the exclusive use of peach blossoms! She
wouldn't do it; she's got too many other things on hand.''

Effie had stretched out over Colville's lap, and with her
elbow sunk deep in his knee, was resting her chin in her
hand and taking the facts of the landscape thoroughly in.
''Do they have just a week?'' she asked.

''Not an hour more or less,'' said Colville. ''If they found
an almond blossom hanging round anywhere after their time
came, they would make an awful row; and if any lazy little
peach-blow hadn't got out by the time their week was up,
it would have to stay in till next year; the pear blossoms
wouldn't let it come out.''

''Wouldn't they?'' murmured the child, in dreamy sympathy with this belated peach-blow.

''Well, that's what people say. In America it would be
allowed to come out any time. It's a free country.''

Mrs. Bowen offered to draw Effie back to a posture of
more decorum, but Colville put his arm round the litle girl.
''Oh, let her stay! It doesn't incommode me and she must
be getting such a novel effect of the landscape.''

The mother fell back into her former attitude of jaded
passivity. He wondered whether she had changed her mind
about having him speak to Mr. Morton; her quiescence
might well have been indifference; one could have said,
knowing the whole situation, that she had made up her mind
to let things take their course, and struggle with them no
longer.

He could not believe that she felt content with him; she
must feel far otherwise; and he took refuge, as he had the
power of doing, from the discomfort of his own thoughts
in jesting with the child, and mocking her with this
extravagance and that; the discomfort then became merely
a dull ache that insisted upon itself at intervals, like a
grumbling tooth.

The prospect was full of that mingled wildness and sub-
ordination that gives its supreme charm to the Italian landscape; and without elements of great variety, it combined
them in infinite picturesqueness. There were olive orchards

and vineyards, and again vineyards and olive orchards. Closer to the farm-houses and cottages there were peaches and other fruit trees and kitchen-gardens; broad ribbons of grain waved between the ranks of trees; around the white villas the spires of the cypresses pieced the blue air. Now and then they came to a villa with weather-beaten statues strutting about its parterres. A mild, pleasant heat brooded upon the fields and roofs, and the city, dropping lower and lower as they mounted, softened and blended its towers and monuments in a sombre mass shot with gleams of white.

Colville spoke to Imogene, who withdrew her eyes from it with a sigh, after long brooding upon the scene. "You can do nothing with it, I see."

"With what?"

"The landscape. It's too full of every possible interest. What a history is written all over it, public and private! If you don't take it simply like any other landscape, it becomes an oppression. It's well that tourists come to Italy so ignorant, and keep so. Otherwise they couldn't live to get home again; the past would crush them."

Imogene scrutinised him as if to extract some personal meaning from his words, and then turned her head away. The clergyman addressed him with what was like a respectful toleration of the drolleries of a gifted but eccentric man, the flavour of whose talk he was beginning to taste.

"You don't really mean that one shouldn't come to Italy as well informed as possible?"

"Well, I did," said Colville, "but I don't."

The young man pondered this, and Imogene started up with an air of rescuing them from each other—as if she would not let Mr. Morton think Colville trivial or Colville consider the clergyman stupid, but would do what she could to take their minds off the whole question. Perhaps she was not very clear as to how this was to be done; at any rate she did not speak, and Mrs. Bowen came to her support from whatever motive of her own. It might have been from a sense of the injustice of letting Mr. Morton suffer from the complications that involved herself and the others. The affair had been going very hitchily ever since they started,

with the burden of the conversation left to the two men and
that helpless girl; if it were not to be altogether a failure she
must interfere.

"Did you ever hear of Gratiano when you were in
Venice?" she asked Mr. Morton.

"Is he one of their new water-colourists?" returned the
young man. "I heard they had quite a school there now."

"No," said Mrs. Bowen, ignoring her failure as well as
she could; "he was a famous talker; he loved to speak an infinite deal of nothing more than any man in Venice."

"An ancestor of mine, Mr. Morton," said Colville. "a
poor, honest man, who did his best to make people forget
that the ladies were silent. Thank you, Mrs. Bowen, for
mentioning him. I wish he were with us to-day."

The young man laughed. "Oh, in the *Merchant of
Venice!*"*

"No other," said Colville.

"I confess," said Mrs. Bowen, "that I *am* rather stupid
this morning. I suppose it's the softness of the air; it's been
harsh and irritating so long. It makes me drowsy."

"Don't mind *us*," returned Colville. "We will call you at
important points." They were driving into a village at which
people stop sometimes to admire the works of art in its
church. Here, for example, is—— What place is this?" he
asked of the coachman.

"San Domenico."

"I should know it again by its beggars." Of all ages and
sexes they swarmed round the carriage, which the driver had
instinctively slowed to oblige them, and thrust forward their
hands and hats. Colville gave Effie his small change to
distribute among them, at sight of which they streamed
down the street from every direction. Those who had received
brought forward the halt and blind, and did not scruple to propose being rewarded for this service. At the same time they did
not mind his laughing in their faces; they laughed too, and
went off content, or as nearly so as beggars ever are. He but-
toned up his pocket as they drove on more rapidly. "I am the
only person of no principle—except Effie— in the carriage,
and yet I am at this moment carrying more blessings out

of this village than I shall ever know what to do with. Mrs. Bowen, I know, is regarding me with severe disapproval. She thinks that I ought to have sent the beggars of San Domenico to Florence, where they would all be shut up in the Pia Casa di Ricovero, and taught some useful occupation. It's terrible in Florence. You can walk through Florence now and have no appeal made to your better nature that is not made at the appellant's risk of imprisonment. When I was there before, you had opportunities of giving at every turn."

"You can send a cheque to the Pia Casa," said Mrs. Bowen.

"Ah, but what good would that do me? When I give I want the pleasure of it; I want to see my beneficiary cringe under my bounty. But I've tried in vain to convince you that the world has gone wrong in other ways. Do you remember the one-armed man who we used to give to on the Lung' Arno? That persevering sufferer has been repeatedly arrested for mendicancy, and obliged to pay a fine out of his hard earnings to escape being sent to your Pia Casa."

Mrs. Bowen smiled, and said, Was he living yet? in a pensive tone of reminiscence. She was even more than patient of Colville's nonsense. It seemed to him that the light under her eyelids was sometimes a grateful light. Confronting Imogene and the young man whose hopes of her he was to destroy at the first opportunity, the lurid moral atmosphere which he breathed seemed threatening to become a thing apparent to sense, and to be about to blot the landscape. He fought it back as best he could, and kept the hovering cloud from touching the earth by incessant effort. At times he looked over the side of the carriage, and drew secretly a long breath of fatigue. It began to be borne in upon him that these ladies were using him ill in leaving him the burden of their entertainment. He became angry, but his heart softened, and he forgave them again, for he conjectured that he was the cause of the cares that kept them silent. He felt certain that the affair had taken some new turn. He wondered if Mrs. Bowen had told Imogene what she had demanded of him. But he could only conjecture and wonder in the dreary undercurrent of thought that flowed evenly and darkly on with the talk he kept going. He made the most he could of the varying views of Florence which the turns and mounting levels of the road gave him. He became affectionately grateful to the young clergyman when he replied promptly and fully, and took an interest in the objects or subjects he brought up.

Neither Mrs. Bowen nor Imogene was altogether silent. The one helped on at times wearily, and the other broke at times from her abstraction. Doubtless the girl had undertaken too much in insisting upon a party of pleasure with her mind full of so many things, and doubtless Mrs. Bowen was sore with a rankling resentment at her insistence, and vexed at herself for having yielded to it. If at her time of life and with all her experience of it, she could not rise under this inner load, Imogene must have been crushed by it.

Her starts from the dreamy oppression, if that were what kept her silent, took the form of aggression, when she disagreed with Colville about things he was saying, or attacked him for this or that thing which he had said in times past. It was an unhappy and unamiable self-assertion, which he was not able to compassionate so much when she resisted or defied Mrs. Bowen, as she seemed seeking to do at every point. Perhaps another would not have felt it so; it must have been largely in his consciousness; the young clergyman seemed not to see anything in these bursts but the indulgence of a gay caprice, though his laughing at them did not alleviate the effect to Colville, who, when he turned to Mrs. Bowen for her alliance, was astonished with a prompt snub, unmistakable to himself, however imperceptible to others.

He found what diversion and comfort he could in the party of children who beset them at a point near the town, and followed the carriage, trying to sell them various light and useless trifles made of straw—fans, baskets, parasols, and the like. He bought recklessly of them and gave them to Effie, whom he assured, without the applause of the ladies, and with the grave question of the young clergyman, that the vendors were little Etruscan girls, all at least twenty-five hundred years old. "It's very hard to find any Etruscans under that age; most of the grown-up people are three thousand."

The child humoured his extravagance with the faith in fable which children are able to command, and said, "Oh, tell me about them!' while she pushed up closer to him, and began to admire her presents, holding them up before her, and dwelling fondly upon them one by one.

"Oh, there's very little to tell," answered Colville. "They're mighty close people, and always keep themselves very much *to* themselves. But wouldn't you like to see a party of Etruscans of all ages, even down to little babies only eleven or twelve hundred years old, come driving into an American town? It would make a great excitement, wouldn't it?"

"It would be splendid."

"Yes; we would give them a collation in the basement of the City Hall, and drive them out to the cemetery. The Americans and Etruscans are very much alike in that—they always show you their tombs."

"Will they in Fiesole?"

"How you always like to burrow into the past!" interrupted Imogene.

"Well, it's rather difficult burrowing into the future," returned Colville defensively. Accepting the challenge, he added: "Yes, I should really like to meet a few Etruscans in Fiesole this morning. I should feel as if I'd got amongst my contemporaries at last; they would understand me."

The girl's face flushed. "Then no one else can understand you?"

"Apparently not. I am the great American *incompris*."*

'I'm sorry for you," she returned feebly; and, in fact, sarcasm was not her strong point.

When they entered the town they found the Etruscans preoccupied with other visitors, whom at various points in the quaint little piazza they surrounded in dense groups, to their own disadvantage as guides and beggars and dealers in straw goods. One of the groups reluctantly dispersed to devote itself to the new arrivals, and these then perceived that it was a party of artists, scattered about and sketching, which had absorbed the

attention of the population. Colville went to the restaurant
to order lunch, leaving the ladies to the care of Mr. Morton.
When he came back he found the carriage surrounded by the
artists, who had turned out to be the Inglehart boys. They had
walked up to Fiesole the afternoon before, and they had been
sketching there all the morning. With the artist's indifference to the conventional objects of interest, they were still
ignorant of what ought to be seen in Fiesole by tourists, and
they accepted Colville's proposition to be of his party in
going the rounds of the Cathedral, the Museum, and the
view from that point of the wall called the Belvedere. They
found that they had been at the Belvedere before without
knowing that it merited particular recognition, and some of
them had made sketches from it—of bits of architecture and
landscape, and of figure amongst the women with straw fans
and baskets to sell, who thronged round the whole party
again, and interrupted the prospect. In the church they dif-
fered amongst themselves as to the best bits for study, and
Colville listened in whimsical despair to the enthusiasm of
their likings and dislikings. All that was so far from him
now; but in the Museum, which had only a thin interest
based upon a small collection of art and archæology, he suffered a real affliction in the presence of a young Italian
couple, who were probably plighted lovers. They went
before a grey-haired pair, who might have been the girl's
father and mother, and they looked at none of the objects,
though they regularly stopped before them and waited till
their guide had said his say about them. The girl, clinging
tight to the young man's arm, knew nothing but him; her
mouth and eyes were set in a passionate concentration of her
being upon him, and he seemed to walk in a dream of her.
From time to time they peered upon each other's faces, and
then they paused, rapt and indifferent to all besides.

The young painters had their jokes about it; even Mr
Morton smiled, and Mrs. Bowen recognised it. But Imogene
did not smile; she regarded the lovers with an interest in
them scarcely less intense than their interest in each other;
and a cold perspiration of question broke out on Colville's
forehead. Was that her ideal of what her own engagement

should be? Had she expected him to behave in that way to her, and to accept from her a devotion like that girl's? How bitterly he must have disappointed her! It was so impossible to him that the thought of it made him feel that he must break all ties which bound him to anything like it. And yet he reflected that the time was when he could have been equal to that, and even more.

After lunch the painters joined them again, and they all went together to visit the ruins of the Roman theatre and the stretch of Etruscan wall beyond it. The former seems older than the latter, whose huge blocks of stone lie as firmly and evenly in their courses as if placed there a year ago; the turf creeps to the edge at top, and some small trees nod along the crest of the wall, whose ancient face, clean and bare, looks sternly out over a vast prospect, now young and smiling in the first delight of spring. The piety or interest of the community, which guards the entrance to the theatre by a fee of certain centesimi, may be concerned in keeping the wall free from the grass and vines which are stealing the half-excavated arena back to forgetfulness and decay; but whatever agency it was, it weakened the appeal that the wall made to the sympathy of the spectators. They could do nothing with it; the artists did not take their sketch-blocks from their pockets. But in the theatre, where a few broken columns marked the place of the stage, and the stone benches of the auditorium were here and there reached by a flight of uncovered steps, the human interest returned.

"I suspect that there is such a thing as a ruin's being too old," said Colville. "Our Etruscan friends made the mistake of building their wall several thousand years too soon for our purpose."

"Yes," consented the young clergyman. "It seems as if our own race became alienated from us through the mere effect of time, don't you think, sir? I mean, of course, terrestrially."

The artists looked uneasy, as if they had not counted upon anything of this kind, and they began to scatter about for points of view. Effie got her mother's leave to run up and down one of the stairways, if she would not fall. Mrs. Bowen sat down on one of the lower steps, and Mr. Morton took his place respectfully near her.

"I wonder how it looks from the top?" Imogene asked this of Colville, with more meaning than seemed to belong to the question properly.

"There is nothing like going to see," he suggested. He helped her up, giving her his hand from one course of seats to another. When they reached the point which commanded the best view of the whole, she sat down, and he sank at her feet, but they did not speak of the view.

"Theodore, I want to tell you something," she said abruptly. "I have heard from home."

"Yes?" he replied, in a tone in which he did his best to express a readiness for any fate.

"Mother has telegraphed. She is coming out. She is on her way now. She will be here very soon."

Colville did not know exactly what to say to these passionately consecutive statements. "Well?" he said at last.

"Well"—she repeated his word—"what do you intend to do?"

"Intend to do in what event?" he asked, lifting his eyes for the first time to the eyes which he felt burning down upon him.

"If she should refuse?"

Again he could not command an instant answer, but when it came it was a fair one. "It isn't for me to say what I shall do," he replied gravely. "Or, if it is, I can only say that I will do whatever you wish."

"Do *you* wish nothing?"

"Nothing but your happiness."

"Nothing but my happiness!" she retorted. "What is my happiness to me? Have I ever sought it?"

"I can't say," he answered; "but if I did not think you would find it——"

"I shall find it, if ever I find it, in yours," she interrupted. "And what shall you do if my mother will not consent to our engagement?"

The experienced and sophisticated man—for that in no ill way was what Colville was—felt himself on trial for his honour and his manhood by this simple girl, this child. He could not endure to fall short of her ideal of him at that moment, no matter what error or calamity the fulfilment involved. "If you feel sure that you love me, Imogene, it will make no difference to me what your mother says. I would be glad of her consent; I should hate to go counter to her will; but I know that I am good enough man to be true and keep you all my life the first in all my thoughts, and that's enough for me. But if you have any fear, any doubt of yourself, now is the time——"

Imogene rose to her feet as in some turmoil of thought or emotion that would not suffer her to remain quiet.

"Oh, keep still!" "Don't get up yet!" "Hold on a minute, please!" came from the artists in different parts of the theatre, and half a dozen imploring pencils were waved in the air.

"They are sketching you," said Colville, and she sank compliantly into her seat again.

"I have no doubt for myself—no," she said, as if there had been no interruption.

"Then we need have no anxiety in meeting your mother," said Colville, with a light sigh, after a moment's pause. "What makes you think she will be unfavourable?"

"I don't think that; but I thought—I didn't know but——"

"What?"

"Nothing, now." Her lips were quivering; he could see her struggle for self-control, but he could not see it unmoved.

"Poor child!" he said, putting out his hand toward her.

"Don't take my hand; they're all looking," she begged.

He forbore, and they remained silent and motionless a little while, before she had recovered herself sufficiently to speak again.

"Then we are promised to each other, whatever happens," she said.

"Yes."

"And we will never speak of this again. But there is one thing. Did Mrs. Bowen ask you to tell Mr. Morton of our engagement?"

"She said that I ought to do so."

"And did you say you would?"

"I don't know. But I suppose I ought to tell him."

"I don't wish you to!" cried the girl.

"You don't wish me to tell him?"

"No; I will not have it!"

"Oh, very well; it's much easier not. But it seems to me that it's only fair to him."

"Did you think of that yourself?" she demanded fiercely.

"No," returned Colville, with sad self-recognition. "I'm afraid I'm not apt to think of the comforts and rights of other people. It was Mrs. Bowen who thought of it."

"I knew it!"

"But I must confess that I agreed with her, though I would have preferred to postpone it till we heard from your family." He was thoughtfully silent a moment; then he said, "But if their decision is to have no weight with us, I think he ought to be told at once."

"Do you think that I am flirting with him?"

"Imogene!" exclaimed Colville reproachfully.

"That's what you imply; that's what she implies."

"You're very unjust to Mrs. Bowen, Imogene."

"Oh, you always defend her! It isn't the first time you've told me I was unjust to her."

"I don't mean that you are willingly unjust, or could be so, to any living creature, least of all to her. But I—we—owe her so much; she has been so patient."

"What do we owe her? How has she been patient?"

"She has overcome her dislike to me."

"Oh, indeed!"

"And—and I feel under obligation to her for—in a thousand little ways; and I should be glad to feel that we were acting with her approval; I should like to please her."

"You wish to tell Mr. Morton?"

"I think I ought."

"To please Mrs. Bowen! Tell him, then! You always cared more to please her than me. Perhaps you stayed in Florence to please her!"

She rose and ran down the broken seats and ruined steps

so recklessly and yet so sure-footedly that it seemed more like a flight than a pace to the place where Mrs. Bowen and Mr. Morton were talking together.

Colville followed as he could, slowly and with a heavy heart. A good thing develops itself in infinite and unexpected shapes of good; a bad thing into manifold and astounding evils. This mistake was whirling away beyond his recall in hopeless mazes of error.* He saw this generous young spirit betrayed by it to ignoble and unworthy excess, and he knew that he and not she was to blame.

He was helpless to approach her, to speak with her, to set her right, great as the need of that was, and he could see that she avoided him. But their relations remained outwardly undisturbed. The artists brought their sketches for inspection and comment, and, without speaking to each other, he and Imogene discussed them with the rest.

When they started homeward the painters said they were coming a little way with them for a send-off, and then going back to spend the night in Fiesole. They walked beside the carriage, talking with Mrs. Bowen and Imogene, who had taken their places, with Effie between them, on the back seat; and when they took their leave, Colville and the young clergyman, who had politely walked with them, continued on foot a little further, till they came to the place where the highway to Florence divided into the new road and the old. At this point it steeply overtops the fields on one side, which is shored up by a wall some ten or twelve feet deep; and here round a sharp turn of the hill on the other side came a peasant driving a herd of the black pigs of the country.

Mrs. Bowen's horses were, perhaps, pampered beyond the habitual resignation of Florentine horses to all manner of natural phenomena; they reared at sight of the sable crew, and backing violently uphill, set the carriage across the road, with its hind wheels a few feet from the brink of the wall. The coachman sprang from his seat, the ladies and the child remained in theirs as if paralysed.

Colville ran forward to the side of the carriage. "Jump, Mrs. Bowen! jump, Effie! Imogene——"

The mother and the little one obeyed. He caught them in

his arms and set them down. The girl sat still, staring at him with reproachful, with disdainful eyes.

He leaped forward to drag her out; she shrank away, and then he flew to help the coachman, who had the maddened horses by the bit.

"Let go!" he heard the young clergyman calling to him; "she's safe!" He caught a glimpse of Imogene, whom Mr. Morton had pulled from the other side of the carriage. He struggled to free his wrist from the curb-bit chain of the horse, through which he had plunged it in his attempt to seize the bridle. The wheels of the carriage went over the wall; he felt himself whirled into the air, and then swung ruining down into the writhing and crashing heap at the bottom of the wall.

XXI

WHEN Colville came to himself his first sensation was delight in the softness and smoothness of the turf on which he lay. Then the strange colour of the grass commended itself to his notice, and presently he perceived that the thing under his head was a pillow, and that he was in bed. He was supported in this conclusion by the opinion of the young man who sat watching him a little way off, and who now smiled cheerfully at the expression in the eyes which Colville turned inquiringly upon him.

"Where am I!" he asked, with what appeared to him very unnecessary feebleness of voice.

The young man begged his pardon in Italian, and when Colville repeatd his question in that tongue, he told him that he was in Palazzo Pinti, whither he had been brought from the scene of his accident. He added that Colville must not talk till the doctor had seen him and given him leave, and he explained that he was himself a nurse from the hospital, who had been taking care of him.

Colville moved his head and felt the bandage upon it; he desisted in his attempt to lift his right arm to it before the attendant could interfere in behalf of the broken limb. He recalled dimly and fragmentarily long histories that he had dreamed, but he forbore to ask how long he had been in his present case, and he accepted patiently the apparition of the doctor and other persons who came and went, and were at his bedside or not there, as it seemed to him, between the opening and closing of an eye. As the days passed they acquired greater permanence and maintained a more uninterrupted identity. He was able to make quite sure of Mr. Morton and of Mr. Waters; Mrs. Bowen came in, leading Effie, and this gave him a great pleasure. Mrs. Bowen seemed to have grown younger and better. Imogene was not among the phantoms who visited him; and he accepted her absence as quiescently as he accepted the presence of the others. There was a cheerfulness in those who came that permitted him no anxiety, and he was too weak to invite it by any conjecture. He consented to be spared and to spare himself; and there were some things about the affair which gave him a singular and perhaps not wholly sane content. One of these was the man nurse who had evidently taken care of him throughout. He celebrated, whenever he looked at this capable person, his escape from being, in the odious helplessness of sickness, a burden upon the strength and sympathy of the two women for whom he had otherwise made so much trouble. His satisfaction in this had much to do with his recovery, which, when it once began, progressed rapidly to a point where he was told that Imogene and her mother were at a hotel in Florence, waiting till he should be strong enough to see them. It was Mrs. Bowen who told him this with an air which she visibly strove to render non-committal and impersonal, but which betrayed, nevertheless, a faint apprehension for the effect upon him. The attitude of Imogene and her mother was certainly not one to have been expected of people holding their nominal relation to him, but Colville had been revising his impressions of events on the day of his accident; Imogene's last look came back to him, and he could not think the situation altogether unaccountable.

"Have I been here a long time?" he asked, as if he had not heeded what she told him.

"About a fortnight," answered Mrs. Bowen.

"And Imogene—how long has she been away?"

"Since they knew you would get well."

"I will see them any time," he said quietly.

"Do you think you are strong enough?"

"I shall never be stronger till I have seen them," he returned, with a glance at her. "Yes; I want them to come to-day. I shall not be excited; don't be troubled—if you were going to be," he added. "Please send to them at once."

Mrs. Bowen hesitated, but after a moment left the room. She returned in half an hour with a lady who revealed even to Colville's languid regard evidences of the character which Mrs. Bowen had attributed to Imogene's mother. She was a large, robust person, laced to sufficient shapeliness, and she was well and simply dressed. She entered the room with a waft of some clean, wholesome perfume, and quiet temperament and perfect health looked out of her clear, honest eyes—the eyes of Imogene Graham, though the girl's were dark and the woman's were blue. When Mrs. Bowen had named them to each other, in withdrawing, Mrs. Graham took Colville's weak left hand in her fresh, strong, right, and then lifted herself a chair to his bedside, and sat down.

"How do you do to-day, sir?" she said, with a touch of old-fashioned respectfulness in the last word. "Do you think you are quite strong enough to talk with me?"

"I think so," said Colville, with a faint smile. "At least I can listen with fortitude."

Mrs. Graham was not apparently a person adapted to joking. "I don't know whether it will require much fortitude to hear what I have to say or not," she said, with her keen gaze fixed upon him. "It's simply this: I am going to take Imogene home."

She seemed to expect that Colville would make some reply to this, and he said blankly, "Yes?"

"I came out prepared to consent to what she wished, after I had seen you, and satisfied myself that she was not mistaken; for I had always promised myself that her choice should be perfectly untrammelled and I have tried to bring her up with principles and ideas that would enable her to make a good choice."

"Yes," said Colville again. "I'm afraid you didn't take her temperament and her youth into account, and that she disappointed you."

"No; I can't say that she did. It isn't that at all. I see no reason to blame her for her choice. Her mistake was of another kind."

It appeared to Colville that this very sensible and judicial lady found an intellectual pleasure in the analysis of the case, which modified the intensity of her maternal feeling in regard to it, and that, like many people who talk well, she liked to hear herself talk in the presence of another appreciative listener. He did not offer to interrupt her, and she went on. "No, sir, I am not disappointed in her choice. I think her chances of happiness would have been greater, in the abstract, with one nearer her own age, but that is a difference which other things affect so much that it did not alarm me greatly. Some people are younger at your age than at hers. No, sir, that is not the point." Mrs. Graham fetched a sigh, as if she found it easier to say what was not the point than to say what was, and her clear gaze grew troubled. But she apparently girded herself for the struggle. "As far as you are concerned, Mr. Colville, I have not a word to say. Your conduct throughout has been most high-minded and considerate and delicate."

It is hard for any man to deny merits attributed to him, especially if he has been ascribing to himself the opposite demerits. But Colville summoned his dispersed forces to protest against this.

"Oh, no, no," he cried. "Anything but that. My conduct has been selfish and shameful. If you could understand all——"

"I think I do understand all—at least far more, I regret to say, than my daughter has been willing to tell me. And I am more than satisfied with you. I thank you and honour you."

"Oh no; don't say that," pleaded Colville. "I really can't stand it."

"And when I came here it was with the full intention of approving and confirming Imogene's decision. But I was met at once by a painful and surprising state of things. You are aware that you have been very sick?"

"Dimly," said Colville.

"I found you very sick, and I found my daughter frantic at the error which she had discovered in herself—discovered too late, as she felt." Mrs. Graham hesitated, and then added abruptly, "She had found out that she did not love you."

"Didn't love me?" repeated Colville feebly.

"She had been conscious of the truth before, but she had stifled her misgivings insanely, and, as I feel, almost wickedly, pushing on, and saying to herself that when you were married, then there would be no escape, and she *must* love you."

"Poor girl! poor child! I see, I see."

"But the accident that was almost your death saved her from that miserable folly and iniquity. Yes," she continued, in answer to the protest in his face, "folly and iniquity. I found her half crazed at your bedside. She was fully aware of your danger, but while she was feeling all the remorse that she ought to feel—that any one could feel— she was more and more convinced that she never had loved you and never should. I can give you no idea of her state of mind."

"Oh, you needn't! you needn't! Poor, poor child!"

"Yes, a child indeed. If it had not been for pity I felt for Her——— But no matter about that. She saw at last that if your heroic devotion to her"—Colville did his best to hang his pillowed head for shame—"if your present danger did not awaken her to some such feeling for you as she had once imagined she had; if they both only increased her despair and self-abhorrence, then the case was indeed hopeless. She was simply distracted. I had to tear her away almost by force. She has had a narrow escape from brain-fever. And now I have come to implore, to *demand*"—Mrs. Graham, with all her poise and calm, was rising to the hysterical key—"her release from a fate that would be worse than death for such a girl. I mean marrying without the love of her whole soul. She esteems you, she respects you, she admires you, she likes you; but——" Mrs. Graham pressed her lips together, and her eyes shone.

"She is free," said Colville, and with the words a mighty load rolled from his heart. "There is no need to demand anything."

"I know."

"There hasn't been an hour, an instant, during—since I—we—spoke together that I wouldn't have released her if I could have known what you tell me now."

"Of course!—of course!"

"I have had my fears—my doubts; but whenever I approached the point I found no avenue by which we could reach a clearer understanding. I could not say much without seeming to seek for myself the release I was offering her."

"Naturally. And what added to her wretchedness was the suspicion at the bottom of all that she had somehow forced herself upon you—misunderstood you, and made you say and do things to spare her that you would not have done voluntarily.'' This was advanced tentatively. In the midst of his sophistications Colville had, as most of his sex have, a native, fatal, helpless truthfulness, which betrayed him at the most unexpected moments and this must now have appeared in his countenance. The lady rose haughtily. She had apparently been considering him, but, after all, she must have been really considering her daughter. ''If anything of the kind was the case,'' she said, ''I will ask you to spare her the killing knowledge. It's quite enough for *me* to know it. And allow me to say, Mr. Colville, that it would have been far kinder in you——''

''Ah, *think*, my dear madam!'' he exclaimed. ''How *could* I?''

She did think, evidently, and when she spoke it was with a generous emotion, in which there was no trace of pique.

''You couldn't. You have done right; I feel that, and I will trust you to say anything you will to my daughter.''

''To your daughter? Shall I see her?''

''She came with me. She wished to beg your forgiveness.''

Colville lay silent. ''There is no forgivenes to be asked or granted,'' he said, at length. ''Why should she suffer the pain of seeing me?—for it would be nothing else. What do you think? Will it do her any good hereafter? I don't care for myself.''

''I don't know what to think,'' said Mrs. Graham. ''She is a strange child. She may have some idea of reparation.''

''Oh, beseech her from me not to imagine that any reparation is due! Where there has been an error there must be blame; but wherever it lies in ours, I am sure it isn't at her door. Tell her I say this; tell her that I acquit her with all my heart of every shadow of wrong; that I am not unhappy, but glad for her sake and my own that this has ended as it has.'' He stretched his left hand across the coverlet to her, and said, with the feebleness of exhaustion, ''Good-bye. Bid her good-bye for me.''

Mrs. Graham pressed his hand and went out. A moment after the door was flung open, and Imogene burst into the room. She threw herself on her knees beside his bed. "I will *pray* to you!" she said, her face intense with the passions working in her soul. She seemed choking with words which would not come; then, with an inarticulate cry that must stand for all, she caught up the hand that lay limp on the coverlet; she crushed it against her lips, and ran out of the room.

He sank into deathly torpor, that physical refusal of his brain to take account of what had passed. When he woke from it, little Effie Bowen was airily tiptoeing about the room, fondly retouching its perfect order. He closed his eyes, and felt her come to him and smooth the sheet softly under his chin. Then he knew she must be standing with clasped hands admiring the effect. Some one called her in whisper from the door. It closed, and all was still again.

XXII

COLVILLE got himself out of the comfort and quiet of Mrs. Bowen's house as soon as he could. He made the more haste because he felt that if he could have remained with the smallest trace of self-respect, he would have been glad to stay there for ever.

Even as it was, the spring had advanced to early summer, and the sun was lying hot and bright in the piazzas, and the shade dense and cool in the narrow streets, before he left Palazzo Pinti; the Lung' Arno was a glare of light that struck back from the curving line of the buff houses; the river had shrivelled to a rill in its bed; the black cypresses were dim in the tremor of the distant air on the hill-slopes beyond; the olives seemed to swelter in the sun, and the villa walls to burn whiter and whiter. At evening the mosquito began to wind his tiny horn. It was the end of May, and nearly everybody but the Florentines had gone out of Florence, dispersing to Villa Reggio by the sea, to the hills of Pistoja, and to the high, cool air of Siena. More than once Colville had said that he was keeping Mrs. Bowen after she ought to have got away, and she had answered that she liked hot weather, and that this was not comparable to the heat of Washington in June. She was looking very well, and younger and prettier than she had since the first days of their renewed acquaintance in the winter. Her southern complexion enriched itself in the sun; sometimes when she came into his room from outdoors the straying brown hair curled into loose rings on her temples, and her cheeks glowed a deep red.

She said those polite things to appease him as long as he was not well enough to go away, but she did not try to detain him after his strength sufficiently returned. It was the blow on the head that kept him longest. After his broken arm and his other bruises were quite healed, he was aware of physical limits to thinking of the future or regretting the past, and this sense of his powerlessness went far to reconcile him to a life of present inaction and oblivion. Theoretically he ought to have been devoured by remorse and chagrin, but as a matter of fact he suffered very little from either. Even in people who are in full possession of their capacity for mental anguish one observes that after they have undergone a certain amount of pain they cease to feel.

Colville amused himself a good deal with Effie's endeavours to entertain him and take care of him. The child was with him every moment that she could steal from her tasks, and her mother no longer attempted to stem the tide of her devotion. It was understood that Effie should joke and laugh with Mr. Colville as much as she chose; that she should fan him as long as he could stand it; that she should read to him when he woke, and watch him when he slept. She brought him his breakfast, she petted him and caressed him, and wished to make him a monster of dependence and self-indulgence. It seemed to grieve her that he got well so fast.

The last night before he left the house she sat on his knee by the window looking out beyond the firefly twinkle of Oltrarno, to the silence and solid dark of the solemn company of hills beyond. They had not lighted the lamps because of the mosquitoes, and they had talked till her head dropped against his shoulder.

Mrs. Bowen came in to get her. "Why, is she asleep?"

"Yes. Don't take her yet," said Colville.

Mrs. Bowen rustled softly into the chair which Effie had left to get into Colville's lap. Neither of them spoke, and he was so richly content with the peace, the tacit sweetness of the little moment, that he would have been glad to have it silently endure forever. If any troublesome question of his right to such a moment of bliss obtruded itself upon him, he did not concern himself with it.

"We shall have another hot day to-morrow," said Mrs. Bowen at length. "I hope you will find your room comfortable."

"Yes: it's at the back of the hotel, mighty high, and wide, and no sun ever comes into it except when they show it to foreigners in winter. Then they get a few rays to enter as a matter of business, on condition that they won't detain them. I dare say I shall stay there some time. I suppose you will be getting away from Florence very soon.''

''Yes. But I haven't decided where to go yet.''

''Should you like some general expression of my gratitude for all you've done for me, Mrs. Bowen?''

''No; I would rather not. It has been a great pleasure—to Effie.''

''Oh, a luxury beyond the dreams of avarice.'' They spoke in low tones, and there was something in the hush that suggested to Colville the feasibility of taking into his unoccupied hand one of the pretty hands which the pale nightlight showed him lying in Mrs. Bowen's lap. But he forbore, and only sighed. ''Well, then, I will say nothing. But I shall keep on thinking all my life.''

She made no answer.

''When you are gone, I shall have to make the most of Mr. Waters,'' he said.

''He is going to stop all summer, I believe.''

''Oh yes. When I suggested to him the other day that he might find it too hot, he said that he had seventy New England winters to thaw out of his blood, and that all the summers he had left would not be more than he needed. One of his friends told him that he could cook eggs in his piazza in August, and he said that he should like nothing better than to cook eggs there. He's the most delightfully expatriated compatriot I've ever seen.''

''Do you like it?''

''It's well enough for him. Life has no claims on him any more. I think it's very pleasant over here, now that everybody's gone,'' added Colville, from a confused resentfulness of collectively remembered Days and Afternoons and Evenings. ''How still the night is!''

A few feet clapping by on the pavement below alone broke the hush.

''Sometimes I feel very tired of it all, and want to get home,'' sighed Mrs. Bowen.

''Well, so do I.''

''I can't believe it's right staying away from the country

so long." People often say such things in Europe.

"No, I don't either, if you've got anything to do there."

"You can always make something to do there."

"Oh yes." Some young men, breaking from a street near by, began to sing. "We shouldn't have that sort of thing at home."

"No," said Mrs. Bowen pensively.

"I heard just such singing before I fell asleep the night after that party at Madame Uccelli's, and it filled me with fury."

"Why should it do that?"

"I don't know. It seemed like voices from our youth—Lina."

She had no resentment of his use of her name in the tone with which she asked: "Did you hate that so much?"

"No; the loss of it."

They both fetched a deep breath.

"The Uccellis have a villa near the baths of Lucca," said Mrs. Bowen. "They have asked me to go."

"Do you think of going?" inquired Colville. "I've always fancied it must be pleasant there."

"No; I declined. Sometimes I think I will just stay on in Florence."

"I dare say you'd find it perfectly comfortable. There's nothing like having the range of one's own house in summer." He looked out of the window on the blue-black sky.

" 'And deepening through their silent spheres,
    Heaven over heaven rose the night,' "

he quoted. "It's wonderful! Do you remember how I used to read *Mariana in the South** to you and poor Jenny? How it must have bored her! What an ass I was!"

"Yes," said Mrs. Bowen breathlessly, in sympathy with his reminiscence rather than in agreement with his self-denunciation.

Colville broke into a laugh, and then she began to laugh too; but not quite willingly as it seemed.

Effie started from her sleep. "What—what is it?" she

asked, stretching and shivering as half-wakened children do.

"Bed-time," said her mother promptly, taking her hand to lead her away. "Say good-night to Mr. Colville."

The child turned and kissed him. "Good night," she murmured.

"Good night, you sleepy little soul!" It seemed to Colville that he must be a pretty good man, after all, if this little thing loved him so.

"Do you always kiss Mr. Colville good-night?" asked her mother when she began to undo her hair for her in her room.

"Sometimes. Don't you think it's nice?"

"Oh yes; nice enough."

Colville sat by the window a long time thinking Mrs. Bowen might come back; but she did not return.

Mr. Waters came to see him the next afternoon at his hotel. "Are you pretty comfortable here?" he asked.

"Well, it's a change," said Colville. "I miss the little one awfully."

"She's a winning child," admitted the old man. "That combination of conventionality and *naïveté* is very captivating. I notice it in the mother."

"Yes, the mother has it too. Have you seen them to-day?"

"Yes; Mrs. Bowen was sorry to be out when you came."

"I had the misfortune to miss them. I had a great mind to go again to-night."

The old man said nothing to this. "The fact is," Colville went on, "I'm so habituated to being there that I'm rather spoiled."

"Ah, it's a nice place," Mr. Waters admitted.

"Of course I made all the haste I could to get away, and I have the reward of a good conscience. But I don't find that the reward is very great."

The old gentleman smiled. "The difficulty is to know conscience from self-interest."

"Oh, there's no doubt of it in my case," said Colville. "If I'd consulted my own comfort and advantage, I should still be at Palazzo Pinti."

"I dare say they would have been glad to keep you."

"Do you really think so?" asked Colville, with sudden seriousness. "I wish you would tell me why. Have you any reason—grounds? Pshaw! I'm absurd!" He sank back into the easy-chair from whose depths he had pulled himself in the eagerness of his demand, and wiped his forehead with his handkerchief. "Mr. Waters, you remember my telling you of my engagement to Miss Graham?"

"Yes."

"That is broken off—if it were ever really on. It was a great mistake for both of us—a tragical one for her, poor child, a ridiculous one for me. My only consolation is that it *was* a mistake and no more; but I don't conceal from myself that I might have prevented it altogether if I had behaved with greater wisdom and dignity at the outset. But I'm afraid I was flattered by an illusion of hers that ought to have pained and alarmed me, and the rest followed inevitably, though I was always just on the point of escaping the consequences of my weakness—my wickedness."

"Ah, there is something extremely interesting in all that," said the old minister thoughtfully. "The situation used to be figured under the old idea of a compact with the devil. His debtor was always on the point of escaping, as you say, but ɪ recollect no instance in which he did not pay at last. The myth must have arisen from man's recognition of the inexorable sequence of cause from effect, in the moral world, which even repentance cannot avert. Goethe tries to imagine an atonement for Faust's trespass* against one human soul in his benefactions to the race at large; but it is a very cloudy business."

"It isn't quite a parallel case," said Colville, rather sulkily. He had, in fact, suffered more under Mr. Waters's generalisation than he could from a more personal philosophy of the affair.

"Oh no; I didn't think that," consented the old man.

"And I don't think I shall undertake any extended scheme of drainage or subsoiling in atonement for my little dream," Colville continued, resenting the parity of outline that grew upon him in spite of his protest. They were both silent for a while, and then Colville cried out, "Yes, yes; they are alike. *I* dreamed, too, of recovering and restoring my own lost and broken past in the love of a young soul, and it was in essence the same cruelly egotistic dream; and it's nothing in my defence that it was all formless and undirected at first, and that as soon as I recognised it I abhorred it."

"Oh yes, it is," replied the old man, with perfect equanimity. "Your assertion is the hysterical excess of Puritanism in all times and places. In the moral world we are responsible only for the wrong that we intend. It can't be otherwise."

"And the evil that's suffered from the wrong we didn't intend?"

"Ah, perhaps that isn't evil."

"It's pain!"

"It's pain, yes."

"And to have wrung a young and innocent heart with the anguish of self-doubt, with the fear of wrong to another, with the shame of an error such as I allowed, perhaps encouraged her to make——"

"Yes," said the old man. "The young suffer terribly. But they recover. Afterward we don't suffer so much, but we don't recover. I wouldn't defend you against yourself if I thought you seriously in the wrong. If you know yourself to be, you shouldn't let me."

Thus put upon his honour, Colville was a long time thoughtful. "How can I tell?" he asked. "You know the facts; you can judge."

"If I were to judge at all, I should say you were likely to do a greater wrong than any you have committed."

"I don't understand you."

"Miss Graham is a young girl, and I have no doubt that the young clergyman—what was his name?"

"Morton. Do you think—do you suppose there was anything in that?" demanded Colville, with eagerness, that a more humorous observer than Mr. Waters might have found ludicrous. "He was an admirable young fellow, with an excellent head and a noble heart. I underrated him at one time, though I recognised his good qualities afterward; but I was afraid she did not appreciate him.''

''I'm not so sure of that,'' said the old man, with an astuteness of manner which Colville thought authorised by some sort of definite knowledge.

''I would give the world if it were so!'' he cried fervently.

''But you are really very much more concerned in something else.''

''In what else?''

''Can't you imagine?''

''No,'' said Colville; but felt himself growing very red in the face.

''Then I have no more to say.''

''Yes, speak!'' And after an interval Colville added, ''Is it anything about—you hinted at something long ago—Mrs. Bowen?''

''Yes;'' the old man nodded his head. ''Do you owe her nothing?''

''Owe her nothing? Everything! My life! What self-respect is left me! Immeasurable gratitude! The homage of a man saved from himself as far as his stupidity and selfishness would permit! Why, I—I love her!'' The words gave him courage. ''In every breath and pulse! She is the most beautiful and gracious and wisest and best woman in the world! I have loved her ever since I met her here in Florence last winter. Good heavens! I must have always loved her! But,'' he added, falling from the rapture of his confession, ''she simply loathes *me!*''

''It was certainly not to your credit that you were willing at the same time to marry some one else.''

''Willing! I wasn't willing! I was bound hand and foot! Yes—I don't care what you think of my weakness—I was not a free agent. It's very well to condemn one's-self, but it may be carried too far; injustice to others is not the only injustice, or the worst. What I was willing to do was to keep my word—to prevent that poor child, if possible, from ever finding out her mistake.''

If Colville expected this heroic confession to impress his listener he was disappointed. Mr. Waters made him no reply, and he was obliged to ask, with a degree of sarcastic impatience, "I suppose you scarcely blame me for that?"

"Oh, I don't know that I blame people for things. There are times when it seems as if we were all puppets, pulled this way or that, without control of our own movements. Hamlet was able to browbeat Rosencrantz and Guildenstern* with his business of the pipe; but if they had been in a position to answer they might have told him that it required far less skill to play upon a man than any other instrument. Most of us, in fact, go sounding on without any special application of breath or fingers, repeating the tunes that were played originally upon other men. It appears to me that you suffered yourself to do something of the kind in this affair. We are a long time learning to act with commonsense or even common sanity in what are called matters of the affections. A broken engagement *may* be a bad thing in some cases, but I am inclined to think that it is the very best thing that would happen in most cases where it happens. The evil is done long before; the broken engagement is merely sanative, and so far beneficent."

The old gentleman rose, and Colville, dazed by the recognition of his own cowardice and absurdity, did not try to detain him. But he followed him down to the outer gate of the hotel. The afternoon sun was pouring into the piazza a sea of glimmering heat, into which Mr. Waters plunged with the security of a salamander. He wore a broad-brimmed Panama hat, a sack coat of black alpaca, and loose trousers of the same material, and Colville fancied him doubly defended against the torrid waves not only by the stored cold of half a century of winters at Haddam East Village, but by an inner coolness of spirit, which appeared to diffuse itself in an appreciable atmosphere about him. It was not till he was gone that Colville found himself steeped in perspiration, and glowing with a strange excitement.

XXIII

COLVILLE went back to his own room, and spent a good deal of time in the contemplation of a suit of clothes, adapted to the season, which had been sent home from the tailor's just before Mr. Waters came in. The coat was of the lightest serge, the trousers of a pearly grey tending to lavender, the waistcoat of cool white duck. On his way home from Palazzo Pinti he had stopped in Via Tornabuoni and bought some silk gauze neckties of a tasteful gaiety of tint, which he had at the time thought very well of. But now, as he spread out the whole array on his bed, it seemed too emblematic of a light and blameless spirit for his wear. He ought to put on something as nearly analogous to sackcloth as a modern stock of dry-goods afforded; he ought, at least, to wear the grave materials of his winter costume. But they were really insupportable in this sudden access of summer. Besides, he had grown thin during his sickness, and the things bagged about him. If he were going to see Mrs. Bowen that evening, he ought to go in some decent shape. It was perhaps providential that he had failed to find her at home in the morning, when he had ventured thither in the clumsy attire in which he had been loafing about her drawing-room for the past week. He now owed it to her to appear before her as well as he could. How charmingly punctilious she always was herself!

As he put on his new clothes he felt the moral support which the becomingness of dress alone can give. With the blue silk gauze lighty tied under his collar, and the lapels of his thin coat thrown back to admit his thumbs to his waistcoat pockets, he felt almost cheerful before his glass. Should he shave? As once before, this important question occurred to him. His thinness gave him some advantages of figure, but he thought that it made his face older. What effect would cutting off his beard have upon it? He had not seen the lower part of his face for fifteen years. No one could say what recent ruin of a double chin might not be lurking there. He decided not to shave, at least till after dinner, and after dinner he was too impatient for his visit to brook the necessary delay.

He was shown into the salotto alone, but Effie Bowen came running in to meet him. She stopped suddenly, bridling.

"You never expected to see me looking quite so pretty," said Colville, tracing the cause of her embarrassment to his summer splendour. "Where is your mamma?"

"She is in the dining-room," replied the child, getting hold of his hand. "She wants you to come and have coffee with us."

"By all means—not that I haven't had coffee already, though."

She led the way, looking up at him shyly over her shoulder as they went.

Mrs. Bowen rose, napkin in lap, and gave him a hand of welcome. "How are you feeling to-day?" she asked, politely ignoring his finery.

"Like a new man," he said. And then he added, to relieve the strain of the situation, "Of the best tailor's make in Florence."

"You look very well," she smiled.

"Oh, I always do when I take pains," said Colville. "The trouble is that I don't always take pains. But I thought I would to-night, in calling upon a lady."

"Effie will feel very much flattered," said Mrs. Bowen.

"Don't refuse a portion of the satisfaction," he cried.

"Oh, is it for me too?"

This gave Colville consolation which no religion or philosophy could have brought him, and his pleasure was not marred, but rather heightened, by the little pangs of expectation, bred by long custom, that from moment to moment Imogene would appear. She did not appear, and a thrill of security succeeded upon each alarm. He wished her well with all his heart; such is the human heart that he wished her arrived home the betrothed of that excellent, that wholly unobjectionable young man, Mr. Morton.

"Will you have a little of the ice before your coffee?" asked Mrs. Bowen, proposing one of the moulded creams with her spoon.

"Yes, thank you. Perhaps I will take it in place of the coffee. They forgot to offer us any ice at the *table d'hôte* this evening."

"This is rather luxurious for us," said Mrs. Bowen. "It's a compromise with Effie. She wanted me to take her to Giacosa's this afternoon."

"I *thought* you would come," whispered the child to Colville.

Her mother made a little face of mock surprise at her. "Don't give yourself away, Effie."

"Why, let us go to Giacosa's too," said Colville, taking the ice. "We shall be the only foreigners there, and we shall not even feel ourselves foreign. It's astonishing how the hot weather has dispersed the tourists. I didn't see a Baedeker on the whole way up here, and I walked down Via Tornabuoni across through Porta Rosso and the Piazza della Signoria and the Uffizzi. You've no idea how comfortable and home-like it was—all the statues loafing about in their shirt sleeves, and the objects of interest stretching and yawning round, and having a good rest after their winter's work."

Effie understood Colville's way of talking well enough to enjoy this; her mother did not laugh.

"Walked?" she asked.

"Certainly. Why not?"

"You are getting well again. You'll soon be gone too."

"I've *got* well. But as to being gone, there's no hurry. I rather think I shall wait now to see how long you stay."

"We may keep you all summer," said Mrs. Bowen, dropping her eyelids indifferently.

"Oh, very well. All summer it is, then. Mr. Waters is going to stay, and he is such a very cool old gentleman that I don't think one need fear the wildest antics of the mercury where he is."

When Colville had finished his ice, Mrs. Bowen led the way to the salotto; and they all sat down by the window there and watched the sunset die on San Miniato. The bronze copy of Michelangelo's David, in the Piazzale below the church, blackened in perfect relief against the pink sky and then faded against the grey while they talked. They were so domestic that Colville realised with difficulty that this was an image of what might be rather than what really was; the very ease with which he could apparently close his hand upon the happiness within his grasp unnerved him. The talk strayed hither and thither, and went and came aimlessly. A sound of singing floated in from the kitchen, and Effie eagerly asked her mother if she might go and see Maddalena. Maddalena's mother had come to see her, and she was from the mountains.

"Yes, go," said Mrs. Bowen; "but don't say too long."

"Oh, I will be back in time," said the child, and Colville remembered that he had proposed going to Giacosa's.

"Yes; don't forget." He had forgotten it himself.

"Maddalena is the cook," explained Mrs. Bowen. "She sings ballads to Effie that she learned from her mother, and I suppose Effie wants to hear them at first hand."

"Oh yes," said Colville dreamily.

They were alone now, and each little silence seemed freighted with a meaning deeper than speech.

"Have you seen Mr. Waters to-day?" asked Mrs. Bowen, after one of these lapses.

"Yes; he came this afternoon."

"He is a very strange old man. I should think he would be lonely here."

"He seems not to be. He says he finds company in the history of the place. And his satisfaction at having got out of Haddam East Village is perennial."

"But he will want to go back there before he dies."

"I don't know. He thinks not. He's a strange old man, as you say. He has the art of putting all sorts of ideas into people's heads. Do you know what we talked about this afternoon?"

"No, I don't," murmured Mrs. Bowen.

"About you. And he encouraged me to believe—imagine —that I might speak to you—ask—tell you that—I loved you, Lina." He leaned forward and took one of the hands that lay in her lap. It trembled with a violence inconceivable in relation to the perfect quiet of her attitude. But she did not try to take it away. "Could you—do you love me?"

"Yes," she whispered; but here she sprang up and slipped from his hold altogether, as with an inarticulate cry of rapture he released her hand to take her in his arms.

He followed her a pace or two. "And you will—will be my wife?" he pursued eagerly.

"Never!" she answered, and now Colville stopped short, while a cold bewilderment bathed him from head to foot. It must be some sort of jest, though he could not tell where the humour was, and he could not treat it otherwise than seriously.

"Lina, I have loved you from the first moment that I saw you this winter, and Heaven knows how long before!"

"Yes; I know that."

"And every moment."

"Oh, I know that too."

"Even if I had no sort of hope that you cared for me, I loved you so much that I must tell you before we parted——"

"I expected that—I intended it."

"You intended it! and you do love me! And yet you won't—— Ah, I don't understand!"

"How could *you* understand? I love you—I blush and burn for shame to think that I love you. But I will never marry you; I can at least help doing that, and I can still keep some little trace of self-respect. How you must really despise me, to think of anything else, after all that has happened. Did you suppose that I was merely waiting till that poor girl's back was turned, as you were? Oh, how can you be yourself, and still be yourself? Yes, Jenny Wheelwright was right. You are too much of a mixture. Theodore Colville"—her calling him so showed how often she had thought of him so—"too much for her, too much for Imogene, too much for me; too much for any woman except some wretched creature who enjoys being trampled on and dragged through the dust, as you have dragged me.''

''I dragged *you* through the dust? There hasn't been a moment in the past six months when I wouldn't have rolled myself in it to please you.''

''Oh, I knew that well enough! And do you think that was flattering to me?''

''That has nothing to do with it. I only know that I love you, and that I couldn't help wishing to show it even when I wouldn't acknowledge it to myself. That is all. And now when I am free to speak, and you own that you love me, you won't—— I give it up!'' he cried desperately. But in the next breath he implored, ''*Why* do you drive me from you, Lina?''

''Because you have humiliated me too much.'' She was perfectly steady, but he knew her so well that in the twilight he knew what bitterness there must be in the smile which she must be keeping on her lips. ''I was here in the place of her mother, her best friend, and you made me treat her like an enemy. You made me betray her and cast her off.''

''I?''

''Yes, you! I knew from the very first that you did not really care for her, that you were playing with yourself, as you were playing with her, and I ought to have warned her.''

''It appears to me you did warn her,'' said Colville, with some resentful return of courage.

''I tried,'' she said simply, ''and it made it worse. It made it worse because I knew that I was acting for my own sake more than hers, because I wasn't—disinterested.'' There was something in this explanation, serious, tragic, as it was to Mrs. Bowen, which made Colville laugh. She might have had some perception of its effect to him, or it may have been merely from a hysterical helplessness, but she laughed too a little.

''But why,'' he gathered courage to ask, ''do you still dwell upon that? Mr. Waters told me that Mr. Morton—that there was——''

''He is mistaken. He offered himself, and she refused him. He told me.''

"Oh!"

"Do you think she would do otherwise, with you lying here between life and death? No: you can have no hope from that."

Colville, in fact, had none. This blow crushed and dispersed him. He had not strength enough to feel resentment against Mr. Waters for misleading him with this *ignis fatuus*.

"No one warned him, and it came to that," said Mrs. Bowen. "It was of a piece with the whole affair. I was weak in that too."

Colville did not attempt to reply on this point. He feebly reverted to the inquiry regarding himself, and was far enough from mirth in resuming it.

"I couldn't imagine," he said, "that you cared anything for me when you warned another against me. If I could——"

"You put me in a false position from the beginning. I ought to have sympathised with her and helped her instead of making the poor child feel that somehow I hated her. I couldn't even put her on guard against herself, though I knew all along that she didn't really care for you, but was just in love with her own fancy for you. Even after you were engaged I ought to have broken it off; I ought to have been frank with her; it was my duty; but I couldn't without feeling that I was acting for myself too, and I would not submit to that degradation. No! I would rather have died. I dare say you don't understand. How could you? You are a man, and the kind of man who couldn't. At every point you made me violate every principle that was dear to me. I loathed myself for caring for a man who was in love with me when he was engaged to another. Don't think it was gratifying to me. It was detestable; and yet I did let you see that I cared for you. Yes, I even *tried* to make you care for me—falsely, cruelly, treacherously."

"You didn't have to try very hard," said Colville, with a sort of cold resignation to his fate.

"Oh no; you were quite ready for any hint. I could have told her for her own sake that she didn't love you, but that

would have been for my sake too; and I would have told you
if I hadn't cared for you and known how you cared for me
I've saved at least the consciousness of this from the wreck.''

"I don't think it's a great treasure," said Colville. "I
wish that you had saved the consciousness of having been
frank even to your own advantage."

"Do you dare to reproach me, Theodore Colville? But
perhaps I've deserved this too."

"No, Lina, you certainly don't deserve it, if it's unkindness, from me. I won't afflict you with my presence: but will
you listen to me before I go?''

She sank into a chair in sign of assent. He also sat down.
He had a dim impression that he could talk better if he took
her hand, but he did not venture to ask for it. He contented
himself with fixing his eyes upon as much of her face as he
could make out in the dusk, a pale blur in a vague outline
of dark.

"I want to assure you, Lina—Lina, my love, my dearest,
as I shall call you for the first and last time!—that I *do*
understand everything, as delicately and fully as you could
wish, all that you have expressed, and all that you have left
unsaid. I understand how high and pure your ideals of duty
are, and how heroically, angelically, you have struggled to
fulfil them, broken and borne down by my clumsy and
stupid selfishness from the start. I want you to believe, my
dearest love—you must forgive me!—that if I didn't see
everything at the time, I do see it now, and that I prize the
love you kept from me far more than any love you could
have given me to the loss of your self-respect. It isn't logic—
it sounds more like nonsense, I am afraid—but you know
what I mean by it. You are more perfect, more lovely to me,
than any being in the world, and I accept whatever fate you
choose for me. I would not win you against your will if I
could. You are sacred to me. If you say we must part, I
know that you speak from a finer discernment than mine,
and I submit. I will try to console myself with the thought
of your love, if I may not have you. Yes, I submit."

His instinct of forbearance had served him better than the
subtlest art. His submission was the best defence. He rose

with a real dignity, and she rose also. "Remember," he said, "that I confess all you accuse me of, and that I acknowledge the justice of what you do—because you do it." He put out his hand and took the hand which hung nerveless at her side. "You are quite right. Good-bye." He hesitated a moment. "May I kiss you, Lina?" He drew her to him, and she let him kiss her on the lips.

"Good-bye," she whispered. "Go——"

"I am going."

Effie Bowen ran into the room from the kitchen. "Aren't you going to take——" She stopped and turned to her mother. She must not remind Mr. Colville of his invitation; that was what her gesture expressed.

Colville would not say anything. He would not seize his advantage, and play upon the mother's heart through the feelings of her child, though there is no doubt that he was tempted to prolong the situation by any means. Perhaps Mrs. Bowen divined both the temptation and the resistance. "Tell her," she said, and turned away.

"I can't go with you to-night, Effie," he said, stooping toward her for the inquiring kiss that she gave him. "I am—going away, and I must say good-bye."

The solemnity of his voice alarmed her. "Going away!" she repeated.

"Yes—away from Florence. I'm afraid I shall not see you again."

The child turned from him to her mother again, who stood motionless. Then, as if the whole calamitous fact had suddenly flashed upon her, she plunged her face against her mother's breast. "I can't *bear* it!" she sobbed out; and the reticence of her lamentation told more than a storm of cries and prayers.

Colville wavered.

"Oh, you must stay!" said Lina, in the self-contemptuous voice of a woman who falls below her ideal of herself.

XXIV

IN the levities which the most undeserving husbands permit themselves with the severest of wives, there were times after their marriage when Colville accused Lina of never really intending to drive him away, but of meaning, after a disciplinary ordeal, to marry him in reward of his tested self-sacrifice and obedience. He said that if the appearance of Effie was not a *coup de théâtre** contrived beforehand, it was an accident of no consequence whatever; that if she had not come in at that moment, her mother would have found some other pretext for detaining him. This is a point which I would not presume to decide. I only know that they were married early in June before the syndic of Florence, who tied a tricolour sash round his ample waist for the purpose, and never looked more paternal or venerable than when giving the sanction of the Italian state to their union. It is not, of course, to be supposed that Mrs. Colville was contented with the civil rite, though Colville may have thought it quite sufficient. The religious ceremony took place in the English chapel, the assistant clergyman officiating in the absence of the incumbent, who had already gone out of town.

The Rev. Mr. Waters gave away the bride, and then went home to Palazzo Pinti with the party, the single and singularly honoured guest at their wedding feast, for which Effie Bowen went with Colville to Giacosa's to order the ices in person. She has never regretted her choice of a step-father, though when Colville asked her how she would like him in that relation she had a moment of hesitation, in which she reconciled herself to it; as to him she had no misgivings. He has sometimes found himself the object of little jealousies on her part, but by promptly deciding all questions between her and her mother in Effie's favour he has convinced her of the groundlessness of her suspicions.

In the absence of any social pressure to the contrary, the Colvilles spent the summer in Palazzo Pinti. Before their fellow-sojourners returned from the *villeggiature** in the fall, however, they had turned their faces southward, and they are now in Rome, where, arriving as a married couple, there was no inquiry and no interest in their past.

It is best to be honest, and own that the affair with Imogene has been the grain of sand to them. No one was to blame, or very much to blame; even Mrs. Colville says that. It was a thing that happened, but one would rather it had not happened.

Last winter, however, Mrs. Colville received a letter from Mrs. Graham which suggested, if it did not impart, consolation. "Mr. Morton was here the other day, and spent the morning. He has a parish at Erie, and there is talk of his coming to Buffalo."

"Oh, Heaven grant it!" said Colville, with sudden piety.

"Why?" demanded his wife.

"Well, I wish she was married."

"You have nothing whatever to do with her."

It took him some time to realise that this was the fact.

"No," he confessed: "but what do you think about it?"

"There is no telling. We are such simpletons! If a man will keep on long enough—— But if it isn't Mr. Morton, it will be some one else—some *young* person."

Colville rose and went round the breakfast table to her. "I hope so," he said. "*I* have married a young person, and it would only be fair."

This magnanimity was irresistible.

EXPLANATORY NOTES

3 *Ponte Vecchio*: It. old bridge. Reputedly on the site of a Roman bridge, it was reconstructed in the fourteenth century.

4 *when the Democrat-Republican bolted the nomination of a certain politician of its party*: bolt (US) means to break away from, withhold support from. An incident during Howells's editorship of the *Atlantic Monthly* (1871–80) is illuminating—'Appalled by the corruption and barbaric ineptitude of the first Grant (Republican) administration, Republican idealists, and notably those of Howells's Cambridge acquaintanceship, tried to bolt the regular party and nominate Charles Francis Adams on a good government, civil service, free trade, and reconciliation with the South platform in 1872. Howells was a Liberal Republican, threw the *Atlantic* behind the party and felt crushed when the Cincinnati Convention of the Liberals was captured by Horace Greeley, who was then also nominated by the Democrats. There was nothing to do but go back to Grant' (Edwin H. Cady, *The Road to Realism*, Syracuse, 1956).

6 *his Ruskin in his hand, among the masterpieces of Italian Gothic*: John Ruskin's three-volume *The Stones of Venice* (1851–3) celebrates Gothic architecture at the expense of the Renaissance style of which the city provides so many examples.

9 *scaldino*: It. earthenware brazier.

festa: It. holiday.

11 *Bernhardtesque*: in the manner of the French actress Sarah Bernhardt (1844–1923), who first achieved fame in tragic roles in the 1860s.

13 *my little Effie*: Howells gives Mrs Bowen's daughter the name of Ruskin's young bride, Effie Gray, whom he married in 1848 and separated from in 1854.

the India shawl sacque: alternative spelling of 'sack', in this case a loose coat, hanging down at the back.

15 *where Romola lived*: the heroine of George Eliot's novel *Romola* (1863), set in Florence at the end of the fifteenth century, when the city was divided between supporters of the recently expelled Medici family and the popular party, led by the Dominican prior Girolamo Savonarola (see below, note to

p. 36). The novel traces, *inter alia*, the fall of Savonarola, whom Romola comes to know.

17 *Psyches and Hebes and Graces*: statuettes of female figures in Greek mythology. Hebe, the daughter of Zeus and Hera, was the goddess of youth; Psyche overcame the envious schemes of Aphrodite with the aid of her lover Eros; the three Graces were personifications of grace and beauty.

a figure of primo tenore: a man with the bearing of a first tenor in opera.

22 *a member of Parliament, and a republican*: the Risorgimento (see below, note to p. 27) ended with the compromise of an Italy governed by a constitutional monarchy. Many, however, still adhered to the pure republicanism of the nationalist prophet Giuseppe Mazzini (1805–72), who was not allowed to take up his parliamentary seat in the last decade of his life.

23 *a crush hat*: a collapsible opera hat.

24 *the yellow Abruzzi blanket portière*: a *portière* is a curtain over a doorway to prevent draughts; the Abruzzi is a mountainous region to the east of Rome.

25 *Junonian*: more usually 'Junoesque', a stately beauty, like that of Zeus' wife Juno.

26 *those exquisite great Du Maurier women*: refers to the society women George du Maurier (1834–96) drew for *Punch*, rather than the characters in his novels, which include *Trilby* (1894).

27 *a bitterly ironical comparison of the achievements of Italy and America in the last ten years*: the Italian achievements Colville has in mind are presumably the events completing the Risorgimento, the movement for the independence and unification of the country. The Kingdom of Italy was proclaimed in 1861 after the defeat of the Austrians in the north and Garibaldi's victory over Neapolitan Bourbons in the south; Venetia joined the kingdom in 1866 and Rome in 1870. The same period in the USA saw the Civil War, the failure of Southern Reconstruction, and the corruption of the 'Gilded Age', although great economic progress also occurred. The crucial 'comparison' is clearly between the integration of one nation and the disintegration of the other.

28 *our international novelists*: including the Henry James of *Roderick Hudson* (1875), *The American* (1877), *Daisy Miller* (1878), and

The Portrait of a Lady (1881); and Howells himself in *A Foregone Conclusion* (1875), *A Fearful Responsibility* (1881), and the last chapters of *The Lady of the Aroostock* (1879).

the ennobling influences of society in Newport: Newport, Rhode Island, the principal summer resort for New York society in the period. Edith Wharton describes the Newport of the 1870s in *The Age of Innocence*, Ch. 21 *et seq.*

32 *that passage somewhere in Heine's Pictures of Travel*: an inaccurate recollection of an experience described in Ch. 15 of the *Journey from Munich to Genoa* in Heine's *Italy* (1829), the third volume of the *Pictures of Travel*.

33 *Do the girls of Buffalo . . . the old negro minstrel song*: Colville is alluding to the chorus of the famous minstrel song of the 1840s, 'Buffalo Gals' by Cool White. The negro Jim sings it in Ch. 2 of Mark Twain's *Adventures of Tom Sawyer*.

the end of the war: Lee surrendered to Grant on 9 April 1865, ending the American Civil War.

36 *rather Low Church*: a member of the Anglican or Episcopal Church with views close to those of Nonconformists, i.e. ascribing relatively little importance to the authority of priests and bishops and to the role of ritual.

Savonarola: Fra Girolamo Savonarola (1452–98), a Dominican prior, was a powerful preacher against the corruption associated with the Medici. He became the leader of the popular party in Florence, and established a theocratic republic after the family's expulsion. He antagonized Pope Alexander VI, however, and was eventually executed for heresy.

40 *facchini*: It. porters.

42 *the Inglehart boys*: based on the 'Duveneck boys', art students at the Munich Academy taught by the artist Franck Duveneck, who took them to Florence and Venice for two years in 1879.

Tourguéneffish . . . Read Lisa: Ivan Turgenev (1818–83) was greatly admired by Howells, particularly for the absence of sentimentality in his treatment of love. He reviewed *Lisa* (1859) in the *Atlantic Monthly* of February 1873, praising its combination of 'artistic impartiality' and 'deep moral earnestness', and calling it 'a tragedy written by a man of great genius'. The story concerns a man's love for a much younger woman.

43 *the Giottos . . . the Cimabues*: Cimabue (1240–1302) was a

Florentine painter who remained close to the Byzantine tradition; his student Giotto (1266–1337) anticipated elements of the Renaissance style of a century later.

43 *Santa Coce . . . Alfieri's monument*: Santa Croce is a Franciscan church containing frescos by Giotto and several tombs, including that of the eighteenth-century dramatist Alfieri.

44 *Santa Maria Novella*: a Dominican church which, as Colville says, contains Cimabue's *Madonna*.

those frescoes of Ghirlandajo's: frescos on the theme of the Lives of the Virgin and St John the Baptist by Domenico Ghirlandaio (1449–94), the teacher of Michelangelo.

having the convents suppressed: the 'Josephinism' of the Holy Roman Emperor Joseph II (ruled 1765–90) subordinated Church to State. One outcome was the suppression of a large number of monasteries in the Austrian possessions in Italy. Few were left after the Napoleonic era.

55 *remise*: Fr. carriage, hired from a livery stable.

the Lancers: form of quadrille, i.e. a square dance for four couples with several sections.

58 *the interminable german*: a cotillion, a set of round dances with many variations.

61 *the Etruscan wall at Fiesole*: now a small town five miles north of Florence, Fiesole was an Etruscan and Roman city. The disastrous carriage expedition in Forster's *A Room with a View*, Ch. 6, is to Fiesole.

Hoosier: an inhabitant of Indiana, from a slang word for bumpkin or hayseed.

62 *an extended course of sprouts*: colloquial, a flogging, course of discipline.

63 *Villari's book*: *The Life and Times of Girolamo Savonarola* (1859–61) by Pasquale Villari, one of the major sources of *Romola*.

my ancestral puritanism . . . the puritanism of Savonarola: Howells's use of upper and lower case in the [following] passage is somewhat confusing, but Waters essentially compares Savonarola, a fifteenth-century Catholic, with the seventeenth-century Protestant Puritans in England and New England, from which his own 'pale Unitarianism' (see below, note to p. 86) is descended. The parallels are not with specific Puritan doctrines (predestination of the elect, the conversion experience) but with the establishment of a theocratic state and the strictness of 'puritanical' morality. The 'beauty' of puritanism is a theme of *Romola*, where Savonarola is flawed but heroic.

64 *Arrabiati*: It. the rabid ones, opponents of Savonarola.

Malignants: term used by the English Puritans for their ecclesiastical and Royalist opponents.

65 *Cascine*: an eighteenth-century park laid out around the ducal dairy farms (*casine*).

66 *Boboli Gardens*: sixteenth-century terraced gardens near the Arno, with an abundance of statues.

67 *that sonnet of Longfellow's*: Henry Wadsworth Longfellow's 'Il Ponte Vecchio di Firenze' (1874), which he translated as 'The Old Bridge at Florence'.

Hawthorne: in 1858 the novelist Nathaniel Hawthorne rented a villa on a hill overlooking the city, where he began the novel generally known as *The Marble Faun* (1860), which concerns American artists in Rome.

68 *'I remember, when I think . . . divine'*: Tennyson's 'The Vision of Sin', from which the lines come, was published in 1842.

69 *Bianchi and Neri*: It. Whites and Blacks, feuding factions in fourteenth-century Florentine politics.

'It was the nightingale and not the lark': *Romeo and Juliet*, III. v. 2. Juliet tries to prevent Romeo leaving her at daybreak by pretending that the call they hear is not that of 'the herald of morn'.

70 *Hazel Kirke*: Steele Kaye's melodrama, which had a long New York run. As it was first produced in 1880, the reference is a useful indication of the (otherwise unspecified) date when *Indian Summer* is set.

Alexander Smith: a Scottish poet (1830–67) and member of the verbose and obscure 'Spasmodic School'; the reputations of this group never recovered from William Aytoun's parody 'Firmilian' (1854).

71 *that story of Heine's*: in the first part of Heine's *Florentine Nights* (1837).

Bellini: Vincenzo Bellini (1801–35), the Italian composer of operas, notably *La Sonnambula* (1831), *Norma* (1832), and *I Puritani* (1834).

72 *the very worst rococo*: unnecessarily ornate in style. The rococo manner in painting, architecture, and decoration flourished in the middle of the eighteenth century.

eternal fêtes champêtres: Fr. an outdoor entertainment or festival.

The Newcomes: a novel by Thackeray published serially in 1853–5, dealing with the career and marriage of Clive Newcome, the son of an officer in the Indian army. Colonel Newcome's death-bed scene, after he has been reduced to poverty, is open to Colville's charge of sentimentality.

73 *Browning's 'The Statue and the Bust'*: a poem published in *Men and Women* (1855), based on a legend about the equestrian statue of Ferdinando de' Medici in the Piazza dell' Annunziata in Florence. Robert and Elizabeth Barrett Browning were based in Florence throughout their married life (1846–61).

the 'Legend of Pornic': Browning's 'Gold Hair: A Story of Pornic', published in *Dramatis Personae* (1847).

75 *old Piloty's things at Munich*: Karl von Piloty, a painter and professor at the Munich Academy.

76 *Poe's 'Ullalume'*: actually 'Ulalume', a poem about a visit to a woman's tomb, published in 1847.

83 *forestiere*: It. foreigner.

86 *the dolce lume of print*: It. sweet light, alluding to a line in Dante's *Inferno*, x. 69, 'Non fiere gli occhi suoi lo dolce lome?'

the old Socinian: Mr Waters formerly professed faith in Unitarianism, a version of Protestantism with many adherents in New England, including at one time Emerson and other Transcendentalists. Affirming that God is one, Unitarians thereby reject the doctrine of the Trinity and the divinity of Christ. These views are often traced back to the sixteenth-century Italian theologians Laelius and Faustus Socinus: hence Waters is 'the old Socinian', looking out on the 'old convent' of San Marco, where Savonarola was prior.

87 *the example of Mr Emerson . . . the pale Unitarianism*: the American essayist Ralph Waldo Emerson (1803–82) resigned his position as a Unitarian minister in 1832 when he found himself unable to subscribe to orthodox doctrine.

88 *the wicked old Carnival, that he tried so hard to kill*: Carnival was a festival associated in Catholic countries with the last days or

hours before Lent. The Florentine Carnival under the Medici involved wild and elaborate revelry; unable to suppress it, Savonarola attempted to convert pagan activities into Christian ones. *Romola*, Ch. 49, describes the famous Burning of the Vanities in 1497, when a pyramid of costumes, books, pictures, etc. was set ablaze.

93 *corso*: It. race.

97 *a battery on exhibition*: the battery was invented by the Italian Volta in 1800.

98 *veglione*: It. masked ball.

99 *dominoes*: masks, or black cloaks with hoods.

102 *two or three Mephistos*: devils, from Mephistopheles in the Faust story.

104 *a passage from Swedenborg*: Emanuel Swedenborg (1688–1772) was a Swedish mystic and philosopher with many American followers, including Howells's father.

110 *squeaking and gibbering masks*: alludes to *Hamlet*, I. i. 115–16, 'the sheeted dead / Did squeak and gibber in the Roman streets.'

117 *You've heard of the Buondelmonti*: one of the leading families of medieval Florence, engaged on the side of the Guelphs and the Pope in their struggle against the Ghibellines, who supported the Emperor.

123 *lucerna*: It. oil-lamp.

131 *'Grazie; sto bene'*: It. 'Thank you; I am well.'

143 *Avanti!*: It. 'Come in!'

148 *Rigoletto*: a tragic opera (1851) by Giuseppe Verdi.

154 *the moment when Lorenzino killed Alessandro*: Alessandro de' Medici, the first Medici ruler of Florence, was assassinated by his cousin in 1537 at the Ricciardi Palace, where Colville comes upon Waters. His successor, Cosimo I, had Lorenzino assassinated in turn.

155 *the great siege*: Charles V, the Holy Roman Emperor, besieged Florence in 1529, and appointed Alessandro when it capitulated.

156 *Michelangelo's bastions*: *Baedeker's Handbook to Northern Italy*, 1877, directed travellers to the south-east of the city, where they could find 'the gateway of the old fortifications, created

by Michael Angelo in 1529 as engineer to the republic, and . . . defended by him during an eleven months siege of the city by the Imperial troops'.

157 *the great frate*: It. friar, i.e. Savonarola, who was executed in 1498, as described in the passage that follows.

'*the riddle of the painful earth*': allusion to Tennyson's 'The Palace of Art' (1832), ll. 213–14, 'Full oft the riddle of the painful earth . . . Flashed through her as she sat alone.'

162 *its statues by Bandinelli*: a Florentine sculptor (1493–1560) and rival of Michelangelo.

171 *One of Mr James's . . . I should have said Howells*: see note to p. 28 on 'our international novelists', above. Howells established his early reputation by making use of his travels and his period as American Consul in Venice (1861–5).

175 *convenances*: Fr. social conventions.

179 *salotto*: It. drawing-room, parlour.

197 *salsa agradolce*: It. bitter-sweet sauce.

199 *Isis and Osiris*: Egyptian deities. Osiris, the god of the dead, was killed by his brother Set. The nature-goddess Isis, his sister and wife, avenged him and reassembled the scattered parts of his body.

207 *buonamano . . . giovane*: It. tip, waiter.

218 *a copy of The Marble Faun*: Hawthorne's Italian novel (1860). See above, note to p. 67.

220 *Gibbon's report*: In *Memoirs of My Life* (1796), Chs. 4 and 8. The historian Edward Gibbon, author of *The Decline and Fall of the Roman Empire* (1776–88) was sent to Lausanne by his father for Calvinist instruction after converting to Catholicism. He returned there late in his life.

223 *the poor young Indian prince*: the Monument marks the place where the body of the Maharajah of Kohlapore was burned on a pyre in 1870.

226 *a course of Kingsley*: Charles Kingsley (1819–75) was an Anglican priest and historian who published both sermons and novels, including *Alton Locke* (1850) and *Westward Ho!* (1855).

a course of Carlyle: Thomas Carlyle (1795–1881), a Scottish essayist and historian, was a leading Victorian man of letters who inspired younger writers on both sides of the Atlantic, including Emerson.

240 *Gratiano . . . in The Merchant of Venice*: a friend of Antonio,
Gratiano 'speaks an infinite deal of nothing, more than any
man in all Venice' (I. i. 118). He eventually marries Nerissa,
Portia's maid.

243 *the great American incompris*: Fr. a misunderstood person.

249 *hopeless mazes of error*: an echo of Milton's *Paradise Lost*, ii. 561,
'And found no end, in wand'ring mazes lost', quoted in Gibbon's *Memoirs*, Ch. 4.

261 *Mariana in the South*: a poem by Tennyson, published in 1832,
which adopts the persona of the forsaken Mariana in *Measure
for Measure*. Colville slightly misquotes ll. 91–2, 'And deepening through the silent spheres / Heaven over Heaven rose the
night.'

263 *Goethe tries to imagine an atonement for Faust's trespass*: at the end
of Part I of Goethe's verse drama *Faust* (1808) the hero faces
damnation as a consequence of his pact with the devil
Mephistopheles. In Part II (1832) he wins salvation by an act
of service to humanity, reclaiming land from the sea.

266 *Hamlet was able to browbeat Rosencrantz and Guildenstern*: cf.
Hamlet, III. ii. 66–9—'blest are those / Whose blood and
judgement are so well co-medled, / That they are not a pipe
for Fortune's finger / To sound what stop she please . . .'

276 *coup de théâtre*: Fr. a theatrical stroke; a sensational develop-
ment, as in the theatre.

277 *villegiature*: It. country holidays.

THE WORLD'S CLASSICS

A Select List

Robinson Crusoe
Edited by J. Donald Crowley

Roxana
Edited by Jane Jack

THOMAS HARDY: A Pair of Blue Eyes
Edited by Alan Manford

Jude the Obscure
Edited by Patricia Ingham

Under the Greenwood Tree
Edited by Simon Gatrell

The Well-Beloved
Edited by Tom Hetherington

The Woodlanders
Edited by Dale Kramer

SIR WALTER SCOTT: The Heart of Midlothian
Edited by Claire Lamont

Redgauntlet
Edited by Kathryn Sutherland

Waverley
Edited by Claire Lamont